Beyond the Battlefields: New Perspectives on Warfare and Society in the Graeco-Roman World,
Edited by Edward Bragg, Lisa Irene Hau and Elizabeth Macaulay-Lewis

This book first published 2008 by

Cambridge Scholars Publishing

15 Angerton Gardens, Newcastle, NE5 2JA, UK

British Library Cataloguing in Publication Data
A catalogue record for this book is available from the British Library

ISBN (10): 1-84718-516-9, ISBN (13): 9781847185167

Beyond the Battlefields:
New Perspectives on Warfare and Society
in the Graeco-Roman World

Edited by

Edward Bragg, Lisa Irene Hau
and Elizabeth Macaulay-Lewis

Cambridge Scholars Publishing

Beyond the Battlefields

TABLE OF CONTENTS

LIST OF ILLUSTRATIONS

Figure 9-1. Attic black-figure neck-amphora, attributed to the Painter of London, E543. About 540 BC. H. 36.2 cm (14 ¼ in.); D. (body) 28.6 cm (11 ¼ in.) Malibu, California, the J. Paul Getty Museum 86.AE.73. Photograph courtesy of the J. Paul Getty Museum, Villa Collection, Malibu, California.

Figure 9-2. Attic red-figure calyx-krater from Vulci, attributed to the Tyszkiewicz Painter. About 490-480 BC. H. 45.2 cm (17 13/16 in.); D. 51.3 cm (20 3/16 in.) Boston, Museum of Fine Arts, Catharine Page Perkins Fund 97.368. Photograph © 2008, Museum of Fine Arts, Boston.

Figure 9-3. Protocorinthian aryballos from Thebes, attributed to the Chigi Group. 670-630 BC. H. 6.8 cm (2 ¾ in.) Paris, Musée du Louvre CA 931. Photograph courtesy of Musée du Louvre/M. et P.Chuzeville.

Figure 9-4. Attic black-figure hydria, attributed to the Painter of Louvre, F6. 560-540 BC. H. 46 cm (18 in.) Paris, Musée du Louvre F6. Photograph courtesy of Musée du Louvre/M. et P.Chuzeville.

Figure 9-5. Attic black-figure calyx-krater, from the north slope of the Acro*polis*, Athens, attributed to Exekias. 550-525 BC. H. 44.5 cm (17.5 in.), D. (max) 53 cm (20.9 in.) Athens, Agora Museum AP1044. Image after *Hesperia* 25 (1956), pl. 50, courtesy of the American School of Classical Studies in Athens: Agora Excavations.

Figure 9-6. Attic black-figure amphora, type A, from Vulci, attributed to the Leagros Group. 530-500 BC. H. 63 cm (24.8 in.) London, British Museum B199. Photograph © the Trustees of the British Museum.

Figure 9-7. Attic black-figure cup from Kameiros 575-550 BC. H. 15 cm (6 in.); D. 24 cm (9 ½ in.) Berlin, Antikensammlung F1679. Photograph: David Saunders.

Figure 9-8. Attic black-figure amphora, type A, from Orvieto, attributed to Exekias. 550-525 BC. H. 58.3 cm (23 in); D. (max.) 37.5 cm (14.8 in.) Philadelphia, University of Pennsylvania Museum MS 3442. Image: 164219, courtesy of University of Pennsylvania Museum.

Figure 9-9. Attic black-figure neck-amphora from Vulci, attributed to the Group of London B145. 550-500 BC. H. 35.7 cm (14.1 in.) London, British Museum B251. Photograph © the Trustees of the British Museum.

Figure 11-1. A *sestertius* with Head of Vespasian on the obverse and on the reverse, Victory standing inscribing a shield attached to a palm tree (*BMC* 2.638 (p. 141), Plate 25, No. 4.) Photograph © the Trustees of the British Museum.

Figure 11-2. A Vespasianic *quandrans*, a lone palm tree appears on the obverse (with the inscription *IMP VES PASIAN AVG)* and a *vexillum* on the reverse (with the inscription *P M TR P P P COS III* and *SC.* Photograph © the Trustees of the British Museum.

Figure 11-3. A Vespasianic *sestertius* with a victory on the reverse, inscribing a shield which is fixed to a palm tree. The inscription on the reverse reads *VICTORIA AUGUSTI.* Photograph © the Trustees of the British Museum.

Figure 12-1. Solidus of Constantine, Trier mint, c. 317. (*RIC* VII, 192). Image courtesy of Numismatik Lanz München (Auction 112, Lot 866, 25 Nov. 2002).

Figure 12-2. Solidus of Constantine, Siscia mint, 317. (*RIC* VII, 28). (ANS 1001.1.22131). Photograph by author.

Figure 12-3. Valerius Victorinus Funerary Inscription, Ulmetum, after 324. (*AE* 1976, 631). Histria Museum in Istria, Romania; photograph by author.

Figure 12-4. Medallion of Magnentius, Aquileia mint, c. 351. (*RIC* VIII, 122). Image courtesy of Numismatica Ars Classica (Auction 33, Lot 605, 6 April 2006).

Figure 12-5. Æ2 of Vetranio, Siscia mint, 350. (*RIC* VIII, 287). (ANS 1984.146.1096.) Photograph by author.

LIST OF TABLES

ABBREVIATIONS

All abbreviations of ancient sources are according to the *Oxford Classical Dictionary*[3].

ABV	Beazley 1956 *Attic Black-figure Vase-painters* (Oxford).
Add²	Carpenter, Mannack, and Mendonça. 1989 *Beazley Addenda: Additional References to ABV, ARV² and Paralipomena* 2nd ed. (Oxford).
ARV²	Beazley, 1963 *Attic Red-figure Vase-painters* (second edition) (Oxford).
AHB	*Ancient History Bulletin*
AJA	*American Journal of Archaeology. The Journal of the Archaeological Institute of America*
AJP	*The American Journal of Philology*
AK	*Antike Kunst*
AM	*Mitteilungen des Deutschen Archäologischen Instituts, Athenische Abteilung*
Antike Welt	*Antike Welt (Zeitschrift für Archäologie und Kulturgeschichte)*
ArtB	*The Art Bulletin*
BAD	Beazley Archive Database number (www.beazley.ox.ac.uk).
BICS	*Bulletin of the Institute of Classical Studies, London*
BMC	*Coins of the Roman Empire in the British Museum*
Byz	*Byzantion*
Byz. Forsch.	*Byzantinische Forschungen*
CAH	*Cambridge Ancient History*
Chiron	*Chiron (Mitteilungen der Kommission für alte Geschichte und Epigraphik des deutschen archäologischen Instituts)*
C&M	*Classica et Mediaevalia*
CP	*Classical Philology*
CQ	*Classical Quarterly*
CR	*The Classical Review*
CVA	*Corpus Vasorum Antiquorum*
CW	*Classical World*

EJ	Ehrenberg and Jones, 1976, *Documents Illustrating the Reigns of Augustus and Tiberius*, 2nd ed.
FGrH	Jacoby *Die Fragmente der Griechischen Historiker*
G&R	*Greece and Rome*
GRBS	*Greek, Roman and Byzantine Studies*
Hermes	*Hermes. Zeitschrift für klassische Philologie*
Hesperia	*Hesperia. The Journal of the American School of Classical Studies at Athens*
HZ	*Historische Zeitschrift*
JdI	*Jahrbuch des Deutschen Archäologischen Instituts*
JHS	*The Journal of Hellenic Studies*
JGH	*Journal of Garden History*
JRA	*The Journal of Roman Archaeology*
JRS	*The Journal of Roman Studies*
LIMC	*Lexicon Iconographicum Mythologiae Classicae* I-VIII (Zürich 1981-1999).
LTUR	Steinby (ed.), 1993 *Lexicon topographicum urbis romae* (Rome)
LCM	*Liverpool Classical Monthly*
LSJ	Liddell, Scott, and Jones, *Greek-English Lexicon*, 9th ed. (Oxford 1940)
Mnemos.	*Mnemosyne*
MRR	*The Magistrates of the Roman Republic Volumes I-II & Supplement*
NC	*Numismatic Chronicle*
OCD	*Oxford Classical Dictionary*
ORF[3]	Malcovati (ed.) 1967[3] *Oratorum Romanorum Fragmenta Liberae Rei Publicae*. Turin
PAPS	*Proceedings of the American Philosophical Society*
Para	Beazley, 1971 *Paralipomena: Additions to Attic Black-figure Vase-painters and to Attic Red-figure Vase-painters* (Oxford).
PBSR	*Papers of the British School at Rome*
Philologus	*Philologus: Zeitschrift fur Klassische Philologie*
PLRE	Jones, Martindale, and Morris (eds.) 1971, *The Prosopography of the Later Roman Empire*, vol. I, AD 260-395.
PME	Casson (ed.) 1989 *Periplus Maris Erythraei*, Princeton.
RIC	Mattingly et al. (eds.) 1923-94 *The Roman Imperial Coinage*.
RhM	*Rheinisches Museum für Philologie*

RM   *Römische Mitteilungen (Mitteilungen des Deutschen*
              Archäologischen Instituts, Römische Abteilung)
TAPA   *Transactions of the American Philological Association*
YCS   *Yale Classical Studies*
ZPE   *Zeitschrift für Papyrologie und Epigraphik*

FOREWORD

In February 2005, Edward Bragg was fortunate enough to attend a classics conference at the University of South Africa, Johannesburg, entitled "Battlefields in Antiquity". This three-day conference, organised by Dr Richard Evans, involved a series of cross-disciplinary papers. One of these was a comparison between the Battle of Asculum of 279 BC, where Pyrrhus won a bloody victory over Rome, and the Battle of Isandlwana of AD 1879, where the Zulus overcame a British force. Following this conference a few of the delegates travelled north to the Pilansburg game reserve, and, while driving around on this safari in a dusty, hot black Nissan with Craig Caldwell, Richard Evans and Kate Gilliver, the idea for this conference arose.

Ancient warfare has long been a major focus of modern scholars; with the study of tactics and battles traditionally attracting most scholarly interest. However, there is much more to the study of ancient warfare than researching how phalanxes or cohorts made mutual kebabs of each other.[1] We believe that it is in the contexts that lie beyond the ancient battlefield that a number of scholars and postgraduates are producing some of today's most exciting and innovative research.

This was a primary reason for holding the postgraduate conference "Beyond the Battlefields of the Graeco-Roman World" at Oxford in July 2nd–4th 2006, which Edward Bragg organised, and where eleven of the thirteen papers in this collection were originally presented. This volume not only expands upon this new area of scholarship, but also brings new methods to bear on the study of ancient warfare and society in the Graeco-Roman world. The contributors have been inspired by contemporary events and the attention given by scholars and in the media to contemporary military activities outside the context of the battlefield, such as intelligence, propaganda, and the treatment of prisoners of war.

Rather than addressing warfare and society solely from a literary, historical or archaeological perspective, the articles in this volume address all classes of evidence for warfare and its relation with society in the

---

[1] The mutual kebab expression comes from Philip Sabin 2000 "The face of Roman battle" (*JRS* 90, 9).

Graeco-Roman world.[2] The wide sprectrum of the papers speaks to the tremendous impact of warfare on culture and society in the ancient world.

The range of papers also shows the large variety of angles from which the subject of ancient warfare and its interface with society can be seen. Despite classical scholars' interest in the same time period, there is often little exchange between archaeologists, historians, art historians, and philologists, and for this reason opportunities to move debate forward are often missed. This volume hopes to go some way towards remedying that.

Thus, this work offers a new occasion for advancing scholarly debate. Rather than focusing on one theme, such as tactics, strategy, or the representation of war, as other works have done so well, this volume takes a holistic approach to the study of ancient warfare and its effect on society, politics, and art, everything that lies "beyond the battlefield".

Edward Bragg, London
Lisa Irene Hau, Bristol
Elizabeth Macaulay-Lewis, Oxford
March 2008

---

[2] This is discussed further below in the Introduction.

ACKNOWLEDGEMENTS

Thanks are owed to a number of people who helped the editors with this book. First and foremost to Professors Brian Campbell and Hans van Wees, whose interest in the conference and willingness to read papers and to contribute to the volume were of paramount importance. Professor Jonathan Powell, Dr Ed Bispham, Dr Richard Evans, Dr Alison Cooley, Dr Shaun Tougher and Dr Adrian Kelly all read papers and provided support along the way. Professor Nick Fisher kindly supplied Ed Bragg with information about AHRC grants for postgraduate conferences, which made the conference possible. All of the second readers, many of whom are mentioned in the individual contributions, greatly improved the papers in this volume. Cambridge Scholars Publishing has been very supportive of this whole project and we are pleased to have worked with them on this book.

We would also like to thank the organisations and people whose support made the conference not only a possibility but a success: the Arts and Humanities Research Council for its financial support as well as the Faculty of Classics and Wadham College at the University of Oxford for the generous use of their facilities. The conference would never have been successful without the support of: Miss Erica Clarke, Mrs Ghislaine Rowe, Mr Ido Israelowich, Miss Lindsay Driediger, Miss Annelies Cazemier, Mr Ryan Wei, Dr Bob Cowan, and finally the late, and sorely missed, Dr Peter Derow for not only supporting the successful application to the AHRC, but also for his invaluable advice on where to go for food and drink in Oxford during the hot evenings of July 2006. This book is dedicated to Peter's memory.

E.B., L.I.H, and E.M.L.

INTRODUCTION

BRIAN CAMPBELL AND HANS VAN WEES

The study of ancient warfare is moving beyond the battlefields farther and more frequently than ever before. Beyond the experience of combat, beyond the tactics and strategy which have been of such absorbing interest to so many for so long, lie fields of historical enquiry which are only just beginning to be systematically explored. War left its mark everywhere in ancient social, economic, political and cultural life, and was in turn shaped by countless cultural, political, economic, and social forces. The interaction between these spheres is the focus of some of the most promising current research, which addresses such fundamental problems as what motivated war and other forms of collective violence, how representations of war in art and literature reflected cultural trends, and whether war ever dominated life to such an extent that any ancient state – even Sparta or Rome – deserves to be called 'militaristic'.

This volume represents a new wave of interest in warfare as a far more than merely military phenomenon. It contains most of the papers delivered at a conference entitled 'Beyond the Battlefields of the Graeco-Roman World', held in Oxford 2-4 July 2006. The organizers were postgraduate students at the Universities of Oxford and London and the participants were postgraduates from Britain, Europe and the USA. Many excellent and innovative presentations, enthusiastic debate, and a friendly atmosphere ensured that this excellently organized conference was both memorable and a significant contribution to scholarship.

The papers collected here range widely both chronologically and in subject matter. Of the chapters concerned with the Greek world, two are concerned with military practices which existed not just beyond the battlefield but behind the scenes. Woolmer adds to what little we know about spying in classical Greece by reassessing the role of merchants in information-gathering. Building on the argument, developed in his PhD thesis, that traders were not the marginalised figures often described by modern scholars but fully integrated into their communities, he suggests that they had both the connections and the authority to be valuable and respected sources of information about enemy strengths and movements in time of war. This might explain, for example, the Spartans' indiscrimate slaughter, without burial, of all merchants caught sailing around the Peloponnese in 431 BC: perhaps this was an attempt to eliminate spies rather than an almost random atrocity. Behind-the-scenes activity also accounts, Asmonti suggests, for the success and fame of the admiral Conon, instrumental in securing Athens' return as a major player in international relations after its defeat in the Peloponnesian War. Conon's record of commanding naval campaigns was good, but not outstanding, and it was probably his record as an organiser, as a builder of warships and naval infrastructures, especially in Cyprus, rather than as an admiral which brought him to the attention of the Persian authorities and won him the backing which enabled him to restore Athens' fortunes.

The other four Greek papers all address representations of war in art and literature, studying not so much the actual military landscape beyond the battlefield as the conventions and interests of those who painted the surviving pictures of that landscape, in words or images. Saunders' careful examination of the figures of fallen warriors which are so common in Athenian vase painting concludes that surprisingly these did not primarily convey the much-discussed concept of the 'beautiful death'. In all their variety, their dominant interest is in the warriors fighting over the body, rather than in the corpse itself which tends to remain marginal to the scene. And the iconography of men fighting to protect a comrade or to humiliate a defeated enemy, respectively, does not necessarily mirror a common or important feature of real contemporary combat, but encapsulates in a single image some of the key values shared by archaic Greek elites. Another aspect of these values is explored by Kozak, who identifies a subtle discourse of peace which pervades the *Iliad*, where one might have expected a glorification of war. It is above all the story and character of Hector which allows the poet to develop the tension between martial ideals and a full appreciation of the joys of peace, and which puts paid to any notion that the *Iliad* adopts a simple, unambiguous 'heroic code' centred on war.

The complexity of Greek ethics regarding warfare is also a central theme of the papers by Hau and Nevin. The former surveys the development of a striking literary motif, the description of the behaviour of the victor after his victory, which is exploited to point moral messages about fate, self-knowledge and self-control, which from Herodotus to Polybius and Diodorus become increasingly explicit. The interest of ancient authors in this theme – rather than for example the care of the wounded, the consolidation of conquests, or any other practical dimension of the aftermath of war – demonstrates that the historiography of war has a strong moral dimension, but also that the ethics of war were nor uncontroversial but subject to divergent interpretations and active debate. This point is reinforced by Nevin's analysis of the accounts of the campaign of Delium in 424 BC in Thucydides and Diodorus. She demonstrates that the two authors differ fundamentally in their moral evaluation of this campaign, with Thucydides strongly hinting at acts of sacrilege which Diodorus chose to ignore. This was not a matter of Thucydides neutrally reporting acts which were generally regarded as outrages and Diodorus abbreviating them out of his story, but of two authors imposing their own agendas on their accounts and accordingly playing up or down ethical issues as they saw fit. These chapters warn us that ancient views on the morality of warfare could vary dramatically from one context to another.

Among the papers dealing with the Roman world major themes include the recruiting and organization of the army of the early Roman republic, which was crucial to the survival and development of the Roman state. Armstrong undermines the idea of the Servian military constitution as a viable model for understanding the early Roman army. The military provision was forced to rely on groups outside the existing procedure. So, although there was a timocratic system it was flexible enough for the process to accommodate itself to military needs. The early army was the product of immediate and evolving social and military circumstances. In a different way recruiting remained crucial in the late empire, though part of the recruiting process now consisted in winning over the troops of other military leaders or usurpers. Caldwell deals with recruitment and loyalty in the third and fourth centuries, which he relates to the character of the civil wars. Recruitment was related to motivation and civil war battles saw the absorbing of defeated forces through imperial clemency – an important source of manpower. Constantine was a potent symbol of total victory with his army of the Rhine, and regional loyalty was to continue to be important as well as the inevitable financial inducements. The Danubian and Balkan provinces were crucial as a source of soldiers and were also a major theatre of civil war battles. Everywhere those to who sought power had to win over other troops and keep the loyalty of their own.

The celebration and exploitation of military success was of perennial importance. Bragg examines how during the republic in the permanent jury courts great aristocratic figures talked up their record of military service to defend or justify themselves or attack others those who were defendants. It was also common to denigrate the achievements of opponents. In these tussles battle scars could be mentioned or even revealed. The context was that in Roman society military *virtus* was highly prized and military success was frequently publicly announced and celebrated. So, it could be argued that to convict a good soldier would damage the *Res Publica*. Cicero could even make a point in favour of his client Archias because he had written movingly about Roman wars. It was no different for emperors in the propagation of military achievement, and Augustus made the military success that ended civil war a central feature of the *Res Gestae*. Lange argues that the apparently negative elements of the *Res Gestae* serve to emphasize a change for the better, since all success was now to depend on Augustus and therefore his participation in the civil wars was justified, since by ending them he allowed the Roman Empire to assume its rightful place in the world. Consequently the founding of colonies (*Res Gestae* 28) should be seen as part of the end of the civil wars since soldiers were now settled in an organized way. Another element in military celebration appeared in the mastery of the natural environment as portrayed in the Roman triumph. Macaulay-Lewis examines how rulers displayed control over famous plants as part of the celebration of military victory. Representations of plants and also living specimens were displayed in triumphal processions. The Flavian triumph over Judaea was particularly notable with its emphasis on balsam, which was highly valuable, and also date palm trees. There was an economic element here since the display was not only a victory symbol but also an indication of the fruits of victory brought under Rome's control.

The theme of celebrating military success is related to the emperor's role with his troops and the increasing tendency to assume personal leadership and even take risks. Levithan argues that soldiers liked their leaders to have some measure of military accomplishment; this could be displayed to best advantage in siege operations, which gave the emperor the chance to appear as leader in full view in a controlled situation. So, in contrast to open battle conditions emperors sometimes exposed themselves to fire; it was a useful leadership technique and to be shot at or even slightly wounded could inspire men to acts of revenge against the enemy. By the later empire being a good emperor was tantamount to being a good general and Whately suggests that one imperial quality was the ability to control the troops and keep firm discipline, which in turn guaranteed the success of Roman arms. He describes the presentation by contemporary, largely civilian, ancient writers of indiscipline and insubordination in the 550s to the 620s. This is related to ancient generalship because discipline was described in terms of generalship; a failure by a commander to control his men could lead to problems since a good general eliminated indiscipline. So for Agathias the poor condition of the army amounted to poor leadership. Military treatise writers like Syrianus and Maurice also emphasize the connection between generalship and discipline. Therefore there was not necessarily a decline in discipline in the later Roman army but a failure in generalship; and the didactic purpose of the writers was to correct this.

From this bare summary of the chapters the richness and variety of the present volume will already be clear, and there is much to enjoy in the details of the discussions as well. If in this volume we see the future of the study of warfare, then we can say without hesitation that, yes, it works.

CHAPTER ONE

"SHOW US YOUR SCARS, MANIUS AQUILLIUS." THE MILITARY RECORD OF MAGISTRATES IN DEFENCE SPEECHES DURING THE ROMAN REPUBLIC*

EDWARD BRAGG

> I have gone to the law, not about assault or killing with a weapon or poisoning, but about three nanny goats. I claim that they are missing because a neighbour has stolen them. The judge requires proof. In loud tones, using your whole stock of gestures, you boom about Cannae and the Mithridatic War, and the perjuries of Punic rage and Sullas and Mariuses and Muciuses. Postumus, it is time you said something about my three nanny goats.[1]

The poet Martial satirises the tendency of Roman advocates to employ elaborate historical digressions within their speeches, including at times famous military conflicts, in order to appeal to the patriotic nostalgia of the jury. Unlike modern Western courts, in which lawyers on the whole are obliged to keep to material relevant to the case, Roman legal oratory could, and frequently did, entail a wide breadth of digressive and emotive information to move and persuade the assembled court.[2] This paper

---

*I would like to thank Professor Jonathan Powell, Dr. Edward Bispham, and Dr. Richard Evans for reading and commenting on earlier versions of this paper. All translations are my own except for those taken from the Loeb editions of Cicero's *Pro Fonteio* and *Pro Sestio*, and Berry's Oxford edition of Cicero's *Pro Archia*.
[1] Mart., 6.19, "*Non de vi neque caede nec veneno, sed lis est mihi de tribus capellis: vicini queror has abesse furto. Hoc iudex sibi postulat probari: tu Cannas Mithridaticumque bellum et periuria Punici furoris et Sullas Mariosque Muciosque magna voce sonas manuque tota. Iam dic, Postume, de tribus capellis.*"
[2] Powell and Paterson 2004, 4, point out that in the late Republic "Roman advocates regularly used arguments on apparently extraneous questions to

demonstrates how one prominent type of forensic digression, that of the military record of Roman magistrates, was employed in a diversity of ways within the defence speeches of the middle and late Republic.[3]

There were two legal tribunals within which prominent legal cases of the middle and late Republic were held.[4] Firstly, there was the *iudicium populi*, before which prosecutions were brought in the third and second century. This involved three separate *anquisitiones* (investigations) before a *contio*, and then, finally, after a *trinundium* (a gap of three market days) there was a formal vote of the assembled people.[5] Although the *iudicium populi* continued to function in the first century, as demonstrated by the trial of Rabirius for *perduellio* (harm to the state) in 63 BC, it became largely obsolete, and it was before the *quaestiones perpetuae* that prosecutions were primarily brought during the late Republic.[6] Assembled juries of between roughly 50 and 70 men now decided the outcome, and the first of these permanent standing courts to be established was the *quaestio de repetundis* in around 149 BC by the *lex Calpurnia*.[7] This *quaestio* aimed to provide redress to provincials who had suffered illegal exactions by unscrupulous Roman governors. Further *quaestiones* developed in the subsequent decades, including amongst others: one for *ambitus* (electoral malpractice), one for *peculatus* (embezzlement of public money), and also one for *maiestas populi Romani minuta* (diminishing of the majesty of the Roman people).[8] These *quaestiones perpetuae* were overseen by praetors in the Roman Forum, and it was before these courts that most of Cicero's forensic oratory was delivered.

---

reinforce their cases"; Nicolet 1980, 378, emphasises the frequently emotive and dramatic nature of the law-courts during the late Republic: "the reading of the indictment, the examination of witnesses, the presentation of exhibits, speeches for the prosecution and defence—all lent itself admirably to theatrical performances by great advocates who were also great artists".

[3] Canter 1931, 352-3, 360, identifies a considerable number of *digressiones* in the 57 extant or near extant speeches of Cicero. It should be stressed that the term digression is employed throughout this paper in a broad modern sense and not *digressio*, which scholars such as Canter correctly identify as a specific rhetorical mechanism.

[4] See Cloud 1994 "The constitution and public criminal law" *CAH IX*[2], 491-530.

[5] Cic. *Dom.* 45; Cloud 1994, 501-2.

[6] Cic. *Rab. Perd.* 15-18; Cass. Dio, 37.26.1-28.4.

[7] Lintott 2004, 75, cites the varying jury numbers with 70 votes in the trials of both Gabinius and Scaurus in 54 BC (Cic. *Att.* 4.18.1; *Q.Fr* 3.4.1) and only 56 votes cast during Clodius' trial for *incestum* (Cic. *Att.* 4.18.4); see Cloud 1994, 505-6, on the establishment of the *quaestio de repetundis*; Cic. *Brut.* 106.

[8] See Lintott 1999, 158.

Unsurprisingly, due to the nature of the sources, the majority of evidence concerning the employment of the military record comes from Cicero. Nonetheless, we do have some details of its pre-Ciceronian use, with the fragments of one of the Elder Cato's speeches being the most illuminating. This oration was entitled *Dierum dictarum de consulatu suo*, and, according to Astin, it was probably delivered in around late 191 or 190 BC before a *contio* of the *iudicium populi* when Cato defended himself against a tribunician prosecution.[9] The fragments that survive demonstrate how Cato informed the court of his military service, in particular his Spanish campaign of 195.[10]

First of all, a number of the fragments detail the preparations and the voyage to Spain of the consular expedition, and it was through this that Cato informed his audience of the logistical requirements and the distances crossed in mounting such an overseas operation. For instance, Cato says that:

> They praise me to the skies, saying no one would ever have thought that one man could have raised so great a fleet, so great an army and so many provisions; while I succeeded in raising them in the shortest time possible.[11]

Although it is difficult to judge who allegedly praised Cato, this is an effective rhetorical mechanism that would nowadays be termed a "man of straw." This is the technique where the orator sets up a supposed belief held by people or critics and then knocks it down by citing real achievement—a persuasive mechanism frequently employed by Tony Blair in his political oratory.[12] One wonders who exactly the people are,

---

[9] *ORF³*, Cato frs. 21-55; Astin 1978, 60.

[10] Livy, 34.8.4-21.8; Plut. *Cat. Mai.* 10: detail Cato's Spanish achievements.

[11] *ORF³*, Cato fr. 28; Charisius *Gramm.* 266 B: "*Laudant maximis laudibus, tantum navium, tantum exercitum, tantum [com]meatum non opinatum esse quemquam hominem comparare potuisse; id me tam maturrime comparavisse.*" A significant rhetorical point about the fragment is the sense of flowing rhythm through the triple use of *tantum*, which gives breadth to Cato's campaign preparations.

[12] For example, the following excerpt from the Prime Minister's speech to the Labour Party conference at Brighton on October 2, 2001 demonstrates the use of a "man of straw." "People say: we are only acting because it's the USA that was attacked. Double standards, they say. But when Milosevic embarked on the ethnic cleansing of Muslims in Kosovo, we acted. The sceptics said it was pointless, we'd make matters worse, we'd make Milosevic stronger; and look what happened, we won, the refugees went home, the policies of ethnic cleansing were reversed and

who supposedly make these critical comments of Cato, but of course without a specific reference the audience is subtly, yet deliberately left in the dark.

In a later fragment of his defence speech Cato goes on to detail the military campaign itself including one engagement, and at the end of this battle Cato describes how he personally praised his men by means of a military *contio*. "If any man performed courageously, I rewarded him handsomely, and praised him with many words when the soldiers were paraded."[13] Cato, doubtless conscious of his trial audience, which was very probably a crowd of citizens gathered somewhere within Rome, was astutely informing them of his generous treatment of Roman troops, so pointing to his role as a good traditional paternal commander.

One other fragment which stands out from Cato's speech involves the recent Roman campaign against Antiochus in 191 BC, in which Cato was a military tribune to the consul M'. Acilius Glabrio with the Censor playing a major part in the decisive battle at Thermopylae.[14] In the following fragment Cato appears to over-emphasise his role in this achievement: "Likewise when very recently I dispersed and settled the greatest of threats from Thermopylae and Asia."[15] Without the adjoining sentences it is difficult to judge the extent of the self-promotion here. Nonetheless, it is clear that Cato is highlighting his personal participation in the defeat of Antiochus, very possibly playing on that other well-known achievement at Thermopylae in 480 BC when the Spartans alongside other Greek troops withstood that other great threat from the East, the Persian forces of Xerxes.[16] This interpretation does, however, depend on how well the story of Leonidas was known amongst the people of second century BC Rome. For this question it is probably significant that Cato in his *Origines* specifically compares the heroic sacrifice of a Roman military tribune during the Hannibalic War to Leonidas's defiant stand, thus

---

one of the great dictators of the last century will see justice in this century." See Guardian Unlimited for the full speech:
<http://politics.guardian.co.uk/labour2001/story/0,1414,562006,00.html>, accessed December 13th 2007.
[13] *ORF*[3], Cato fr. 35: "si *quis strenue fecerat, donabam honeste, ut alii idem vellent facere, atque in contione verbis multis laudabam.*"
[14] For Cato's role in the Thermopylae engagement, see Plut. *Cat. Mai.* 12-14; Livy 36.17-21; *MMR* 1.354-5.
[15] *ORF*[3], Cato fr. 49: "*Item ubi ab Thermopuleis atque ex Asia maximo tumultus maturissime disieci atque consedavi*".
[16] See Hdt. 7.204-39 for the best account of the Battle of Thermopylae.

demonstrating that Cato himself believed that the Roman audience for his historical work knew about the Spartan King's heroism.[17]

Overall, in the fragments of Cato's *Dierum dictarum de consulatu suo* one already senses a diversity of martial self-advertisement, in which the active and correct personal behaviour of the commander is frequently emphasised, a theme reiterated throughout many of Cicero's later defence speeches. Although the remaining evidence of such second century defence speeches before the *iudicium populi* is poor and frequently of an indirect, fragmentary and confusing nature, as demonstrated by the "Trial of the Scipios" in the 180s BC and the prosecution of Gaius Gracchus for dereliction of duty in 124, the subject of military service was undoubtedly still a significant aspect of such prosecution cases and so very likely part of the resultant defence speeches.[18]

Fortunately with the rise and establishment of the *quaestiones perpetuae* in the late Republic, the literary sources provide significant details about the forensic context in which the military record was employed. One of its most dramatic and stereotypical uses occurred during the trial of Manius Aquillius, an ex-consul who was charged with *repetundae* in about 95 BC. Aquillius had been legate to Marius at the start of the Cimbrian campaign in 103; later as consul in 101, he had overseen the suppression of a slave revolt in Sicily, during which he apparently killed the rebel leader and subsequently won an ovation.[19] Aquillius was, therefore, a defendant with a good service record, details of which his advocate Marcus Antonius doubtless elaborated on in court. According to Cicero's dialogue *De Oratore* the most memorable part of Antonius' defence was when he ripped open Aquillius' tunic in order to expose the

---

[17] Livy, 36.15 describes, prior to the 191 BC engagement, how "it [Thermopylae] is renowned for the deaths of the Spartans in the struggle against Persia, deaths more famous than the engagement which was fought there"; Cato *Orig.* fr. 83; Gell. 3.7.1-20.

[18] The principal sources for the "Trial of the Scipios" are Livy, 38.50-60; Gell. 4.18, 6.19; and Polyb. 23.14. The sources, however, provide a confusing and fragmentary picture of the political attacks on Publius and Lucius Scipio. Nonetheless it is clear that their behaviour during the campaign against Antiochus the Great was of central importance in the disputes, in particular the issue of moneys received from the Syrian king. Stockton 1979, 219; *ORF³*, 180-2; upon returning to Rome from his quaestorship in Sardinia, Gracchus was charged with dereliction of duty, and there are fragments from one or perhaps two speeches in which Gracchus defended himself.

[19] *MRR* 1.564; 571; Plut. *Mar.* 14.7: Aquillius was placed in charge of the army in Gaul when Marius returned to Rome to hold elections; *MMR* 2.2; Posidonius *FGrH* 87 F36 (= Ath. 5.213b). Diod. Sic. 36.10.1 details his Sicilian successes.

scars on the front of the ex-consul's body.[20] This display, according to Cicero's account, was so moving that it apparently brought tears to Marius' eyes.[21] Antonius' action was aimed at inducing sympathy amongst the jurors for Aquillius, by displaying evidence of the wounds which the ex-consul had received when putting his body on the line for Rome.

Matthew Leigh highlights how battle scars were a recognised means of self-promotion within Roman Republican politics. He counters the argument that they might be a literary *topos* by pointing out how the artwork of the late Republic favoured verism, where every wrinkle and physical defect was displayed and that there was a propensity to admire the marked, modified, and worked body.[22] In addition, Leigh cites the Elder Cato's comment on how political candidates for office wore togas without a tunic in order to show their scars; there is also the famous display of Servilius' scars in 167 BC as part of his speech supporting Aemilius Paullus' triumph. Both of these cases demonstrate that the positive value of advertising one's scars went back at least to the middle second century.[23] Richard Evans, on the other hand, argues that their overt display from the mid-second century onwards was not always positively viewed, and he cites Terence's play *The Eunuch*, in which a slave character portrays the display of battle-scars as boorish.[24] In addition, barring Aquillius' case, it was through the *reference* to honourable or dishonourable scars, not their actual display, that scars were usually exploited to promote or denigrate a military reputation during the late Republic.[25] Taking Leigh's and Evans' arguments into account, I do not

---

[20] Cic. *De Orat.* 2.194-6: "Assuredly I [Antonius speaking within the Ciceronian dialogue] felt that the Court was deeply affected when I called forward my unhappy old client, in his garb of woe, and when I did those things approved by yourself, Crassus—not by way of technique, as to which I know not what to say, but under stress of deep emotion and indignation—I mean my tearing open his tunic and exposing his scars. While Gaius Marius, from his seat in the court, was strongly reinforcing by his weeping the pathos of my appeal, and I, repeatedly naming him, was committing his colleague to his care…"

[21] Cic. *De Orat.* 2.196.

[22] Leigh 1995, 207-8.

[23] Leigh 1995, 195-6; Plut. *Quaest. Rom.* 49; Livy, 45.39.

[24] Evans 1999, 90; Ter. *Eun.* 480-5: the slave Parmeno to the courtesan Thais: "and the donor of these gifts is not making demands on you to live with him alone, to the exclusion of everybody else. He doesn't recount battles and display his scars or lie in wait for you like someone else I know."

[25] Evans 1990, 83; for example, Cic. *Verr.* 2.5.32 has Cicero claiming that Verres had received some scars on his chest from one of his female lovers, thus playing on the stereotype of honourable scars.

want to argue that the display of scars was the norm and one of the primary means by which the military record was exploited. This is in contrast to the simplistic approach taken by Vasaly. In her article on Cicero's early speeches, she makes this statement about the challenge facing Roman prosecutors:

> "The worst that a prosecutor had to fear in such cases was for the defence counsel suddenly to disrobe his client, revealing his scars that testified to his battlefield heroics on Rome's behalf."[26]

As has already been demonstrated by the Elder Cato and will be made even more evident by the following analysis of some of Cicero's defence speeches, this paper argues that the military record was employed in a variety of ways as the gathered people and juries were not only targeted by dramatic displays, but by more nuanced rhetoric as well.

For example, the prosecution of Aquillius demonstrates one significant tactic that is frequently overlooked, namely the exploitation of the martial ethos of others present in the court, in Aquillius' case Gaius Marius. Now Marius was following the practice of friends and family by sitting near to the defendant, and according to Cicero he cried following Antonius' theatrics.[27] These tears, whether real or pre-meditated, would have, together with Antonius' naming of Marius, drawn attention to this pre-eminent commander. Thus, one man's physical display of his *virtus* induced a subsequent focus on one of the most well-known Roman *imperatores* of the period, someone with immense *auctoritas*. Later, in his defence of Murena in 63 BC, Cicero employed the same tactic, when he pointed to the presence in court of Murena's commander during the Mithridatic War, the renowned L. Licinius Lucullus.[28] Furthermore, one could argue that the personal appearance of such illustrious and formidable personalities was also a means of intimidating the jurors.

As stated earlier, the most detailed information concerning the forensic employment of a defendant's military record occurs within the speeches of Cicero, with the orations defending Fonteius, Murena, Archias, Flaccus, Balbus, Sestius, and Plancius, all of which include extensive digressions.[29]

---

[26] Vasaly 2002, 99.

[27] Cic. *De Orat.* 2.196; the individuals who on the day of the trial lend assistance to the defendant by either practical measures or simply by their presence near to him in court are termed in general *advocati*.

[28] Cic. *Mur.* 20: "this I venture to assert in Lucius Lucullus' presence…"

[29] See Cic. *Mur.* 11-2, 15-22, 31-34, 89; *Flacc.* 6, 27-33, 60-63, 101-103; *Balb.* 5-6, 9, 63-64; *Planc.* 28, 61; it should be stated that a number of the surviving

For brevity and to demonstrate the diversity of this practice, only the *Pro Fonteio*, *Pro Archia* and *Pro Sestio* will be given detailed analysis in this paper. Prior to this, it should be stressed that Cicero was a new man with a meagre military record who was acutely aware of both his personal and his ancestral lack of military *auctoritas*, and this was a factor in the way he approached military achievements in his speeches.[30] For example, at times he himself attempts to adopt military *auctoritas*, as demonstrated in the speeches against Catiline, and on other occasions he emphasises the military records of his clients or their supporters as a means of associating himself with their martial successes.[31]

The first case is that of Marcus Fonteius. Fonteius had been the praetorian governor of Transalpine Gaul from around 74-72 BC and was later prosecuted for *repetundae* in either 70 or 69.[32] Throughout his defence speech Cicero paints a dutiful and virtuous portrait of Fonteius, someone with a good military record; and early on in the oration he provides this general description of how Fonteius policed his apparently troublesome *provincia*.

> Marcus Fonteius was in charge of the province of Gaul, which comprises a type of men and communities which (to say nothing of ancient times) have either within our own memory waged long and bitter wars with the people of Rome, or have been quite recently subdued by our generals, subjugated in war, brought to notice by the triumphs and memorials of which their conquest has been the occasion, and have lately had their lands and cities made forfeit by the senate; in some cases they have met in armed encounter with Marcus Fonteius himself, and have, at cost of much strenuous effort to him, been brought beneath the power and dominion of the Roman people.[33]

Ciceronian speeches are likely to have been revised prior to publication and therefore are perhaps not exactly the orations actually delivered.

[30] May 1988, 13.

[31] Cic. *Cat.* 2.12-16; cf. May 1988, 56-7; for example, in Cicero's *Pro Lege Manilia* we see Cicero's efforts to associate himself with the recent military successes of Pompey.

[32] *MRR* 2.104.

[33] Cic., *Font.*, 12: "*Provinciae Galliae M. Fonteius praefuit, quae constat ex eis generibus hominum et civitatum qui, ut vetera mittam, partim nostra memoria bella cum populo Romano acerba ac diuturna gesserunt, partim modo ab nostris imperatoribus subacti, modo bello domiti, modo triumphis ac monumentis notati, modo ab senatu agris urbibusque multati sunt, partim qui cum ipso M. Fonteio ferrum ac manus contulerunt multoque eius sudore ac labore sub populi Romani imperium dicionemque ceciderunt.*"

On the surface this digression makes Fonteius appear like an active military governor. Cicero achieves this by alluding to past Roman victories against the Gauls in order to provide a positive backdrop to Fonteius' recent military activities, emphasising how the Gauls, in both distant and present times, had been a bitter enemy of Rome, as demonstrated by their famous sacking of the city in 386 and then by their participation in the more recent Hannibalic and Cimbric wars.[34] Hence, Fonteius was continuing the long established Roman fight against the Gauls. Cicero's description, however, of both Fonteius' and the earlier Roman victories is intentionally vague, since by not detailing or labelling the past successes through the names of specific *imperatores*, tribes, and places, he is, in a sense, under no subsequent rhetorical obligation to detail Fonteius' actions, which in reality were very probably not that memorable. Unsurprisingly, though not all of its sections have come down to us, there are no details in Cicero's speech of Fonteius performing frontline military service, something one might expect considerable emphasis on, or reference to, throughout the oration if Fonteius had been an active and successful *homo militaris* during his governorship.[35]

The next tactic related to Fonteius' military service comes when Cicero justifies the magistrate's various exactions from the Gauls:

> ...he requisitioned large troops of cavalry to serve in the wars then being waged all over the world by the people of Rome, large sums of money to provide these with pay, and enormous quantities of corn to enable us to carry on the war in Spain.[36]

Cicero's explanation plays on the heavy logistical requirements faced by Rome in the mid 70s BC, particularly during the long and bitter Sertorian War of 77-72.[37] In doing so he is presenting Fonteius' activities to the jurors as a functional part of Rome's war machine, where pay, horses, and corn were all needed, requirements that a number of the jurors would have been aware of through their military and commercial experiences. Thus,

---

[34] Polyb. 1.6.1, 3.60.11; Plut. *Mar.* 11-27; Cornell 1995, 313-4.

[35] Cic. *Font.* 20 does mention the *Bellum Vocontii* in a passing reference, which makes it appear that a section or reference to this war was omitted from the published version of the speech. However, we do not know what the *Bellum Vocantii* was or whether Fonteius was personally involved in it.

[36] Cic. *Font.* 13: "....*magnos equitatus ad ea bella quae tum in toto orbe terrarum a populo Romano gerebantur, magnas pecunias ad eorum stipendium, maximum frumenti numerum ad Hispaniense bellum tolerandum imperavit.*"

[37] The principal sources for the Sertorian War: Plut. *Sert.* 10-27; App. *BC* 1.108-115.

Fonteius' apparent illegal exactions from the Gallic provincials, as alleged by the prosecution, were being painted by Cicero as having taken place not for personal gain, but as a necessary part of Fonteius' military responsibilities.

Finally, Cicero in winding up his speech creates an impression that there was a current dearth of military men in Rome, so pushing the jury to believe that the conviction of Fonteius would undermine the state's capability to wage war.

> And today how should you act, now that the profession of arms has fallen out of fashion among our youth; when our best men and our greatest generals have been wasted either by age or by civil dissension and public calamity; when wars so numerous are either unavoidably undertaken by us, or sprung upon us with unforeseen suddenness?[38]

This generalisation is then supported by Cicero naming "past masters of warfare holding praetorian rank," such as Sulla, Marius, Catulus, and Crassus, "men who gained their military knowledge not from textbooks but from their operations and their victories."[39] This gives the impression that, following Fonteius' alleged suppression of the Gauls, this experienced ex-praetor would soon be pursuing a similarly illustrious career. Thus, Cicero points to the potential of Fonteius' future military service on behalf of Rome, an invaluable duty that will be cut short if they, the jury, find him guilty. To emphasise the point further Cicero then goes on to make the jury consider the welfare of their families with or without this skilful and dutiful *homo militaris*:

> View carefully these considerations, gentlemen, and you will assuredly prefer to retain at home in the service of yourselves and your children a man tireless in the toils of war, so valiant in the face of its perils, so skilled in its theory and its practice, so wise in its strategy, so fortunate in its accidents and its chances....[40]

---

[38] Cic. *Font.* 42: "*Quid nunc vobis faciendum est studiis militaribus apud iuventutem obsoletis, fortissimis autem hominibus ac summis ducibus partim aetate, partim civitatis discordiis ac rei publicae calamitate consumptis, cum tot bella aut a nobis necessario suscipiantur aut subito atque improvisa nascantur?*"

[39] Cic. *Font.* 43: "*scietis fuisse....praetorios homines, belli gerendi peritissimos.....non litteris homines ad rei militaris scientiam, sed rebus gestis ac victoriis eruditos.*"

[40] Cic. *Font.* 43: "*Quae si diligenter attendetis, profecto, iudices, virum ad labores belli impigrum, ad pericula fortem, ad usum ac disciplinam peritum, ad consilia prudentem, ad casum fortunamque felicem domi vobis ac liberis vestris retinere....*"

There is a parallel here, and throughout the speech, to the various idealised martial virtues that a top-notch Roman commander should possess, as espoused by Cicero during his 66 BC oration *Pro Lege Manilia* that supported Pompey's appointment to the Mithridatic command.[41] There is a marked difference, however, in that Pompey's achievements were well known unlike those of Fonteius, a fact that causes Cicero to pass over Fonteius' fighting record by such means as deliberate blurring, something that he hoped the jury would not pick up on.

The second Ciceronian speech to be analysed is the defence of Archias, a Syrian-born poet who was prosecuted in 62 BC over the illegal possession of Roman citizenship. The *Pro Archia*, above all, demonstrates the extent to which the promotion of Roman military achievements influenced criminal advocacy, since it provided Cicero with the means to defend a poet, someone who was not a *homo militaris*. The speech highlights in particular how a Roman orator could play on the poetical commemoration of Roman military history to woo the nostalgic patriotism of the jury. Berry, for instance, points out how Cicero in the *exordium* established "an atmosphere of culture and sophistication….in which the jury are flattered into fancying that they also belong".[42] Thus, Cicero was warmly preparing his audience for the upcoming literary citations that they believed they should know.

It is the military achievements of Archias' patron L. Licinius Lucullus, which Cicero above all employs, by highlighting the poet's role in their promotion:

> The Mithridatic War, a great and difficult undertaking pursued with many changes of fortune on land and sea, has been treated by Archias in its entirety. The books he wrote on it cast glory not only on the valiant and illustrious Lucius Lucullus, but also on the reputation of the Roman people.[43]

Cicero then continues to play on how the combined role of the Roman people under the command of Lucullus produced this success, attributing

---

[41] Cic. *Leg. Man.* 28-9.

[42] Cic. *Arch.* 3: "…I trust….that you will allow me, speaking as I am on behalf of an eminent poet and a most learned man and before the crowd of highly educated people, this civilized jury, and such a praetor as is now presiding, to speak rather more freely on cultural and literary matters….;" Berry 2004, 297-8.

[43] Cic. *Arch.* 21: "*Mithridaticum vero bellum, magnum atque difficile et in multa varietate terra marique versatum, totum ab hoc expressum est: qui libri non modo L. Lucullum, fortissimum et clarissimum virum, verum etiam populi Romani nomen inlustrant.*"

specific well-known victories to the citizen body, of which the jurors and
the whole court of course were members. For example he states:

> That astonishing naval battle off Tenedos, when Lucius Lucullus killed the
> enemy commanders and sank their fleet, will always be spoken of and
> proclaimed as ours: ours are the trophies, ours the monuments, ours the
> triumphs.[44]

Berry points out that Cicero is taking a liberty here, since according to the
second century AD Pontic historian Memnon, it was Lucullus' legate C.
Triarius who was responsible for the victory at Tenedos in 72 BC, not
Lucullus.[45] Cicero's claim, however, might simply be reflecting Archias'
poem, which like later Roman imperial literature and art probably
bestowed the honours on the senior commander at the expense of his more
active subordinates.[46] Cicero then concluded this section of the speech by
saying how "those who use their talents to write about such events serve
therefore to increase the fame of the Roman people."[47] Cicero here, by
pressing Archias' service on behalf of the Roman people, is pointing to
someone who, though his actual status was questionable, undoubtedly
deserved to be a Roman citizen.

Cicero adds further support to Archias' services to Rome by detailing
previous and current members of other *imperatores*' entourages,
individuals who had publicised their patrons' military deeds. These
included the poet and dramatist Ennius, who was believed to have
accompanied the consul Marcus Fulvius Nobilior during his Ambracian
campaign in the early second century BC, and there are also references to
the historian Theophanes of Mytilene, who had accompanied Pompey

---

[44] Cic. *Arch.* 21: "*Nostra semper feretur et praedicabitur L. Lucullo dimicante,
cum interfectis ducibus depressa hostium classis, et incredibilis apud Tenedum
pugna illa navalis: nostra sunt tropaea, nostra monimenta, nostri triumphi.*"

[45] *FGrH* 434 F29 (= Phot. *Bibl.* 224). Within the surviving part of the books that
Memnon wrote on the history of his city of Heraclea in Pontus, there is a long
digression on the rise of Rome (Berry 2004, 309).

[46] For example, Fronto *Ep.* 2.1, 2.3: the Emperor Lucius Verus was in nominal
command of the Roman military forces against Parthia in AD 162-6, and he
remained for the most part behind in Syria as Avidius Cassius and Statius Priscus
brought the war to a successful conclusion. Nonetheless, Verus saw the campaign
as a way of establishing a military reputation for himself back in Rome, and from
AD 163 onwards he wrote to Fronto asking his old tutor to write a history of the
war, which eulogised him.

[47] Cic. *Arch.* 21: "*Quae quorum ingeniis efferuntur, ab eis populi Romani fama
celebratur*".

during his Eastern wars; both of these men subsequently produced works commemorating their patrons.[48] Thus, Archias, as Berry says, "is firmly set within the serious, masculine, and Roman context of Roman warfare, rather than the frivolous and self-regarding world of Greek poetry."[49] Cicero was also creating a concept here of an established tradition of Roman martial publicists. For instance, he says that "ought we not greatly to prefer to leave behind us a representation of our designs and characters, moulded and finished by artists of the highest ability?"[50] And it is amongst this genre of artists that Cicero was placing Archias; in doing so he hoped to further persuade the jury of this poet's artistic and patriotic worth.

Finally, there is the case of Publius Sestius. Sestius had held the quaestorship in 63 BC and then the tribunate in 57, and it was during this later office that he became involved in the political street fighting that affected Rome that year.[51] As a consequence he was charged with *vis* (violence), the trial occurring in 56. During his defence of Sestius, Cicero primarily emphasised his own *auctoritas* as part of his various efforts to re-establish himself following his return from exile. He achieved this by creating for the jury and watching public, as May says, "a stunning manifesto of his political philosophy", including his famous analogy of being the helmsman of the ship of state.[52] Nonetheless, within one early digression in *Pro Sestio* Cicero promotes the martial *virtus* of his client. This is when he harks back to the Catilinarian Conspiracy and Sestius' role as quaestor in dealing with the rebellion outside Rome:

> Also, after that conspiracy had burst out from its hiding place in the darkness and was openly winging its way in arms, he [Sestius] went with an army to Capua, since we suspected that that city might be made the object of a sudden attack by that villainous band of rascals owing to the many advantages of its military situation. He drove headlong out of Capua Gaius Mevulanus, Antonius' military tribune, a desperate man, who had openly taken part in that conspiracy at Pisaurum and in other parts of the Gallic territory. He also saw to it that Gaius Marcellus was expelled from

---

[48] Cic. *Arch.* 24, 27; Cic. *Tusc.* 1.3 cites a speech of the Elder Cato in which the censor criticized Nobilior for taking Ennius to Aetolia. On Theophanes, see Strabo 13.2.3 and Plut. *Vit. Pomp.* 37, 42.

[49] Berry 2004, 308-9.

[50] Cic. *Arch.* 30: "...*consiliorum relinquere ac virtutum nostrarum effigiem nonne multo malle debemus, summis ingeniis expressam et politam?*"

[51] *MRR* 2.168, 202.

[52] Cic. *Sest.* 20, 45-6; May 1989, 90.

Capua, since he had not only come there, but had joined a large band of gladiators under the pretext of exercising himself in the use of arms.[53]

Capua was a major centre of gladiatorial schools and the place where the Spartacus revolt had started in 73 BC, and as a consequence Sestius' actions against Gaius Mevulanus and Gaius Marcellus would have seemed to the jury as an extremely laudable and sensible military operation.[54] In order to support the veracity of these statements Cicero cites a letter from the decurions of Capua (local senators) which detailed the services Sestius had given them and their public vote of thanks to him. The recognition and honouring of *virtus* was a central feature of Roman aristocratic society, and although the decurions of Capua might not be the Senate of Rome voting on *supplicationes*, nonetheless Cicero was still following the traditional Roman process of recounting and subsequently praising martial endeavour. He then takes this recollection one step further by asking Sestius' son to come forward:

> Read out, I beg you, O Lucius Sestius, what the decurions of Capua decreed, in order that your boyish voice may now give a hint to the enemies of your family what it seems likely to accomplish when it shall have grown stronger. [The decree of the decurions is read.]....I am reading out a record of danger undergone, a declaration of a most signal favour rendered, an expression of present gratitude, a testimony from a time that is past.[55]

By disclosing this positive information through the defendant's young son, Cicero was providing flesh and blood evidence to the jury of what Sestius would lose if they convicted him. Cicero here has combined the mechanism of filial pathos, something the prosecuted commander Servius

---

[53] Cic. *Sest.* 9: "*Idem, cum illa coniuratio ex latebris atque ex tenebris erupisset palamque armata volitaret, venit cum exercitu Capuam, quam urbem propter plurimas belli opportunitates ab illa impia et scelerata manu temptari suspicabamur; C. Mevulanum, tribunum militum Antoni, Capua praecipitem eiecit, hominem perditum et non obscure Pisauri et in aliis agri Gallici partibus in illa coniuratione versatum; idemque C. Marcellum, cum is non Capuam solum venisset, verum etiam se quasi armorum studio in maximam familiam coniecisset, exterminandum ex illa urbe curavit.*"

[54] Kaster 2006, 132-4; App. *BC* 1.116.

[55] Cic. *Sest.* 10: "*Recita, quaeso, L. Sesti, quid decrerint Capuae decuriones, ut iam puerilis tua vox possit aliquid significare inimicis vestris, quidnam, cum se conroborarit, effectura esse videatur....recito memoriam perfuncti periculi, praedicationem amplissimi benefici, vocem offici praesentis, testimonium praeteriti temporis.*"

Sulpicius Galba had exploited in 149 BC through the display of his children in court, together with the detailing of the defendant's military record, thus producing a powerful means of persuasion.[56] Although this is only a precursory digression within a much more complex speech, it nonetheless illustrates the lengths an orator would go to in order to create a martial ethos for his client, and thus demonstrates his belief in its persuasive value before the court.

Overall, within the extant speeches of Cicero and earlier orations there is a repeated and diverse employment of the military record as a means of creating images of dutiful, brave and unselfish Roman magistrates for the various juries. During his defence of Gnaeus Plancius in 54 BC on a charge of *ambitus*, Cicero even plays on this practice, pointing towards the expectation of the jury that they would receive such information: "You ask what active service he has seen (*rogas, quae castra viderit*)".[57] In achieving this end, Cicero utilised all sorts of rhetorical mechanisms and tactics to ensure that his audience accepted his positive characterisations of these *homines militares*. These included both the blurring and detailing of specific engagements as well as the exploitation of the presence in court of distinguished ex-commanders. Furthermore, as demonstrated by the fragmented and indirect evidence of the pre-Ciceronian period, the digression on military endeavour was a recurring practice. If we consider the extensive and varied nature by which Cicero in his surviving orations over 25 years followed this practice, I believe it was an oratorical means that was frequently employed throughout the middle and late Republic to counter the numerous prosecutions that ex-magistrates and others faced in this period.

To conclude, the question of why the military record was employed in the ways we have seen needs addressing. First of all, it was a product of the innate militarism of Roman Republican society, in which martial *virtus* was highly valued, particularly amongst the Roman aristocracy, as argued by scholars like Harris and Wiseman.[58] Thus, in the case of Sestius, a magistrate who had had few opportunities of displaying such *virtus*, Cicero still found a small, yet convincing example of military service that his client had performed during the Catilinarian revolt.[59]

Secondly, the employment of the military record through these digressions frequently arose in response to the preceding prosecution

---

[56] Livy *Per.* 49.
[57] Cic. *Planc.* 61.
[58] Harris 1979, 10-41; Wiseman 1985, 3-19.
[59] Cic. *Sest.* 12. In addition to his swift actions at Capua, Cicero also emphasises Sestius' presence in the army that finally defeated Catiline near Pistoria in 62 BC.

speeches, especially those which denigrated the behaviour and achievements of governors and military leaders such as Fonteius and Murena. For example, when defending Murena Cicero tells how the younger Cato, one of the prosecutors, asserted that "the whole of that war against Mithridates was only fought against a load of little women".[60] Cato here, by feminizing the enemy whom the defendant had fought, was debasing Murena's most distinguished claims of *virtus*. This, alongside other similar criticisms, was what caused Cicero to promote the credibility of Murena's eastern endeavours, and this included his promotion of Lucullus's official dispatches to Rome, in which Murena's actions were positively cited.[61]

Finally, this type of digression was a result of the nature, frequency, and location of where military achievements were publicised in Rome. The middle and late Republic saw considerable and frequent dissemination of martial success via dispatches and speeches often within the Forum, the very environment in which these defence speeches were being delivered.[62] Hence, the forensic references to military engagements and endeavours were playing on established Roman communication practices, customs which many of the jurors themselves had undoubtedly experienced. That is why in the *Pro Archia* we have the rhetoric about the Roman naval victory over Mithridates: "That astonishing naval battle off Tenedos when Lucius Lucullus killed the enemy commanders and sank their fleet, will always be spoken of and proclaimed as ours: ours are the trophies, ours the monuments, ours the triumphs."[63] Just as in the dispatches and speeches, individual successes and achievements were again being promoted on behalf of the Roman people.

---

[60] Cic. *Mur.* 31: "*...bellum illud omne Mithridaticum cum mulierculis esse gestum.*"

[61] Cic. *Mur.* 20.

[62] For example, Livy, 27.50 tells how, following the defeat of Hasdrubal at the river Metaurus in 207 BC, the consuls' victorious dispatches were read out in a *contio* very possibly held in the Forum; Livy, 45.1 likewise tells of Paullus' victorious Pydna dispatch being disseminated in 168.

[63] Cic. *Arch.* 21: "*Nostra semper feretur et praedicabitur L. Lucullo dimicante, cum interfectis ducibus depressa hostium classis, et incredibilis apud Tenedum pugna illa navalis: nostra sunt tropaea, nostra monimenta, nostri triumphi.*" Cf. note 45.

Bibliography

Astin, A. E. *Cato the Censor*. Oxford: Clarendon Press, 1978.

Berry, D. H. *Cicero. Defence Speeches*. Oxford: Oxford University Press, 2000.

——. "Literature and Persuasion in Cicero's *Pro Archia*." In *Cicero the Advocate*, edited by J. G. F. Powell and J. J. Paterson, 293-311. Oxford, Oxford University Press, 2004.

Brunt, P. A. and Moore, J. M. *Res Gestae Divi Augusti: the Achievement of the Divine Augustus*. Oxford: Oxford University Press, 1967.

Canter, H. V. "*Digressio* in the orations of Cicero" *AJP* 52 (1931): 351-61.

Cloud, D. "The Constitution and Public Criminal Law." In *CAH IX²* (1994): 491-530.

Cornell, T. J. *The Beginnings of Rome—Italy and Rome from the Bronze Age to the Punic Wars (c. 1000 — 264 BC)*. London and New York: Routledge, 1995.

Evans, R. J. "Displaying Honourable Scars: a Roman gimmick." *Acta Classica* 42 (1999): 77-94.

Harris, W. V. *War and Imperialism in Republican Rome 327-70 BC*. Oxford: Clarendon Press, 1979.

Kaster, R. A. (ed.) *Cicero: Speech on behalf of Publius Sestius* Oxford: Oxford University Press, 2006.

Leigh, M. "Wounding and popular rhetoric at Rome." *BICS* 40 (1995): 195-212.

Lintott, A. *The Constitution of the Roman Republic* Oxford: Clarendon, 1999.

——. "Legal Procedure in Cicero's Time" in *Cicero the Advocate*, edited by J. G. F. Powell and J. J. Paterson, 61-78. Oxford: Oxford University Press, 2004.

May, J. M. *Trials of Character: The Eloquence of Ciceronian Ethos*. Chapel Hill (North Carolina) and London: University of North Carolina, 1988.

Nicolet, C. *The World of the Citizen in Republican Rome*, translated by P. S. Falla London: Batsford, 1980.

Powell, J. G. F. and Paterson, J. J. "Introduction." In *Cicero the Advocate*, edited by J. G. F. Powell and J. J. Paterson, 1-57. Oxford: Oxford University Press, 1-57, 2004.

Stockton, D. *The Gracchi*. Oxford: Clarendon, 1979.

Vasaly, A. "Cicero's early speeches" in *Brill's Companion to Cicero: Oratory and Rhetoric,* edited by J. M. May, 71-111. Leiden: Brill, 2002.

Wiseman, T. P. "Competition and Co-operation" in *Roman Political Life
     90 BC-AD 69*, edited by T. P.Wiseman, 3-19. Exeter: Exeter
     University Press, 1985.
Tony Blair's speech to the Labour party conference at Brighton on
     October 2nd 2001, Guardian Unlimited
     http://politics.guardian.co.uk/labour2001/story/0,1414,562006,00.html

CHAPTER TWO

EMPERORS, SIEGES, AND INTENTIONAL EXPOSURE

JOSH LEVITHAN[1]

Roman emperors ruled at the sufferance of the army. Distance and discipline protected them from their troops, but the best policy was to make sure that the army loved their *imperator*, and felt loved in return. Augustus realized this, and not only donned an eagle-recovering breastplate, but personally funded the world's first large-scale pension fund in order to support his troops. The unmilitary Claudius obtained the purple by means of the Praetorian Guard's loyalty to his family, and he depicted his welcome to their barracks on one of his first coin issues. Hadrian toured the empire constantly, speaking to hundreds of army units. Emperors paid larger and larger donatives, until Septimius Severus could advise, realistically enough, "enrich the soldiers and despise the rest."

To ensure the loyalty of the troops, the emperor and his family lurked in every military camp: on coins, on the *imagines* that were carried into battle, in many of the religious observances on the official calendar. But the camps were far-flung: any major campaign was an opportunity to be seen by thousands of soldiers at once. The emperor had the rare chance to act as an actual *imperator*, a commander-in-chief in the flesh as well as ideological principle. Therefore, the presence of the emperor on a major campaign was, after the Julio-Claudian period, *de rigeur*. Once he was with the troops, monopolizing the glory of the campaign and bidding for their affections, he was faced with a decision: how much of the campaign would he share? Would he risk the safety of his own person in order to demonstrate solidarity with his troops and inspire them to greater efforts?

Two generalizations on warfare and society narrow the range of possibilities: First, soldiers everywhere prefer to see their leaders sharing

---

[1] I would like to thank Professor John Matthews for his advice on earlier versions of this paper.

some of the hardships and dangers of war, and they will fight more
enthusiastically and effectively if they do. Nearly every society connects
social and military prestige, and people have traditionally preferred their
ruler or foremost leaders to possess—or seem to possess—some measure
of military accomplishment.[2] Second, no complex society can long survive
if its leaders habitually participate in the most dangerous phases of
combat.

There were efforts to avoid this political-military conundrum. The
innovation of the centurionate as a prestigious, career-tracked officer class
helped: the centurions were personally connected to the emperor, at least
in theory, and took his place at the head of his soldiers, accepting the risks
that a supreme commander could not. Augustus and Tiberius dared to step
away from a personal role, staying at Rome and rarely appearing before
their armies. This was a striking achievement given the near-constant
campaigning of Caesar and many of his warlord predecessors, but it did
not survive even a hint of dynastic strife. Despite the enormous efforts to
impose the emperor's presence on his far-flung legions, it was again by the
end of the first century the normal practice for an emperor to accompany
his army on major campaigns. The questioned remained: when the fighting
started, where should the emperor stand?

----

[2] Harris 1979 and Rosenstein 1990 are among the most important discussions of
the role that military prestige played in the aristocratic politics of the Roman
Republic. For the empire, the most important work is Campbell 1984. Some of the
best examples of Roman leaders sharing the hardships of war will be discussed
below. An excellent source for the feelings of a traditional long-service
infantryman toward his officers is the memoir of "Frank Richards" 1933, 185, 204.
Richards praises the voluntary heroics of Siegfried Sassoon, arguing that he should
have been awarded the VC for personally leading trench raids. "It would have done
your eyes good to have seen young Sassoon in that bombing stunt." Another
officer, called only "The Peer," loses his status as one of the book's villains after
ostentatiously declining to take shelter during a bombardment: "He showed he had
guts and went up twenty holes in my estimation." For a recent invocation of the
moral effect of the personal appearance of senior officers on the battlefield, see
Howard 1997, 118.

Actual military accomplishment in the leader of a modern democracy is rare,
although Britain and the U.S. have put Wellingtons and Eisenhowers in power, to
say nothing of pre-war failures such as Grant. Yet even though kings and
presidents are not today engaged in military activity, they, as well as other
members of their families and of the ruling classes, have sought to *seem* military,
often through dress. Appropriations of military costume by rulers range widely,
from Castro's fatigues to the uniforms worn by royals, the bemedalled chests of
various dictators, and even to the political display of helmets and naval flightsuits.

A. K. Goldsworthy's examination of the positioning of commanders during battles found three possibilities: leading from the front, observing from well behind, and moving amidst the troops but behind the closely-engaged fighters. This last option had the most to recommend it and was the normal practice of Caesar, among others, although some (e.g. Agricola) usually kept to the rear.[3]

But the emperor was no ordinary general, and both the reality of imperial administration and the evolving ideology of empire separated him from the traditional model of the aristocratic commander. Even though Caesar only once in all his campaigns as commander in chief found it necessary to pick up a shield and enter the fray,[4] this was not a risk that most reigning emperors would ever choose to run. It is difficult to imagine Hadrian or Marcus Aurelius in such a position; behind the front lines, surrounded by a horse guard and various servants, friends, and handlers, emperors were usually only endangered by catastrophic routs.[5]

I wish, however, to focus here on sieges, and sieges are very different from battles, for three reasons in particular. First, a siege is a much more controlled situation. The enemy is contained and accounted for: sorties can only come from a few points, and any danger can be quickly perceived and countered.[6]

Second, tactical developments were generally linear, and events unfolded much more slowly than in an open field battle. Therefore, the close proximity of the commander to his troops was not essential. It is useful to adopt here the distinction between generalship, namely tactical control, and leadership. Siege warfare required little on-the-spot generalship: after an initial reconnoiter, sieges became matters for engineers and artillery specialists. If an assault took place, its objective was obvious and the most important preparation was the stimulation of reckless aggression in the assault troops. For both reasons—the lack of

---

[3] Goldsworthy 1996, 149-63.

[4] Or perhaps twice: Caes. *B Gall.* 2.25; App. *B Civ.* 2.104.

[5] I am grateful to Brian Campbell for the reminder that later emperors did occasionally fight in battle, including Maximinus, who used this evidence of personal valor as one argument for the overthrowing of Alexander Severus. See SHA *Max.* 12. As with Julian (see below), such behavior was considered rash. Indeed, the author of the biography in the *Historia Augusta* considers it un-Roman, commenting that Maximinus, "*habuit enim hoc barbaricae temeritatis, ut putaret imperatorem manum etiam sua semper debere*—for he had that barbaric rashness that made him think that even the emperor always owed the help of his own hand."

[6] Of recent monographs on Roman warfare only Gilliver 1999 treats siege warfare as a separate entity. My dissertation (Yale, 2007) addresses the linear, progressive, and static aspects of siege warfare.

demand for quick operational decisions and the paramount importance of morale—leadership was far more important than generalship.

Third, sieges provided unequalled visibility: the enemy did not move, there were many vantage points, and much less dust was kicked up. Josephus describes an assault on Jerusalem as "like a battle on the stage; nothing throughout the engagement escaped the eyes of Titus or of those around him."[7] A large portion of the army was always arrayed before the city, guarding against sallies, and if an emperor chose to interpose himself between his men and their objective, many, even most, could observe what transpired.

The siege, then, provided an opportunity for the emperor to appear as a leader, in a controlled situation, and in full view of his army. Emperors were often on display during sieges. This paper will argue that they sometimes went a step further, seeking to emphasize their leadership and their solidarity with the army by exposing themselves to enemy fire. There is a remarkable number of incidents in the literary sources in which an emperor or other royal personage strays close enough to a city wall to be hit, or nearly hit, with a missile. Too many, it would seem, to demand the conclusion that this exposure was accidental. Rather, these were demonstrations to the troops of a shared risk.

Unlike the potential chaos of a battle, the danger posed by missile fire in a siege situation was relatively slight: hits on the emperor himself—compared to the area of armor, clothing, horse, and his suite of attendants—were unlikely, and if a proper distance was observed, nearly spent missiles might wound slightly but could hardly kill. Just as in the carefully controlled appearances of modern politicians, an emperor's handlers could minimize surprises and be reasonably certain of his security, while appealing directly to the most important constituency.

The risk was acceptable, I think, because the reward was very great: the fact that the emperor had been physically involved (and physically endangered) was worth a good deal to the morale of his troops. Getting shot at was terrific public relations: if the army had been grumbling, it made the point that their leader was with them, and if they already loved him, it provoked them to stoke their aggression to the point where an assault on fortifications might succeed.[8]

There is no overt statement in the sources as to the intentional exposure of an emperor for purposes of morale or political theater. Rather, it is the

---

[7] Joseph. *BJ* 6.146.
[8] Loitering at extreme missile range involves minimal-yet-appreciable-danger, seems like a warlike deed but in practice is not, and makes for a great visual—much like landing on the deck of an aircraft carrier in order to give a short speech.

accumulation of "near-misses" within the overlapping contexts of imperial leadership and siege warfare that will make the case. The concluding part of this paper will examine the evidence for the exposure of the Roman and Persian emperors to missile fire, especially in Ammianus Marcellinus. Before turning to the examples, however, we must consider the ways in which the practice of military leadership and the staging of siege warfare made this behavior both worthwhile and reasonably practical.

First, the practice of combat leadership. Roman emperors could choose between the Greek-rationalist model of a general as commander, who rarely acted as a leader other than to exhort his men, and the Roman emphasis on personal heroism, remembering the ancient practice of taking the *spolia opima* from the opposing commander after victorious single combat. There was, of course, a broad middle ground, and there were several already-established patterns.

Alexander was the quintessential heroic leader, habitually leading his army from the very front and collecting at least four missile wounds, at the siege of Gaza and in India. Alexander's exploits bothered many Roman commanders, including Caesar, and they influenced Julian in both his invasion of Persia and the manner in which he fought. Julian's desire for personal involvement in combat led eventually to his fatal wounding during a skirmish with Persian forces.[9]

Roman heroes in a similar mode were legion. Livy repeatedly gives his heroes un-ironic speeches about actions being louder than words. Valerius Corvinus exhorts his men "to follow my deeds not my words, and to look to me not only for the word at command but also for example." We also read of Caeso Fabius telling his brother that "it is our duty as leaders... to raise the morale of our men rather by fighting than by speaking." These and many other semi-legendary Republican generals fought in the front line.[10]

While Livy was telling exemplary stories and relating tall tales from the murky past, Rosenstein and Harris, among others, have demonstrated the real importance of valor for Republican aristocrats. Marius, who like Livy's Corvinus was facing an especially intimidating enemy (Gauls rather than Samnites) and needed to make a statement to raise the morale

---

[9] Caesar: Plut. *Vit. Caes.* 11; Suet. *Iul.* 7. For *imitatio Alexandri* among Roman emperors, see Campbell 1984, 391-2. Gaius (Suet. *Calig.* 52), Caracalla (Cass. Dio 78.1.1), Alexander Severus (Cass. Dio 75.13.2), and even Augustus himself (Suet. *Aug.* 18) all either visited Alexander's tomb or wore equipment attributed to him. Julian: Matthews 1989, 137-8.

[10] Corvinus: Livy 7.32.5; Caeso: Livy 2.46: *ut... pugnando potius quam adhortando accendamus militum animos.*

of his men, fought in the front lines at Aquae Sextiae—but he was the last to do so. Roman soldiers continued to witness heroic leadership in the old style as it was practiced by Germans and Gauls. Hirtius, for instance, notes the element of display in the exemplary leadership of the chieftain Correus, and Tacitus describes German war-leaders as chosen *ex virtute*, as a reward for fighting aggressively and conspicuously in front of the main battle line.[11]

Writers in Greek, however, commenting upon military leadership for the benefit of a Roman audience, were generally more interested in generalship than leadership. They insisted, with arguments eminently logical, yet somewhat incomplete, that supreme commanders should take no part in actual fighting.

Polybius is scathing in his account of the consul Claudius Marcellus, who died in an ambush sprung when he went forward to reconnoiter an enemy camp. To take risks in minor operations Polybius considered a mark of gross incompetence, and, tellingly, he thought it a very basic principle that "the commanders-in-chief should not expose themselves to danger until a large number of their company have fallen."[12] Plutarch passes along a colorful anecdote from the bitter war between Sertorius and Metellus in Spain: when Sertorius, fed up with a grinding campaign, challenges Metellus to single combat, Metellus is man enough to flatly refuse without blemish to his reputation. Plutarch approves of Metellus, citing Theophrastus for the opinion that "a general should die like a general, and not a common targeteer."[13] Onasander, the author of a first century AD handbook on generalship, insists that the commander should never enter a hand-to-hand fight, and rather pedantically asserts that the general should be satisfied with "the honor of his intellectual successes."[14] Josephus, a client-propagandist prone to flattery and exaggeration of Flavian derring-do, depicts Titus as constantly in the thick of the fighting around Jerusalem, slaying many men with his own hand. Yet he does not dare assert that Titus personally led an assault on the walls—an obvious untruth—and contents himself by crediting Titus with that heroic instinct, claiming that his friends had to hold him back and convince him not to "act the part of a common soldier."[15] At the far end of the Graeco-Roman world, Procopius echoes Polybius in scolding Belisarius for "fighting in

---

[11] Caes. *B Gall.* 8.18: Correus shows himself—*se ostendit*. See also Tac. *Germ.* 7: *ex virtute. si prompti, si conspicui, si ante aciem agant.*

[12] Polyb. 10.32.1-7.

[13] Plut. *Vit. Sert.* 13.

[14] Onasander 13.

[15] Joseph. *BJ* 6.88.

the front ranks like a soldier" and thus risking the whole cause for little benefit.[16]

Heroism aside, Roman culture still demanded that leaders be worthy, courageous men—men of *virtus*. The best way to demonstrate *virtus* as a senior commander was to point to valorous youthful deeds.[17] But most children of the imperial family did not wage their own wars, and they—or those who were managing their reputation—settled for ersatz combat leadership: Nero's introduction into public life, for instance, involved leading the praetorians in a sort of march or drill, "shield in hand." Suetonius preserves reminders that both Tiberius and Claudius descended from men who had proved themselves in single combat—Tiberius did have considerable military experience, but not of personal combat, and he still apparently needed to draw on his ancestors for the *virtus*-cachet of actually having killed.[18]

In addition to proving their manhood, the emperors strove to show a closeness with the troops that had also, in reality, evaporated with the end of active command. Augustus and Tiberius partially made up for their absence from the battlefield by falling back on a more rhetorical identification with their "fellow soldiers." This term, *commilitiones*, seems to have subsequently fallen out of fashion, as Caligula—his very nickname deriving from close association with the troops—and Claudius made ridiculous appearances with their armies in Germany and Britain. During the tumultuous year 69, "fellow soldiers" were everywhere as various generals made a bid for the loyalty of the armies in the post-Julio-Claudian

---

[16] Procop. *Goth.* 5.18.4.

[17] The great warlords had all served as subordinate commanders in their youth. Marius was said to have distinguished himself at Numantia (Plut. *Vit. Mar.* 3), drawing the eye of Scipio Africanus; Pompey killed the opposing commander in a cavalry engagement while he was still a teenager (Plut. *Vit. Pomp.* 7), and Caesar received the *corona civica* at the storming of Mytilene (Suet. *Iul.* 2). On *virtus* in Roman culture see McDonnell 2006.

As for the emperors, Josephus' many breathless accounts of the dashing heroism of the young Titus are exceptional, but Suetonius (*Tit.* 5) picks up a more restrained tradition of his prowess—perhaps equally unlikely—as an archer, claiming that he killed twelve of the defenders of Jerusalem with twelve arrows.

[18] The animal-slaughtering proficiency which certain "bad emperors" liked to demonstrate should be considered a warped version of the same desire for ersatz prowess.

world. Yet by the end of the century words were not enough, and once again the emperors felt the need to join their army on major campaigns.[19]

The absence of a claim to the aggressive *virtus* which traditionally justified military command was not among the emperors' most important problems. It would be overstating the case to make it appear as if every emperor was wracked by doubts over how to act around his troops, or to deny that the emperor functioned more in the style of a late-Republican senator than that of a war-band chieftain. Nor was comportment on campaign or on the battlefield a particularly thorny problem. The privilege of autocracy had long since established that the emperor, unlike a senator or a chieftain, could order men into battle without himself following. He steered clear of the hazards of battle, and there was a settled understanding of what comprised good leadership in camp and on the march.

The well-regarded emperor set an example of physical endurance. Marius and Caesar were the classic exemplars of toughness and austerity, and Tiberius followed in sharing the hardships of his men.[20] Trajan and Hadrian both deliberately dismounted to lead their men on the march. Indifference to weather was a point of emphasis, and Septimius Severus won respect for marching bareheaded in the snow. Several writers indicate the importance of such examples as a supplement to the harsher motivations of army discipline. Of Severus, Herodian writes that he "set his men an example of determination and bravery. In this way he made them persevere during a difficult march not just by fear of breaking regulations, but by encouraging them to imitate their emperor."[21] This explanation goes to the egalitarian roots of the culture, however attenuated in the professional army of an imperial state—Roman soldiers do not like to be compelled to work while their commander stands idle. Marius did an ordinary soldier's share of labor because he believed, anticipating the anthropological discovery of the "shame culture," that it embarrassed his men, goading them more effectively than the fear of punishment.[22]

---

[19] In the third century and after, of course, personal military leadership became a necessity, and the entire focus of the imperial office shifted away from Rome and toward the provincial armies.

[20] Marius: Plut. *Vit. Mar.* 7.4-5; Caesar: Suet. *Iul.* 57; Tiberius: Vell. Pat. 2.104.

[21] Hadrian: Cass. Dio 69.9; Trajan: Cass. Dio 68.23; Septimius Severus: Hdn. 3.6.10. (ζ•λος for encourage, προθυμ•α and •νδρε•α for determination and bravery).

[22] Marius: Sall. *Iug.* 100: *pudore magis quam malo exercitum coercebat.* Onasander 42.2, speaking to the role of the commanding general rather than that of the emperor specifically, also recommends exemplary labor, since "shame breeds eagerness, and the feeling of slavery is replaced by the feeling of common purpose." See also Julian. *Or.* 2.88A.

The personal touch was also important. Marius and Caesar again set the pattern, seeing to everything in person, and being seen. When his men were intimidated by Moorish cavalry, Caesar displayed confidence, demonstrating "his energy and remarkable cheerfulness... high and buoyant morale." Onasander writes that "the duty of the general is to ride by the ranks on horseback, show himself to those in danger, praise the brave, threaten the cowardly, and encourage the lazy."[23]

This sort of leadership was part and parcel of the imperial presence on campaign. Encouragement, in the form of speeches at reviews and pre-battle exhortations, was easily accomplished. Yet riding around on or near the battlefield was at least potentially dangerous, and if danger loomed, a demonstration of imperturbability was essential. Even Onasander, who castigates generals who see value in coming to close quarters with the enemy, agrees that "the general must show himself brave before the army, that he may call forth the zeal of his soldiers." The idea of intentionally seeking danger in order to quietly show off a cool demeanor seems odd, but it is essential to the psychological tool kit of good leaders, and its usefulness has been recognized time and again. Plutarch, for instance, comments on Demetrius' change in demeanor from garrulous to quiet, and Suetonius tells us that Octavian had to be awoken in his tent to attend a battle, so soundly was he sleeping—a crib from the theatrics of Alexander the Great, a master at manipulating morale.[24]

---

[23] Moors: Caes. *B Afr.* 10: *vigore mirabilique hilaritate; animum enim altum et erectum.* Onasander 33.6.

[24] Suet. *Aug.* 16; Plut. *Vit. Dem.* 28.3. Reaching beyond the Greco-Roman world, it may be useful to note that eighteenth and nineteenth century European armies made a fetish of standing still under fire in order to intimidate by showing their confidence; but they carried this well beyond the bounds of reason. In the 20th century, though much changed by the greater firepower of the so-called "empty battlefield," exposure was still seen as a morally impressive act. To add to the examples given in note 1, the most notable feat of leadership performed by the commander of the Gloucesters during their extraordinary holding action on the Imjin river in the Korean War was his "seeming disregard for his own safety" as he walked among their firing positions smoking a pipe with a rifle slung over his back. A 1983 study of U.S combat veterans found that leaders who were judged by their men to be effective took more personally endangering acts than those judged to be ineffective (Frost *et al.*1983). Other studies of American (WWII) and Israeli (1967—in which almost half of all fatalities were officers) soldiers note that the death of so many commanders "had a salutary effect on the morale of the troops," and Israeli soldiers agreed that the most impressive attribute of command leadership was "cool performance" (Ben Ari 1998, 45).

It was especially important for the general or emperor to be visible. The sources provide numerous examples of commanders either wearing highly visible helmets or forsaking headgear entirely in order to be recognizable. Similarly, Caesar is recognized by his cloak, Lucullus by his armor, and Sulla and Belisarius by their white horses. By being recognizable these generals could display their coolness under fire. Should they draw more concerted attacks because they were also recognized by the enemy, this would only enhance their image.

A second basic consideration is the specific relevance of siege warfare to acts of leadership.[25] Siege warfare was demanding: a deadly assault on prepared positions was preceded by weeks, even months of navvying under distant or indirect missile fire. Such activity, more similar to twentieth century warfare than other types of ancient combat, is more psychologically draining than battle, which resolves quickly.[26]

A siege also differed from a battle in that it generally came later in the course of events. A besieged enemy was already defeated, either operationally (they had lost a battle) or morally (they were too unconfident to "come out and fight.") Whatever the extent to which Roman battles were "agonal," sieges were in no way fair or morally instructive events. The besieging army was forced to prolonged labor merely to come to grips with their enemy. There was a punitive character to siege warfare, rooted in the refusal of the defenders to fight without fortifications or concede defeat, and played out in the extreme violence of the sack.

These factors were a drain on morale, and thus a major reason why an emperor might be tempted to make an extraordinary display of leadership before an army arrayed against a city. Not only were extreme demands being made on his men's morale, but no enemy was challenging or offering battle. There might well be a need to concretize the motivation to assault. An attack on the person of the emperor could serve: it was a

---

[25] On sieges in general see Gilliver 1999, 127-160; Goldsworthy 1999, Ziolkowski 1993, Price 1992.

[26] Grinker and Spiegel 1943, identified the psychological difficulties of prolonged, episodic combat; Lord Moran (1945) conceived of a pseudo-medical understanding of courage as a store of moral capital that was inevitably expended by prolonged combat. In addition to the short duration of ancient battle, there was the unanimity of action and the fact that trust could be placed in prowess, since the greatest fears centered on direct conflict with an opponent. Sieges involved passivity, the chance of receiving long-distance wounds from an anonymous opponent, without being able to respond. See also Holmes 1985, 138-140, 216: "Sieges, too... seemed to bruise men's tolerance more than battles in open field." Van Wees 2004, 144: "Sieges were the most demanding form of warfare known to the Greeks."

demonstration that the emperor shared at least some of the danger, and it might qualify as an outrage that demanded vengeance. Given the visibility and theatrical potential of appearing before the walls of a besieged city (see p. 28 above), there was much to be gained from exposing the imperial body to missile fire. Getting shot at, it seems, was a fairly common leadership technique.

The first example[27] concerns Vespasian, shot in the foot during the siege of Jotapata (AD 67).[28] Josephus, of course, is not to be trusted when he writes about the brave deeds of the Flavians, and he is an inveterate exaggerator.[29] Yet the specificity of the incident—the sole of the foot, a spent missile, a minor wound—argues for the historicity of the event. Josephus, even later in the Jewish War, when he had switched sides and accompanied Titus, relied on the details of military notes and reports. For this event, well before his defection, he must have used either such a report or the testimony of a Roman officer. The most plausible aspect of the situation is that Vespasian stood at a prudent range, far enough from the defenders that the missile was nearly spent. The reaction of the soldiers may be exaggerated, but it too is believable: Vespasian was very popular—he would shortly be acclaimed emperor by the legions in Egypt—and when he was wounded, his men took it personally. Anger and vengeance become the moral fuel for a difficult assault.

The second example, the wounding of Agrippa II at Gamala, shows consistency in Josephus: again a very specific wounding, again an immediate, angry increase in combat motivation.[30] That the victim is a minor royal and not a member of the Flavian house should support the case that Josephus is not fabricating these very visible events, but merely amplifying them for the sake of propaganda.[31]

Curiously, since Josephus is at great pains to make Titus the dashing, Alexander-like hero of the siege of Jerusalem, he makes no mention of a

---

[27] See the appendix for the complete range of examples.

[28] Joseph. *BJ* 3.236-9. There is a status dissonance between event and text, of course: historically, Vespasian is a mere general and Josephus a Jewish resister, but by the time of writing, one was emperor and the other his client and professional apologist.

[29] Yavetz 1975.

[30] Joseph. *BJ* 4.14-16.

[31] That Roman soldiers—subjected to much worse during the siege operations—should consider a minor wound to a client king to be "savagery" is not really credible. The wound was most likely well-earned during an attempt to negotiate with the defenders, just as Josephus was wounded in the act of propagandizing at Jerusalem, and not during fighting.

wound that is reported by Cassius Dio.[32] Dio thinks it quite serious: the stone, evidently fired from one of the powerful mural engines possessed by the defenders (they had captured the artillery complement of an entire legion earlier in the war), causes permanent damage to Titus' shoulder. Josephus reports several unlikely heroic escapades[33] in which Titus gallops among Jewish fighters—so why fail to place him more plausibly in harm's way? It is possible that Josephus suppresses the wounding because it took place during one of these skirmishes before the walls: they were not, after all, crucial elements of the siege process, and to gallop heedlessly into the range of mural artillery during a cavalry fight was recklessness. Such rash behavior—*temeritas* overtopping *virtus*—was inappropriate in an imperial princeling in command of several legions. It involved a risk that, unlike the pre-assault wound to Vespasian, could not be quickly transmuted into a source of motivation for the troops. Surely, Josephus would have reported the same event and emphasized the same link if Titus, hero of his story and supreme commander in the Roman east, had been wounded during an assault phase of the long siege.[34] In any case, Josephus' use of two minor woundings as sources of combat motivation for the assault troops demonstrates the culture of leadership and morale that made deliberate exposure a useful leadership technique.

Cassius Dio provides two proper examples of the phenomenon at two different sieges of the Mesopotamian city of Hatra. Trajan, in 117, is shot at as he rides near the walls—a near miss, but a cavalryman among his guard is killed. Septimius Severus, between 198 and 200, is nearly killed by mural artillery, and several of the shield-bearing soldiers protecting him are hit.[35] Although each account is brief, Dio makes clear that these incidents occurred early in the siege, before heavy engineering had begun, when a quick victory was still possible. At that stage of operations—when the relative morale of the opposed forces was still being deliberately tested in preparation for a general assault—emperors could most profitably raise

---

[32] Cass. Dio 65.5.1. See also the close call reported by Suet. *Tit.* 4 that goes unremarked upon by Josephus. See also Jones 1992.

[33] Joseph. *BJ* 5.60ff, 5.88ff. Again, I accuse Josephus of exaggeration, of the danger and distance as well as of the number of enemies and Titus' combat role, rather than of outright falsification of events.

[34] Another, and somewhat more Greek, explanation for the omission is that Josephus may see this as damaging to his repeated assertion that Titus is divinely sanctioned, protected by a powerful personal τ•χη; it would be strange for fortune's darling to be needlessly wounded by a far-off siege engine. See especially Joseph. *BJ* 5.60ff.

[35] Cass. Dio 68.31.3; 76.11.3.

the morale of their men by personal appeal.[36] Dio does not inform us whether the troops reacted with anger and aggression. He does tell us, however, that the Severan siege of Hatra was part of a bungled campaign in which large numbers of troops mutinied or refused to storm the city. It is possible, then, that Severus put himself in harm's way in a more-or-less desperate attempt to inspire an assault from his unwilling troops.[37]

The wounding of Gallienus during a Gallic campaign of 263 can contribute little, unfortunately, to our understanding of the behavior under scrutiny.[38] The brief account in the notoriously unreliable *Historia Augusta* gives no details, other than that an arrow fired from the city under siege caused the wound.

Ammianus Marcellinus, the great historian of the Late Empire, is by far the most important source for our phenomenon. The dramatic narrative of the siege of Amida in 359—at which Ammianus was present as a Roman officer and from which he was able to escape only at the eleventh hour—differs from our previous examples in two important ways. First, this is a Persian siege and a Persian emperor, the city defended by Romans. Second, the long fourth century campaigns between Rome and Persia were waged in a formalized—if not quite "limited" or "agonal"—atmosphere: heralds galloped about, lenient terms of surrender were offered to beleaguered border cities, and both sides indulged in military pageantry.

Sapor approached Amida at the beginning of the summer, hoping for a quick victory to begin his campaign. He intended to overawe the garrison with his huge army, inducing them to capitulate.[39] But the defenders of Amida cut off the first attempt at negotiation by firing a few hopeful missiles in the direction of Sapor's suite. One such projectile tore the cloak of the king of kings himself:

---

[36] The fourth chapter of my dissertation (Yale, 2007) lays out a typology of siege warfare. I demonstrate therein that Roman generals never proceeded with heavy engineering (a siege mound, towers, mines) unless the strength of the site and a relative deficit in morale precluded the quicker expedient of a general assault.

[37] There is a debate, between Speidel 1984 and Kennedy 1986, about the identity and role of certain "Europaean" troops at Hatra which bears indirectly on the issue.

[38] SHA *The Two Gallieni* 4.3.

[39] Intimidation of a garrison suspected to be morally fragile was, of course, common practice in ancient siege warfare, especially at the beginning of campaigns. The imperial frame of mind, though, is presented as slightly irrational: Ammianus informs us that a Roman defector and Sapor's generals urged that the city be bypassed, but the king insisted.

*Portis obequitabat, comitante cohorte regali, qui dum se prope
confidentius inserit, ut etiam vultus eius possit aperte cognosci, sagittis
missilibusque ceteris, ob decora petitus insignia, corruisset, ni pulvere
iaculantium adimente conspectum parte indumenti tragulae ictu discissa,
editurus postea strages innumeras evasisset. Hinc quasi in sacrilegos
violati saeviens templi, temeratumque tot regum et gentium dominum
praedicans, eruendae urbis apparatu nisibus magnis instabat...*

So he (Sapor) rode up to the gates, accompanied by his royal escort, and
had the audacity to approach so near that even his features could be clearly
seen. His conspicuous trappings made him a target for arrows and other
missiles, and he would have been struck down had not the dust hidden him
from the sight of the marksmen, and preserved him, with the loss of part of
his cloak, to be the author of countless massacres at a later time. This
experience caused him to treat his foes as if they had committed sacrilege.
He declared that the master of so many kings and peoples had been
subjected to unhallowed outrage, and devoted himself to preparations for
the utter destruction of the city. [40]

The theatrical scene which follows the near-miss is part of a snide
commentary on the grandiosity of Persian despotism, but it is still very
much in the Roman imperial tradition. It bears a particularly striking
resemblance to Josephus' account of the incident at the siege of Jerusalem
when Titus, enraged at "rebel" perfidy, makes a great show of wishing to
"achieve more... by going down and exposing himself in the forefront"
before he is restrained.[41]

Now, the Persian emperor was heir to a very different tradition of
leadership, and was probably under less pressure to seem pseudo-heroic
than were his Roman counterparts. Nevertheless, the second major stage of
the siege also begins with Sapor entering the missile danger-zone and
being fired upon—this cannot be accidental.[42] Could the first exposure of
Sapor's person to low-risk fire have been a ritual formality? Ammianus'
use of the term "sacrilege" points in that direction. Does Sapor initiate a
formal offense against his person in order to legitimize the siege and to
inspire his soldiers?

Yet even if the first near-miss was staged for the benefit of Sapor's
army, the second constituted a serious attempt at exemplary leadership.
Between his two approaches to the wall, Sapor had sent in a client king to
parley with the defenders.[43] This king, Grumbates of the Chionitae, was

---

[40] Amm. Marc. 19.1.5
[41] Joseph. *BJ* 6.132-4.
[42] Amm. Marc. 19.7.8.
[43] Amm. Marc. 19.1.7.

fired upon, and a ballista missile penetrated the cuirass of his son, killing him. This is the sole fatality among the dozens instances of the phenomenon, but—given that the son rode next to the father—it was also very likely a near-miss. After an interval for the funeral rites of the prince, Sapor, forced to commit to the siege to gain vengeance for Grumbates, initiated a general assault. It was at this point that Sapor exposed himself for a second time, encouraging his troops by his presence and drawing a hail of missiles. There is no report of Sapor being struck, but "many attendants" were slain.[44]

The siege was long and drawn out and prevented the successful continuation of Sapor's campaign, but Amida eventually fell. The following season Sapor was again besieging a Roman city, this time Bezabde. Here we find confirmation that Sapor's near-wounding at Amida was part of the ritual of the thing:

> *Primo igitur impetu, cum agmine cataphractum fulgentium, rex ipse sublimior ceteris castrorum ambitum circumcursans, propre labra ipsa fossarum venit audentius, petitusque ballistarum ictibus crebris et sagittarum, densitate opertus armorum in modum testudinis contextorum, abscessit innoxius. Ira tamen tum sequestrata...*

> In the first assault the king (Sapor) himself, towering in gleaming armor above his cataphracts, made a circuit of the fortress and was rash enough to approach the very lip of the trenches. He was the target of fierce fire from the artillery and the archers, but was protected by a close formation of shields held up tortoise-fashion and got away unscathed. For the moment he suppressed his rage...[45]

This is a good technique: appearing—inspirationally—in the danger zone yet without incurring great danger. Scipio Africanus long before used a screen of shields to approach a city wall safely, and Julian will also do so.[46] An important clue to the ritual character of personal exposure is that

---

[44] Amm. Marc. 19.7.8: Sapor, who is on horseback, is not actually attacking the wall. He may have ridden with the mounted bowmen who provided covering fire for the assault parties, but it is more likely that he simply moved among his own troops as they massed within missile range of the wall. We cannot know for certain if he intended to draw fire again, but it is likely that he did: Ammianus links what he says is the unusual aggressiveness of the attack to the "unheard of" presence of the emperor, who either really is enraged to reckless action, or, more likely, sees the necessity of going the extra mile to motivate his troops.

[45] Amm. Marc. 20.7.2.

[46] Ammianus is aware of the Scipio precedent, and blurs the differences, Amm. Marc. 24.2.16-17.

Ammianus does not mark the rage of Sapor as unreasonable or even unusual: while it would seem rather silly to get angry when, having approached enemy fortifications, one is shot at, Sapor is repeatedly enraged. Ammianus generally only invokes *ira* in order to signify irrational actions or a barbaric ferocity that outstrips reason. Here, though, when the renewed sacrilege does not lead to a successful storming of the city, Sapor merely sends heralds to announce different terms of surrender—business as usual. Thus we might conclude that the rage is staged, a performance of leadership.[47]

The most intriguing of Ammianus' reports of personal exposure is the perplexing incident of Julian's rage during the operations outside Ctesiphon in 363. The young emperor, mired deep in Mesopotamia, has reached the crisis point of an over-ambitious, under-planned campaign. This small fortification is merely an obstacle in the way of greater goals, as Amida was to Sapor. But unlike Sapor, Julian is deep in enemy territory and under great pressure—failure would mean disaster.

> *...ad quod explorandum ausus accedere, obscurior (ut ipse rebatur) cum paucis obequitans muros, pauloque avidius intra ictum telorum repertus, latere non potuit: statimque diversorum missilium nube exagitatus oppetisset tormento murali, ni vulernato armigero, qui lateri eius haerebat, ipse scutorum densitate contectus, evitato magno discrimine, discessisset. Qua causa concitus ira immani, munimentum disposuit obsidere...*

> Believing that he (Julian) would not be recognized he rode with a few companions about the walls to reconnoiter, but when he was rash enough to get within range he could not escape detection. He at once became the target of a rain of missiles and would have met his death from an engine on the walls had he not been protected by a strong screen of shields. His armor-bearer was wounded close beside him, but he himself escaped from this desperate peril and got away unhurt. In a frenzy of rage he decided to besiege the fort...[48]

What happened, here, to Julian? He is the hero of Ammianus' history, broadly admired by the author, usually portrayed as wise and modest, a talented military leader. Yet in his last months (he is killed in a skirmish shortly after this siege, after forgetting to don his armor) he is frankly

---

[47] Similar behaviors persisted for nearly two centuries. At the siege of Antioch in 540, another struggle between Rome and Persia, the defenders fire on the emissary of the Persian king Chosroes, who had come to parley. Enraged, Chosroes decides to immediately assault the city. Proc. *Persian Wars* 2.8.7.

[48] Amm. Marc. 24.5.6.

depicted as increasingly unhinged by hubris. This "frenzy of rage," then, seems to be a pointed tale of recklessness, a desperate act of self-risk that foreshadows the fall of the hero-prince.

Or perhaps not. It is nearly a perfect example of intentional exposure, the play for the motivational near-miss: the highly visible approach, the rain of missiles, the danger minimized by the screen of shields, the near-miss concretized by the wounding of someone directly beside the emperor. Julian is desperate because his strategy is flawed, but his tactics are still sound—he is merely employing the familiar moral stratagem of intentional exposure.

But the task here was too great: a successful nocturnal sally demonstrated that the defenders were confident and Julian's army demoralized. The following day, truly desperate, Julian exceeded even Titus, fighting "among the foremost" in an attempt to inspire his troops not by the formalized risk of long-range exposure, but by his "personal example of courage".[49]

The fort was taken, with Julian among the assault party, "exposing himself valiantly and long to extreme peril," but we are forced to recognize that, like the oft-wounded Alexander, Julian has ceased to be a responsible leader and is only a fortunate gambler. This act is the exception—the over-reaching—that proves the rule. Ordinarily, the small risk of long-range exposure was abundantly repaid by the boost it gave to the all-important morale of the assault troops.

The dozen examples collected below illustrate the long continuity of the practice of intentional exposure, a technique of imperial leadership that has not, to my knowledge, previously been remarked upon. Emperors stage-managed their appearances during a siege, and getting shot at was a way to burnish their image. They were not irresponsibly wandering into danger, they were making a dramatic appeal to their soldiers: we are under fire, we are all in this together… we must attack!

---

[49] Amm. Marc. 24.5.11.

Appendix

1. Josephus *The Jewish War* 3.236-9: Jotapata (AD 67)
        Who: Vespasian.
        Hit?: In the sole of the foot.
        What: A spent missile.
        When: Late in the siege.
        Result: Concern and alarm; a vengeful night assault.

2. Josephus *The Jewish War* 4.14-16: Gamala (AD 67)
        Who: King Agrippa II.
        Hit?: On the right elbow.
        What: A stone (slung).
        When: During construction of earthworks.
        Result: Roman soldiers roused to greater efforts by enemy
        "savagery."

3. Cassius Dio 65.5.1: Jerusalem (AD 70).
        Who: Titus.
        Hit?: On the left shoulder, permanent damage.
        What: A stone, probably from mural artillery.
        When: Apparently early in the siege.
        Result: Unclear.

4. Cassius Dio 68.31.3: Hatra (AD 117).
        Who: Trajan.
        Hit?: Near miss; a cavalryman in his escort is killed.
        What: Unclear.
        When: On horseback during the early phase of assault.
        Result: Unclear.

5. Cassius Dio 76.11.3: Hatra (AD 200)
        Who: Septimius Severus.
        Hit?: Near miss; several of his shield-bearers are hit.
        What: Mural artillery.
        When: Probably before the close assault.
        Result: Unclear; emphasis is on the unnecessary nature of the
        siege.

6. Historia Augusta *The Two Gallieni* 4.3: A town in Gaul (AD 263)
        Who: Gallienus.

Hit?: Wounded.
What: An arrow.
When: Unknown.
Result: Unclear; siege fails and Gallic Empire endures.

7. Ammianus Marcellinus 19.1.5: The siege of Amida (AD 359).
   Who: Sapor, the Persian king.
   Hit?: His cloak; sacrilege/near miss.
   What: An arrow or engine-launched missile, probably the latter.
   When: While approaching to treat with the inhabitants.
   Result: Rage, preparation to destroy city… until dissuaded by generals.

8. Ammianus Marcellinus 19.1.7: Amida (AD 359).
   Who: A prince, son of Grumbates, king of the Chionitae.
   Hit?: In the chest, through the "thorax" cuirass; fatal.
   What: Ballista missile.
   When: During a parley.
   Result: A fight over the corpse. Sapor forced to destroy Amida.

9. Ammianus Marcellinus 19.7.8: Amida (AD 359).
   Who: Sapor.
   Hit?: Near miss; "many attendants" slain.
   What: At least several missiles.
   When: During a general assault.
   Result: None; the participation of the king shows the ferocity of the battle.

10. Ammianus Marcellinus 20.7.2: Bezabde (AD 360)
    Who: Sapor.
    Hit?: Near miss; protective shields held by bodyguard.
    What: Both arrows and artillery.
    When: While riding "in the first assault" among his cataphracts.
    Result: Enraged that he is targeted, but sends heralds in "the usual way".

11. Ammianus Marcellinus 24.5.6: A fort outside Ctesiphon (AD 363)
    Who: Julian.
    Hit?: Near miss; armor-bearer wounded and bodyguards' shields hit.
    What: Mural artillery.

When: During a pre-assault reconnoiter.
Result: Julian besieges "in a frenzy of rage" despite strategic
situation.

12. Procopius *Persian Wars* 2.8.7: Antioch (AD 540)
        Who: Paulus, an emissary of Chosroes, the Persian king.
        Hit?: Near miss.
        What: Several arrows.
        When: Approaching to urge the accept of the demand of an
        indemnity.
        Result: Chosroes, enraged, decides to storm walls.

Bibliography

Ben Ari, E. *Mastering Soldiers: Conflict, Emotions, and the Enemy in an Israeli Military Unit*. New York: Berghahn Books, 1998.

Campbell, J. B. *The Emperor and the Roman Army, 31BC- AD235*. Oxford: Clarendon Press, 1984.

Frost, D., Fiedler, F., and Anderson, J. "The Role of Personal Risk-Taking in Effective Leadership." *Human Relations* 36 (1983): 185-202.

Gilliver, C. *The Roman Art of War*. Stroud, Gloucestershire: Tempus Publishing Ltd., 1999.

Goldsworthy, A. *The Roman Army at War 100BC-AD200*. Oxford: Clarendon Press, 1996.

—. "Community under Pressure: The Roman Army at the Siege of
Jerusalem." In *The Roman Army as a Community*, *JRA Supplemental Series 34*, edited by Goldsworthy and Haynes, 197-210, Journal of Roman Archaeology, 1999.

Grinker, R. and Spiegel, J. *Men under Stress*. Philadelphia: Blakiston, 1945.

Harris, W. *War and Imperialism in Republican Rome*. Oxford: Clarendon Press, 1979.

Holmes, R. *Firing Line*. London: Jonathan Cape, 1985.

Howard, M. "Leadership in the British Army in the Second World War: some personal observations." In *Leadership and Command: the Anglo-American Experience Since 1861*, edited by G.D. Sheffield, 117-128. London: Brassey's, 1997.

Jones, B. W. "The Reckless Titus." In *Studies in Latin Literature and Roman History* 6, 408-420. Brussels: Collection Latomus 217, 1992.

Kennedy, D. " 'Europaean' Soldiers and the Severan Siege of Hatra." In *The Defence of the Roman and Byzantine East*, edited by P. Freeman and D. Kennedy, 397-410. Oxford: B.A.R. International Series 297, 1986.

Matthews, J. *The Roman Empire of Ammianus*. London: Duckworth, 1989.

McDonnell, M. *Roman Manliness: Virtus and the Roman Republic*. Cambridge: Cambridge University Press, 2006.

Price, J. *Jerusalem Under Siege*. Leiden: Brill, 1992.

Richards, F. *Old Soldiers Never Die*. Sydney: Angus & Robertson, 1933.

Sabin, P. "The Face of Roman Battle." *JRS* 90 (2000): 1-17.

Speidel, M. P. " 'Europaeans' — Syrian Elite Troops at Dura-Europos and Hatra." In *Roman Army Studies I*, 301-9. Amsterdam: J.C. Gieben, 1984.

Rosenstein, N. *Imperatores Victi: Military Defeat and Aristocratic Competition in the Middle and Late Republic*. Berkeley: University of California Press, 1990.

van Wees, H. *Greek Warfare: Myths and Realities*. London: Duckworth, 2004.

Wilson, C. (Baron Moran), *Anatomy of Courage*. London: Constable, 1945.

Yavetz, Z. "Reflections on Titus and Josephus," *GRBS* 16 (1975): 411-32.

CHAPTER THREE

BREAKING THE RULES?
IRREGULARITIES IN THE RECRUITMENT
OF THE EARLY ROMAN ARMY
(509-C. 450 BC)*

JEREMY ARMSTRONG

The traditional model of the Roman army of the sixth and fifth centuries BC is based on the tenets of the "Servian Constitution," as described in the works of Livy, Cicero and Dionysius of Halicarnassus.[1] Supposedly created during Rome's Regal period, and still evidently utilized during the early Republic, the "Servian Constitution" presents an ordered image of Roman society whereby the Roman army was recruited and equipped on the basis of a rigid set of socio-economic classes and socio-political divisions. However, as with other aspects of the "Servian Constitution," this tidy military model has proved problematic for scholars as the literary evidence for the early Republic is full of anecdotes and details that seem to contradict this established system.[2] From major discrepancies, like the independent actions of the Fabii at the Cremera River in the early 470s BC (which involved the use of a private, *gens*-based army to conduct state-sanctioned warfare), to minor inconsistencies, such as the recruitment of men in debt in 494 BC, the literary sources for the early Republic often appear to challenge the traditional military model

---

* I would like to thank Prof. C. J. Smith, Dr. R. Sweetman, Dr. J. Coulston, Dr. E. Bispham and Dr. R. Covino for generously reading and commenting on various drafts of this paper. All remaining errors and omissions are, of course, very much my own.
[1] Livy 1.42-43, Dion. Hal. *Ant. Rom.* 4.13- 21, Cic. *Rep.* 2.20.
[2] Several other aspects of the "Servian Constitution" have proved problematic, including the number of rural tribes present at various times and the number of classes that were instituted. See Cornell 1995, 173-197 for a detailed discussion.

more than they support it. Consequently, it is now generally accepted that a Roman army based on the "Servian Constitution" probably did not exist in the sixth and fifth centuries BC, and that the "Servian Constitution" that is presented in the sources in all probability represents a combination of Rome's socio-political institutions as they appeared at a later date, possibly in the third or fourth century BC, coupled with a fair bit of antiquarian research and, in many cases, what amounts to plausible guesswork by later Roman authors.[3]

This situation presents early Roman military historians with a problem. Once this detailed model of early Rome's political and military structure has been removed, scholars are left in the uncomfortable position of trying to find another way to determine what Rome's political and military system actually *did* look like in the fifth and sixth centuries BC.

Fortunately, the situation is not hopeless. The general agreement of the literary sources in ascribing to the sixth century BC the reorganization of Roman society into classes and geographic tribes, coupled with the fact that this type of reform would fit well with what we know about Rome's socio-political development during the period, hints that some form of the geographic/timocratic "Servian Constitution" was in place during the period. Using this as a starting point, scholars such as Nilsson, D'Arms, Sumner, Momigliano, and more recently Cornell have attempted to create revised versions of Rome's early "Servian" system, which either incorporate or explain some of the inconsistencies found in the sources.[4]

By focusing on a small set of contradictions present in the literary evidence, namely those which relate to military recruitment during the first half of the fifth century BC, this paper will endeavor to add to the debate about the actual nature of Rome's military and political system during the early Republic. It will begin by illustrating the inconsistencies which exist between the principles which govern the "Servian" model of recruitment and those which seem to govern the recruitment described in the literary sources. It will then present some new interpretations of the inconsistencies, demonstrate how accounts of recruitment from the early Republic can either support previously existing military models or present new possibilities for revising our understanding of Rome's early "Servian"

---

[3] This skepticism covers a wide range of positions. Some scholars, taking their cue from the hypercriticism common in the nineteenth century (for instance Niebuhr 1811), view large portions of the "Servian Constitution" as suspect (see De Sanctis 1907-1923, 18 ff.; Beloch 1926, 270 f.; Sumner 1970, 76 f.) while others have adopted a slightly more optimistic approach (see Thomsen 1980, 116-117; Cornell 1995, 173-174).

[4] Nilsson 1929, D'Arms 1943, Momigliano 1966a, Sumner 1970, Cornell 1995.

organization, and ultimately address the question of whether the "Servian Constitution" is still a valid model for understanding the early Roman army.[5]

The "Servian Constitution"

In order to orient ourselves in this argument, it is appropriate to begin with a brief analysis of the "Servian Constitution," as presented in the literary evidence. Prior to Servius Tullius' reign, Roman society was apparently organized according to the curiate system, attributed in the sources to Romulus.[6] This archaic tribal system seems to have formed the basis of early Rome's political, military and possibly religious organization, and was based largely on gentilicial ties (i.e. ties of kinship or quasi-kinship).[7] As Roman society evolved during the seventh and sixth centuries BC, this archaic organization evidently became outdated, and a new system was adopted—supposedly under the reign of Servius Tullius—which shifted the focus of organization from kinship or quasi-kinship ties to socio-economic position and geographic location.[8] This new "Servian Constitution" updated the pre-existing tribal structure and divided Roman society horizontally into seven distinct socio-economic classes (table 3-1). The exact relationship between the new tribes and classes is still unknown, although it is likely that the two sets of divisions worked in conjunction with one another.[9] However, it was the new socio-

---

[5] It should be recognized that there are numerous issues relating to the reliability of the literary sources for early Rome. These issues have been discussed at great length in other works; for a representative sample see Ogilvie 1965, 13-108; Dorey 1966; Rawson 1971; Rawson 1976; Thomsen 1980, 9-26; Forsythe 1994; Cornell 1995, 1-26; Walsh 1996; Oakley 1997; Frier 1999; Forsythe 2005, 59-77; Feeney 2005. Although I have not, in this paper, adopted the highly optimistic approach to the literary evidence espoused by some scholars (see particularly Cornell 1995), I do accept that the literary narrative is based, ultimately, on relatively reliable information (be it annalistic, oral, etc.) and as a result, while the vast majority of the detail contained in the narrative is likely to be anachronistic, the core of the literary narrative is assumed to contain at least a kernel of truth.

[6] Livy 1.13, Dion. Hal. *Ant. Rom.* 2.7.

[7] For a detailed discussion of the *curiate* system see Smith 2006, 184-234.

[8] Livy 1.42-1.43, Dion. Hal. *Ant. Rom.* 4.13-16.

[9] Taylor has argued that the tribes must have been utilized during the census (Taylor 1957, 340). However, as Taylor herself astutely noted, "the coordination of tribes and centuries would have required a complete reorganization of the centuriate assembly on each of the five occasions from 387 to 299 [BC] when new tribes were added" (Taylor 1957, 339).

economic classes which were to take the most prominent role in Rome's
new military and political institutions.

These new socio-economic classes were differentiated by a
combination of wealth and social position. Each class was subdivided into
groups called centuries, which together formed the *comitia centuriata*,
Rome's new primary voting assembly. It is worth noting that the centuries
were in no way indicative of actual population figures. The wealth
required for entry into both the *equites* and first class, at least 100,000
asses, would have limited these groups to a relatively small portion of
society, with the result that their centuries would have contained
significantly fewer men than did the centuries of the lower classes.[10]
However, out of the 193 centuries of the centuriate assembly, the *equites*
and first class combined to make up the first 100, which means that,
despite the inclusion of people of varying levels of wealth within the new
political system, both the political and military apparatus of Rome were
dominated by a small social and economic elite.[11]

For military purposes, each class was assigned a particular military
panoply and therefore a particular role in the army; however, despite the
assertion of Spivey and Stoddart, it is likely that at this early equipment
was provided by the soldiers themselves and not the state.[12] Additionally,
the centuries of each class were divided by age into *seniores* and *iuniores*,

---

[10] This figure of 100,000 *asses*, and indeed any of the values given for entry into
the various Servian classes, cannot be viewed with any degree of certainty when
discussing the fifth and sixth centuries BC, as the amounts are given in a coinage
which was not in use in Rome until the fourth century BC. However, the meaning
is still clear, namely that the first Servian class was supposed to represent the
economic elite of Rome (see particularly Dion. Hal. *Ant. Rom.* 4.18 and Cic. *Rep.*
2.39 for descriptions of the first class).

[11] Note the similarity to van Wees' model of early Greek hoplite armies, which he
argued were predominantly composed of the socio-economic elite (van Wees
2004, 60).

[12] Spivey and Stoddart argued that the reforms of Servius Tullius involved the
issuing of armor to citizens, presumably based on the regularity in military
equipment implied by the Servian military classifications (Spivey and Stoddart
1990, 127). However, the sources do not mention the issuing of armor at this point,
and indeed the first reference to the state being responsible for equipping its
soldiers, outside of emergency situations, is associated with Gaius Gracchus in
123-122 BC (see Keppie 1984, 61 for a discussion). Additionally, the personal
nature of arms and armor in early Rome and Latium is supported by its inclusion in
personal ritual contexts throughout the sixth and fifth centuries BC, and
particularly mortuary contexts (see Bietti Sestieri 1992, 221-243 and Cristofani
1990).

with the *iuniores* (the men aged 17 to 44) making up the field army and the *seniores* (those aged 45 and up) making up the "home guard."

Military recruitment under the "Servian Constitution" was a relatively straightforward process. As there was no standing army, when a military need arose, the king—or under the Republic the consuls—held a levy. Unlike later Roman armies, the "Servian" army did not have a set size. Rather, the army size was completely variable, depending on the state's military needs. With Rome's population already divided into classes, centuries, and *iuniores/seniores* during the census, the king or consuls simply decided how large an army was needed and then acquired the requisite number of men from each century, spreading the manpower demand equally across the centuries.[13] While the size of the army was variable, the end result of this recruitment process was an army that was always of the same proportions with regard to class and was therefore always numerically dominated by the combination of the *equites* and first class.

Problems with this Model of Recruitment

In the period between the traditional reign of Servius Tullius and the beginning of the Republic there are only a few references to specific recruitment practices in the literary sources, and those which do exist, like Brutus' raising of an army to face Tarquinius Superbus at Ardea in 510 BC, implicitly support the traditional "Servian" model.[14] The serious problems with the "Servian" model of recruitment only begin with the advent of the Republic when, from the mid 490s BC, the literary sources begin to contradict consistently the model of recruitment presented earlier in the description of the "Servian" reforms. Indeed, out of the 41 instances of warfare in Livy's narrative which occur between 509 and 450 BC, almost half contain references to recruitment practices which do not seem to fit within the "Servian" system.[15] These recruitment irregularities can be

---

[13] This is noted explicitly in Dion. Hal. *Ant. Rom.* 4.19. "For instance, whenever [Servius Tullius] had occasion to raise ten thousand men, or, if it should so happen, twenty thousand, he would divide that number among the hundred and ninety-three centuries and then order each century to furnish the number of men that fell to its share" (trans. Cary).

[14] Livy 1.59 refers to a subdivision of the Servian army, the *iuniores*, although both the levy and the context of the military action are highly irregular.

[15] The chaotic military environment of the first century BC may have had some influence on Livy's and Dionysius' seeming ambivalence about possible irregularities within the "standard" military practices of early Rome. However,

divided into three groups. The first is the recruitment of plebs into the army, the second is the recruitment of indebted men, and the third is the use of clans or *gentes* to perform military actions for the state. Each of these types of recruitment contradicts the basic tenets of the "Servian" military system. By examining *how* they break the rules of the "Servian Constitution" it is possible to get a better understanding of the system which was actually in use during the early Republic.

Plebs vs. the State

The most prominent problem with early Roman recruitment involves the persistent conflict between the state and the plebs over enrollment in the Roman army.[16] From 495 BC, plebeian leaders began to clash with the senate and the consuls over issues of debt, long military service, and general political enfranchisement. As a result of these disputes, the plebeians complained about, opposed, or boycotted 12 different levies between the years 495 and 456 BC.[17]

While there is still some debate about the exact nature of the "plebeians" as a faction in the early Republic, it is likely that the nature of this group in the early fifth century BC was largely misunderstood by historians during the late Republic.[18] Possibly influenced by the power of Rome's plebeian assemblies and the Tribunes of the Plebs in second and first century BC politics, Roman historians of the late Republic and Augustan periods often emphasized the influence of the plebs from their

---

while this may have promoted the validity of these irregularities in the minds of the authors, it did not necessarily preclude the existence of the standard "Servian" model, as the events of the late Republic were notable for their extraordinary nature.

[16] While some of this prominence may be attributed to Livy's desire to use history to contextualize the social and political struggles which affected Rome in the first century BC, the actual existence of the conflict between the plebeians and the state is not in question. See Develin in Raafluab 2005, 293-311, for a discussion of Livy's treatment of the Struggle of the Orders in light of late Republican political developments.

[17] 495 BC (Livy 2.13-25, Dion. Hal. *Ant. Rom.* 6.22- 30); 495 BC (Livy 2.27); 494 BC (Livy 2.32, Dion. Hal. *Ant. Rom.* 6.44- 96); 494 BC (Livy 2.33, Dion. Hal. *Ant. Rom.* 6.44- 96); 491-488 BC (Livy 2.39, Dion. Hal. *Ant. Rom.* 7.2-15); 483 BC (Dion. Hal. *Ant. Rom.* 8.87); 482-480 BC (Livy 2.42); 473 BC (Livy 2.55, Dion. Hal. *Ant. Rom.* 9.44); 461 BC (Livy 3.10); 460 BC (Livy 3.15-20); 458 BC (Livy 3. 25); 457 BC (Livy 3.28).

[18] See Raaflaub 2005 for an overview of this issue.

inception, having them play a major role in both early Roman politics and society.

However, the literary evidence also seems to contain a separate tradition, whereby the plebeians were initially outside of Roman politics and society, and were only gradually integrated during the fifth and fourth centuries BC. This position outside of Rome's early political framework is supported by a wide range of factors including the evident political impotence of the plebs during the early fifth century BC and the fact that plebeians were explicitly barred from holding the consulship until the early fourth century BC. Additionally, the early Republic saw the development of a plebeian "alternate state" within Rome, which included plebeian political assemblies (although largely unofficial at that time) and officials, the plebeian tribunes.[19] This early plebeian position outside of the Roman state may also be remembered in the archaic phrase *populus plebsque*[20] which, as Richard notes, is unlikely simply to refer to the division between patricians and plebs, but rather seems to identify the plebs as being separate from the *populus*, Rome's archaic citizen/soldier body.[21] It may be possible to explain aspects of this plebeian position outside of the state by associating the majority of the plebeians with the *capite censi*, the lowest "Servian" economic classification in the seven class system. However, even this is problematic given the likelihood of the existence of at least some wealthy plebeians in the early Republic and the prohibition on marriage between patricians and plebeians in the Twelve Tables, all of which indicates that the plebeians were a recognizable social group, and hints that they represented much more than just an economic category.[22] Consequently, it is likely that the plebs represented a group which was outside of Rome's official political, military, and possibly social framework during the early Republic (i.e. outside of the *comitia centuriata* and possibly not even included in the *capite censi*),[23] but which was evidently still expected to contribute men to the Roman army. This presents a clear conflict with the "Servian" model of military recruitment because one of the central themes of the "Servian Constitution" is the

---

[19] See Cornell's seminal article "The Failure of the Plebs" (Cornell in Gabba and Momigliano 1983) for a discussion of both the political impotence of the plebs (see also n. 25 below) and the importance of the "alternate state", and Momigliano in Raaflaub 2005 for another detailed argument on the position of the plebeians outside of the early Roman state.

[20] See Momigliano in Raaflaub 2005, 174 for a detailed discussion of this phrase.

[21] Richard in Raaflaub 2005, 120.

[22] Watson 1975, 23.

[23] See below (n. 26).

relationship between military responsibility and political power, at least within Rome's primary voting body, the centuriate assembly. This link between Rome's political assembly and her armed forces was essential to the stability of the state, as it ensured that the political power was in the hands of the same individuals as the military power.

When examining the years in which the plebeians opposed or boycotted levies, it emerges that the plebeians tended to oppose levies only in years where Rome either had expanded military needs or had been at war for several years previously. For instance, in the years between 495 and 488 BC, Rome was at war on an annual basis, often with multiple enemies, and also began to experience trouble from the plebs. The same situation occurred between 482 and 480 BC, and between 463 and 457 BC.[24] However, as the plebs were evidently not supposed to play a major role, either militarily or politically, in the established system based on the *comitia centuriata*, this is a bit of a paradox.[25] If the plebs were supposed to provide a significant contribution to the army, they should, according to the "Servian Constitution," have had compensatory political power, and would therefore have had a political avenue to voice their complaints. Likewise, if the plebs were *not* supposed to provide a significant contribution to the army, the boycotts of the levy should not have been a major issue for the state.

One possible solution to this paradox is the suggestion that, when Rome was put under pressure militarily, she was forced to rely on the plebs, a body of people who had hitherto been outside of the established military and political system, to provide additional manpower for the army.[26] However, while this solution does explain both the plebeian opposition to levies and their political impotence, it also hints that the

---

[24] See above (n. 17) for references. It is possible that aspects of this "plebeian battle-fatigue" represent second century BC anachronisms, as the nature of the struggle contains many late Republican elements, and as many of the details provided to support these sections of Livy's narrative contain evident anachronistic details (see particularly the description of the plebeian veteran, Livy 2.23- 25). However, the sources are unanimous in reporting this "battle-fatigue", and early plebeian military involvement, and subsequent fatigue, would help explain a wide range of developments in early Roman warfare (most notably the sudden problem with discipline in the early fifth century BC). As a result, it would be unwise to discount entirely the authenticity of this early plebeian dissent.

[25] This point is supported by both the evident political impotence of the plebs in the early fifth century BC (see Cornell in Gabba and Momigliano 1983, 101-120) and Appius Claudius' disdain for their military contributions in 494 BC (Dion. Hal. *Ant. Rom.* 6.63).

[26] See Momigliano's argument to this effect in Raaflaub 2005, 175-76.

official military system in Rome during the early fifth century BC might easily be overwhelmed if Rome was faced with numerous opponents or continued warfare, as occurred in the 490s, 480s and 460s BC. Thus, the military may not have been particularly large or have had a deep reserve of manpower, two issues which should not have been problems for the traditional "Servian" military model. In addition, although the plebs were evidently not supposed to contribute men to the army, the regularity with which they served and their importance as an emergency force are marked. This may indicate either that they were able to contribute a large number of men to the army, or that they were reasonably well equipped and therefore possibly well off, although clearly not to the same degree as the first "Servian" class.[27]

A revised version of the "Servian Constitution" which seems to answer these issues was advanced by Momigliano in 1963 and later taken up by Cornell in 1995. They argued for a graduated set of "Servian" reforms, whereby only the top classes existed from the middle of the sixth century BC.[28] Therefore, the official Roman army of the early Republic may have consisted of only the *equites* and first class, with the lower classes being slowly added during the fifth and fourth centuries BC.[29] This model is supported by both Festus (100 L)[30] and Aulus Gellius (*NA* 6.13), who, while quoting a speech by Cato**Error! Bookmark not defined.** in the *Attic Nights*, claims that

---

[27] As a result of the "top-heavy" class structure of the "Servian Constitution" a group could make up a large proportion, numerically, of both Roman society and the Roman army, but play only a minor/secondary role in Roman warfare and politics. The evident military importance of the plebeian contingent in the Roman army would hint that they were equipped, at the very least, to a higher standard than members of the *capite censi* and the fifth Servian class which, according to the Servian military classification, utilized only slings and javelins (fig. 1).

[28] Momigliano 1966a, 596; Cornell 1995, 185.

[29] The lower classes may also have been added quickly. Livy states that the first election of 10 tribunes, in 453 BC, involved choosing two from each class (a practice which was maintained thereafter), which indicates that at least five classes were in existence at the time (Livy 3.30). However, Livy's note that this practice was continued hints that this information was based on the Roman constitution as it existed at a later date and may be an anachronism.

[30] Festus, in his entry for *infraclassem* notes "The *infra classem* are indicated as those which are less than the top [class], which is valued at 120,000 *aes*, having been registered."(Trans. Armstrong). Lindsay 1930. See Momigliano 1966b, 21 for discussion.

> Not all those men who were enrolled in the five classes were called
> classici, but only the men of the first class, who were rated at a hundred
> and twenty-five thousand asses or more. But those of the second class and
> of all the other classes, who were rated at a smaller sum than that which
> I just mentioned, were called infra classem.[31]

Using this model, it can be hypothesized that the plebs either made up or
were part of the early *infra classem*, which would effectively place them
outside of the standard "Servian" political and military system during the
early Republic, but still within the larger Roman social and political
matrix.[32]

The result of this revised version of the "Servian Constitution" is that
the official Roman army of both the Roman monarchy and the early
Republic would have been an army made up entirely of the socio-
economic elite (a supposition which is consistent with what we know
about the social development of Rome during the sixth and early fifth
centuries BC).[33] However, it is possible that the level of warfare in Latium
during the early fifth century BC often overwhelmed this existing system.
Instead of the sporadic and relatively low level warfare which Rome
seems to have faced during the Regal period, in the early fifth century BC
Rome, and indeed all of Latium, experienced an escalation in both the
scale and amount of warfare.[34] This was sparked by a series of population

---

[31] Trans. Rolfe.

[32] Cornell has argued that the formal identification of the plebs as the *infra classem*
is doubtful, noting that the archaic distinction between the *populus* and the plebs,
which is often used as evidence for the plebeian position outside of the army (see
particularly Momigliano in Raaflaub 2005), does not exclude the plebeians from
military service entirely. However, Cornell admits that the plebeian population
"consisted largely of people who were outside of the ranks of the *classis*" (Cornell
1995, 257, 261).

[33] There is both archeological and literary evidence of a powerful aristocratic class
in Latium in the sixth century BC (see Smith 1996, 185-202) which seems to have
been extremely active in military matters, often acting as warlords and
accompanied by a band of followers (Cornell 1995, 143-150; for archaeological
evidence of the martial nature of Latin aristocrats see Gjerstad 1966 and Stary
1981). While it is possible that part of the motivation behind the introduction of the
"Servian" military system was an effort to remove the aristocratic monopoly on
warfare, it is unlikely that the system would have deviated greatly from the
established status quo.

[34] This picture is generally supported by both the archaeology of the region (see
Cornell 1995, 304-305) and the literary evidence (see Livy, e.g. 1.53, 1.55, 2.23,
2.26, 2.30, 2.32, 2.33), although, as noted above, it is wise to be skeptical of all but
the broad outline of it.

movements from the south and east and the decline of the Etruscan city-states in the north, which served to funnel various groups into the region.[35] This escalation would have put the truncated "Servian" army, possibly composed of only the *equites* and the first class, under serious stress, and the socio-economic elite many have struggled to field their necessary allotment of men.[36] As a result, in times of need, and possibly on an increasingly steady basis, the state may have decided to recruit men from the *infra classem* into the army. Therefore, while it is unknown exactly how many classes existed during the early Republic, it is very likely that all of the classes did not, and that the conflict between the state and the plebs arose out of the latter's continued military duty without comparable political compensation.

Recruitment of Men in Debt

The second major recruitment practice that contradicts the established "Servian" system is the enrollment of indebted men into the army. This issue has traditionally been subsumed under the debate around the Struggle of the Orders, as it often pitted plebeians against patricians. However, it does represent an independent issue: the indebted men who were enrolled were poor, but not necessarily unenfrachised, meaning that it is possible that this group may have also contained also patricians and/or members of the *populus*.

The primary evidence for this issue comes from the period surrounding the first plebeian secession in 495 and 494 BC. At this time, the plebeians were complaining about their treatment with regard to debt-bondage.[37] Livy, in 2.23- 25, records the story of a veteran, who bemoans the loss of his property through a series of unfortunate events, and of his subsequent treatment at the hands of his creditors. Although he had evidently fallen below the minimum wealth needed to be eligible for military service, immediately following this speech, in the face of a threat from the Volsci,

---

[35] In the north, the Umbrians emerged from Central Italy and occupied Rimini and Ravenna (Strabo 5.1.7-11), and the Celts came into the region from across the Alps. In the south, Campania experienced the same immigration of peoples from the mountainous exterior as Latium. See Cornell 1995, 304-305 for a general discussion.

[36] Dionysius of Halicarnassus notes the stress which the top Servian classes experienced even under normal circumstances (Dion. Hal. *Ant. Rom.* 4.19).

[37] The issues of debt and debt-bondage are a common trope in agrarian societies from around the Mediterranean. Note particularly the similarities between fifth century BC Rome and Solonian Athens (Arist. *Pol.* 5.10, 1313b-1315b).

he, along with other debtors, was recruited into the army. The issue of debt and *nexum* is then mentioned in connection with a second levy in 495 BC, and in 494 BC indebted plebeians are once again explicitly said to be recruited into the army.[38] It should be noted that there is still some debate over the exact nature of *nexum*, and particularly how it related to military service.[39] In this paper, both *nexum* and debt more generally are taken only as demonstrating that recruitment, regardless of wealth, did take place in the early Republic, leaving to one side the other social and military issues that surround debt in early Rome.

The nature of the evidence for recruitment of indebted men, with its cast of archetypal late Republican characters, has led some to argue that this issue may be an anachronistic invention of late Republican authors who were imposing late Republican social issues on the early Struggle of the Orders.[40] Indeed, the argument for the anachronistic nature of this issue may be supported by the fact that the recruitment of indebted men is not explicitly mentioned after the 490s BC.[41] However, the laws of the Twelve Tables and various plebeian advances in the fifth and fourth centuries BC, including the abolition of *nexum* itself, indicate that at least the debt crisis was probably real.[42]

So, once again, recruitment practices seem to indicate that the early Roman army was occasionally overwhelmed and that, in times of military need, the Roman state was forced to turn to men who were outside of the "Servian" socio-economic classes.[43] While this situation is clearly possible

---

[38] Instances in Livy of debtors being enlisted into the army in 509-450 BC: 495 BC war against the Volsci (Livy 2.23-25), 494 BC war against the Volsci, Aequi and Sabines (Livy 2.30-31), 469 BC war against the Aequi and Volsci (Livy 2.63-3.5), 458 BC war against the Sabines (Livy 3.28).

[39] Ogilvie 1965, 296-298; Watson 1975, 111-124; Cornell 1995, 280-283. It is entirely possible that *nexum* did entail some sort of military obligation although there is no direct evidence to support this hypothesis.

[40] See e.g. Ogilvie 1965, 298.

[41] Cornell has argued that this absence is the result of issues with debt being either an anachronistic interpolation or the result of a defective record for the fifth century BC (Cornell 1995, 267).

[42] Watson 1975, 111-124.

[43] There is also the issue of rich men who may have fallen into debt and therefore out of the *classis*. The length of time between each census during the period from 509 and 450 BC varied between five and 19 years, with the average being seven years (see Frank 1930 for a discussion of the early Roman census), which means that it would have been possible for individuals to have been registered in a certain Servian class during a census, but have subsequently fallen into debt. Nevertheless, given the amount of wealth required for entry and the range of wealth contained in

even within the traditional "Servian" model (as Rome in later periods was not averse to recruiting indebted men and even slaves when in need),[44] the frequency with which this happened in the early Republic (roughly once out of every ten levies between 509 and 450 BC) does indicate a certain flexibility in Rome's relationship with her timocratic system and a willingness to break or bend the standard recruitment rules.

Recruitment of Families and Clans

Finally, there is the recruitment or official use of clans, or *gentes,* to perform military duties for the state. Most of the accounts of *gens*-based military activity concern the activity of the Fabii,[45] and were therefore likely included by the late third century BC historian Quintus Fabius Pictor.[46] Some scholars find his relationship to the Fabius clan problematic, because it is possible that he included and magnified the episodes to bolster his family's reputation.[47] However, the nature of the accounts immediately calls this into question as, despite the victories

---

each class, this phenomenon is likely to have affected only a small portion of the population at the very bottom of the fifth Servian class. However, in a truncated Servian model, this situation may have occurred more frequently.

[44] Dionysius of Halicarnassus has Appius Claudius, in 494 BC, arguing for the use of slaves in the army (Dion. Hal. *Ant. Rom.* 6.63), but this may simply be a literary device. Rome did use slaves during the Second Punic War, in 214 and 210 as rowers (Livy 24.11.5-9, 26.35.1-6), and occasionally even as soldiers (Livy 26.35). Livy explicitly mentions that the *volones*, or slaves employed as legionaries during the Hannibalic War, were freed (Livy 23.35.5, 24.14.3-16); it is unknown whether slaves employed as rowers were freed or returned to their masters after the war (see Rosenstein 2004, 197).

[45] While the activity of the Fabii represents the most obvious cases of *gens*-based warfare, there are several other references to warfare which can be construed as being *gens*-based, perhaps the most notable being the actions of Appius Herdonius and his followers in 460 BC (Livy 3.15-18, Dion. Hal. *Ant. Rom.* 10.14-17).

[46] It is likely that this activity was given its prominence in the historical record by Fabius Pictor, but there is evidence for alternative versions. See particularly Ovid's version of the story of the Fabii at the Cremera River in his *Fasti* (Ov. *Fast.* 2.193-474), which demonstrates a divergence from the narrative as presented in Livy, specifically with regards to date; a point which has sparked debate about the possibility of various alternative sources (see Harries 1991: 150-168).

[47] The links between the narrative of the battle of the Cremera River and the 300 Spartans at the battle of Thermopylae have been well established, particularly with regard to the numbers involved (300 + 4,000 allies). This has made some scholars argue that the entire episode may have been influenced significantly by events in Greece (Ogilvie 1965, 360; Forsythe 2005, 196-197).

recorded, the most notable event is the dramatic defeat and almost complete destruction of the Fabii in 477 BC. This episode, although undoubtedly heroic, is unlikely to be a fabrication by Fabius Pictor for the simple reason that an event of such proportions would likely have been retained in the collective memory of the Roman population. In addition, as Oakley has noted, owing to the strong sense of competition among the Roman elite and the focus on the heroic deeds of their ancestors, it is unlikely that Fabius Pictor would have been able to get away with fabricating large aspects of Roman history, a point supported by the evident respect with which Pictor's work was regarded by later authors of different *gentes*.[48] Indeed, it may very well be the fact that these stories relate to Fabius Pictor's own family history which gives them the most credence, as individual families are known to have kept detailed records of family achievements and notable events.[49] Given the cryptic and often ambiguous nature of many of the sources for early Rome, family histories, despite their possible bias, have been argued to be some of the most reliable.[50]

These references to an archaic, kinship-oriented way of war hint that Rome's timocratic military system may have worked in conjunction with smaller local forces during the Regal and early Republican periods. By the beginning of the Republic, Rome had only recently formed herself into a single urban entity, and many segments of her population lived in areas surrounding the city, presumably in the same kinship-based communities which had existed prior to Rome's emergence as a coherent entity.[51] These

---

[48] Oakley 1997, 22-24. Ridley's article (Ridley 1983) concerning the use of *laudationes* to alter family histories in order to claim false triumphs and consulships demonstrates clearly that the veracity of these family histories should be understood as relative, and cannot be carried down to the most detailed level (see Cic. *Brut.* 62 and Livy 8.40 for ancient criticisms). However, it should be noted that the problems associated with the use of family histories in the ancient sources can usually be understood as elaborations, as opposed to outright fabrications, in that the family historians seem to have, at worst, elaborated their ancestors' role in a set of more generally recognized historical events (i.e. by giving them position of consul or awarding a triumph), as opposed to fabricating entirely spurious wars.

[49] Richard 1990a and 1990b; Smith 2006, 290-295. See Ridley 1983 for possible problems within this tradition.

[50] Cornell 1995, 9-10. See also Culham 1989 for a discussion of the strong archival and documentary tradition in Roman aristocratic families, and Rawson 1976 for a discussion of the first Latin annalists and their sources.

[51] Bietti Sestieri, in her study on the Iron age cemetery at Osteria dell'Osa, has noted that, based on the archaeological evidence, kinship appears to be the most

communities may have been organized to conduct independent, small scale warfare and, while Rome's larger, state-centered conflicts were fought with the official, united army, low level raiding may have continued in the old, time-honored fashion.[52]

Another possibility is that the family units actually formed part of Rome's geographic/timocratic military system itself. Despite the detailed structure given for the recruitment and equipping of the army, the internal organization of Rome's armed forces, particularly while they were in the field, is still largely unknown and may have been based on kinship links. The curiate system, which the "Servian" system replaced, was clearly based on links of kinship or quasi-kinship.[53] While it is evident that the new military structure was designed to create a more state-centered army, it is possible that certain familial links remained in the internal workings of the army.[54] This is supported, albeit tenuously, by the myriad of references to family members fighting together in the early Republic.[55] As a result, the use of family-oriented units may not have been as contradictory to the geographic/timocratic model as is sometimes assumed.[56]

---

likely foundation of community structure in Latium, particularly during the eighth and seventh centuries BC (Bietti Sestieri 1992, 141).

[52] The presence of aristocratic warbands (traditionally dubbed *condottieri*) in central Italy during the sixth and fifth centuries BC is generally accepted and supported by a wide range of evidence including the Lapis Satricanus and the mythic figures of Mastarna and the Vibenna brothers, discussed by the Emperor Claudius in a speech preserved on the Table of Lyon and depicted on the walls of the Francois Tomb. See Cornell 1995, 143-150 and Forsythe 2005, 198-200 for general discussions.

[53] Smith 2006, 184-234.

[54] Ogilvie suggested that the use of the phrase '*e curia egressus*' in Livy's account may indicate a continuation of the archaic curiate organization (1965, 361).

[55] E.g. Livy 2.45-46, 2.48, 2.49, 3.15-20. This may simply represent a particular narrative trope.

[56] This *gens*-based internal organization would mean that the Roman army may have been deployed using a mix of troop types, as all family members (not to mention the poorer followers and "retainers") could not be expected to be in the same Servian class and therefore equipped in the same manner. This would be in contrast to the later "Polybian army" (Polyb. 6.19-46), were the army was clearly deployed according to equipment type.

Conclusions

In conclusion, the consistent irregularities in the accounts of military recruitment during the first half of the fifth century BC indicate that the traditional "Servian" military model does not describe Rome's actual military system during the early Republic. Instead, the evidence suggests that early Rome's military system encompassed a much smaller segment of Roman society than the traditional "Servian model," which was easily overwhelmed by the expanded military requirements of the early fifth century BC and evidently forced to rely heavily on men and groups outside of the existing system to supplement the army on an increasingly regular basis.

Given the amount of evidence that contradicts it, is the "Servian" military model still a viable model for understanding the early Roman army? The answer is unfortunately not as easy as a simple yes or no. While it does seem that a timocratic military system, which may have represented the core of the later "Servian" system, did exist during the late Regal and early Republican periods, it is also clear that the early Roman army was flexible enough to bend this system to suit its military needs. As a result, while aspects of the "Servian" military model can be seen as part of an early Roman military ideal, the early Roman army should not be seen as the product of a particular military model, but rather the result of her immediate and evolving social and military circumstances.

Table

Class	No. of Centuries	Required Wealth (*asses*)	Assigned Military Equipment
Equites	18	100,000(?)[1]	Cavalry
1st	80 + 2[2] (40 *iuniores* and 40 *seniores*)	100,000	Helmet, round shield, greaves, cuirass, sword, and spear
2nd	20 (10 *iuniores* and 10 *seniores*)	75,000	Helmet, oblong shield, greaves, sword, and spear
3rd	20 (10 *iuniores* and 10 *seniores*)	50,000	Helmet, oblong shield, sword, and spear
4th	20 (10 *iuniores* and 10 *seniores*)	25,000	Spear and javelin [Oblong shield, sword][4]
5th	30 +2[3] (15 *iuniores* and 15 *seniores*?)	11,000 [12,500] [4]	Slings and stones [javelin][4]
Capite Censi	1	<11,000 [12,500] [4]	N/A

Table 3-1. The "Servian" Classes (based on the accounts of Livy and Dionysius of Halicarnassus).

1. Equites were required to be of "highest birth" (Dion. Hal. *Ant. Rom.* 4.18) or the "principal men of the State" (Livy 1.43); however, the texts do seem to hint at a required level of wealth as well.

2. The first class included two centuries of engineers, but it is unknown if these represented one century of engineers for the *iuniores* and one century for *seniores*.

3. The fifth class included two centuries of trumpeters and supernumeraries, but it is once again unknown if these represented both *iuniores* and *seniores*.

4. Details in square brackets denote variations present in Dionysius of Halicarnassus' account of the Servian Constitution, but not Livy's.

Bibliography

Beloch, K. J. *Römische Geschichte bis zum Beginn der punischen Kriege.* Berlin and Leipzig, 1926.

Bietti Sestieri, A. M. *The Iron Age Community of Osteria dell'Osa: a study of socio-political development in central Tyrrhenian Italy.* Cambridge: Cambridge University Press, 1992.

Cornell, T. *The Beginnings of Rome: Italy and Rome from the Bronze Age to the Punic Wars (c. 1000-264 BC).* London: Routledge, 1995.

Cristofani, M. (ed.) *La Grande Roma dei Tarquini: Palazzo delle esposizioni, Roma 12 giogno — 30 settembre 1990.* Roma: Catalogo della mostra.

Culham, P. "Archives and Alternatives in Republican Rome." *CP* 84 (1989): 100-115, 1990.

D' Arms, E. F. "The Classes of the 'Servian' Constitution." *AJP* 64 (1943): 424-426.

De Sanctis, G. *Storia dei Romani.* Rome, 1907-1923.

Dorey, T. A. (ed.) *Latin Historians.* London: Routledge & Kegan Paul, 1966.

Feeney, D. "The Beginnings of Literature in Latin." *JRS* 95 (2005): 226-240.

Forsythe, G. *The Historian, L. Calpurnius Piso Frugi, and the Annalistic Tradition.* Lanham: University Press of America, 1994.

—. *A Critical History of Early Rome: From Prehistory to the First Punic War.* Berkeley, Calif.: University of California Press, 2005.

Frank, T. "Roman Census Statistic from 508 to 225 BC." *AJP* 51 (1930): 313-324.

Frier, B. W. *Libri Annales Pontificum Maximorum: the origins of the annalistic tradition.* Ann Arbor, Mich.: University of Michigan Press, 1999.

Gabba, E. and Momigliano, A. (eds.) *Tria corda: scriti in onore di Arnaldo Momigliano.* Como: Edizioni New Press, 1983.

Gjerstad, E. *Early Rome, Volume IV: Synthesis of Archaeological Evidence.* Lund: C. W. K. Gleerup, 1966.

Harries, B. "Ovid and the Fabii: 2.193-474." *CQ* 41 (1991): 150-168.

Keppie, L. *The Making of the Roman Army: From Republic to Empire.* Norman, OK: University of Oklahoma Press, 1984.

Lindsay, W. M., Pirie, J. W., and British, A. (eds.) *Glossaria latina.* Paris: Société anonyme d'edition "Les Belles letters," 1930.

Momigliano 1966a: Momigliano, A. *Terzo Contributo alla storia degli studi classici e del mondo antico*. Roma: Edizioni di Storia e Letteratura, 1966.

—. 1966b. "Procum Patricium." *JRS* 56 (1966): 16-24.

Niebuhr, B. G. *Römische Geschichte I*. Berlin: Realschulbuchhandlung, 1811.

Nilsson, M. P. "The Introduction of Hoplite Tactics at Rome." *JRS* 19 (1929): 1-11.

Oakley, S. P. *A Commentary on Livy, Books 6-10*. Oxford: Clarendon Press, 1997.

Ogilvie, R. M. *A Commentary on Livy, Books 1-5*. Oxford: Clarendon Press, 1965.

Raaflaub, K. (ed.) *Social Struggle in Archaic Rome: New Perspectives on the Conflict of the Orders*. Oxford: Blackwell Publishing, 2005.

Rawson, E. "The Literary Sources for the Pre-Marian Army." *PBSR* 39 (1971): 13-31.

—. "The First Latin Annalists." *Latomus* 35 (1976): 689-717.

Richard, J. C. 1990a. "Les Fabii à la Crémère: Grandeur et decadence de l'organisation gentilice." In *Crise et transformation des sociétés archaïques de l'Italie antique au Ve siècle av. J.-C.*, edited by H. Massa-Pairault, 245-62. Rome: École française de Rome, 1990.

—.1990b. "Historiographie et historie: L'Expédition des Fabii à la Crémère." In *Staat und Staatlichkeit in der frühen römischen Republik: Akten eines Symposiums, 12.-15. Juli 1988, Freie Universität Berlin*, edited by W. Eder, 174-199. Stuttgart: Franz Steiner, 1990

Ridley, R. T. "Falsi Triumphi, Plures Consulatus." *Latomus* 43 (1983): 372-382.

Rosenstein, N. *Rome at War: Farms, Families, and Death in the Middle Republic*. Chapel Hill, NC: University of North Carolina Press, 2004.

Smith, C. J. *Early Rome and Latium: economy and society c.1000 to 500 BC*. Oxford; New York: Clarendon Press: Oxford University Press, 1996.

—. *The Roman Clan: The Gens from Ancient Ideology to Modern Anthropology*. Cambridge: Cambridge University Press, 2006.

Spivey, N. J. and Stoddart, S. *Etruscan Italy: an archaeological history*. London: Batsford, 1990.

Stary, P. F. *Zur eisenzeitlichen Bewaffnung und Kampfesweise in Mittelitalien (ca. 9. bis 6. Jh. v. Chr.)*. Mainz am Rhein: P. von Zabern, 1981.

Sumner, G. V. "The Legion and the Centuriate Organization." *JRS* 60 (1970): 67-78.

Taylor, L. R. 1957. "The Centuriate Assembly before and after the Reform." *AJP* 78 (1957): 337-354.

Thomsen, R. *King Servius Tullius: a historical synthesis*. Copenhagen: Gyldendal, 1980.

Walsh, P. G. *Livy: His Historical Aims and Methods*. London: Bristol Classical Paperbacks, 1996.

Watson, A. *Rome of the XII Tables: Persons and Property*. Princeton, N.J.: Princeton University Press, 1975.

van Wees, H. *Greek Warfare: Myths and Realities*. London: Duckworth, 2004.

CHAPTER FOUR

TINKER, TRADER, SAILOR, SPY?
THE ROLE OF THE MERCANTILE COMMUNITY
IN GREEK INTELLIGENCE GATHERING

MARK WOOLMER

During the autumn of 1917, the American archaeologist Mayanist Sylvanus Morely was about to photograph an old Spanish fort along the Honduran coast when a group of soldiers emerged from within and prevented him from taking his pictures. Morely vehemently protested to the troopers' commanding officer, explaining his position as an eminent archaeologist, but to no avail. Having failed to persuade the unit's commanding officer, Morely next sought the intervention of the regional commander, a military general, but again with no success. Finally, after a great deal of bureaucratic wrangling, he produced a letter of introduction written by President Francisco Bertrand and was reluctantly given permission to take his photos.[1] The ultimate irony of the story is that Morely was using his position as a world-renowned archaeologist to double as a spy, his mission being to identify German agents, short-wave radio positions, and submarine bases. Recently declassified documents show that the US government originally approached Morely because they believed his archaeological credentials gave him a unique and invaluable form of cover. The F.B.I. and C.I.A. have both, in recent years, gone on record stating that archaeologists are useful spies as they can easily move across borders, are familiar with the attitudes and opinions of the indigenous people, and frequently have natural opportunities to observe troop movements, note the distribution of military hardware and bases, and even in extreme situations commit acts of sabotage. This is a striking

---

[1] Price 2003, 30-35.

statement because, as will be demonstrated, ancient inter-regional merchants can be identified as sharing all of these traits.[2]

This paper will therefore argue, in contrast to previous scholarship, that inter-regional merchants were recognised as legitimate sources of political intelligence by the Greek *poleis*. Although inter-regional merchants have long been recognised as the men most likely to come into contact with gossip and information from distant regions, the perception that they had a relatively low social standing has traditionally been seen as a hindrance to their reliability as disseminators of information.[3] This low social status was considered to preclude merchants from being acceptable transmitters of a variety of different types of news and information, including political intelligence, geographic and cartographic information, and social news.

This article has been developed from my research into the role and status of inter-regional merchants in the classical Greek world.[4] The ultimate conclusion I have drawn in my previous research is that, far from being the degenerate and despised figures presented by philosophers such as Aristotle and Plato, many inter-regional merchants were in fact well respected and fully integrated into the social, economic, and political life of the *polis*. Whereas previous scholarship established rigid distinctions between social class and economic activity, my work questions the validity of such an approach. Using a variety of disciplines, most importantly sociology and social theory, economics, anthropology, and archaeology, I have offered an alternative picture of the legal, political, and social status of inter-regional merchants. My research therefore challenges the theory that the mercantile community was in general comprised of foreigners or less affluent citizens, instead suggesting that there was a broader mix of men from various ethnic, social, and economic groups.

I have also reassessed the negative perceptions of the mercantile community and explored why such a diversity of views are found in Greek literature. I propose that rather than being the profit-hungry, immoral, and unscrupulous men depicted by the philosophers, Greek merchants were in general, due to the necessity of finding credit, forced to act in an honourable manner. Furthermore, the existence of large numbers of *proxeny*

---

[2] Much of the surviving evidence for the use of merchants as spies comes from Greek military writers who argue that precautions should be taken against them. For example, Aeneas Tacticus provides a long list of precautionary measures that should be implemented on the outbreak of war; interestingly he includes a number of measures which are aimed primarily towards merchants (Aen. Tact. 10.2-26).

[3] Lewis 1996, 184.

[4] Woolmer 2007.

decrees rewarding merchants for their praiseworthy deeds demonstrates that these men could become highly respected individuals in society.[5]

The institution of *proxenia* is of further significance because it demonstrates that even foreign inter-regional merchants could become highly valued and honoured members of the *polis*. An analysis of the individuals who were awarded with *proxenia* reveals that the title *proxenos* was not bestowed as a way of merely flattering the recipient, but was instead a way of rewarding significant displays of loyalty and public honour. Furthermore, my research has highlighted the fact that there was no significant difference in the types of honours being rewarded to men engaged in commerce and those granted to other occupations. The frequency with which *proxenia* was awarded also indicates that this honour was extended to more than the privileged few.

In light of this more positive interpretation of the social perception and status of the mercantile community, I have examined the political status of merchants within the Greek *polis*, dispelling the theories, firstly, that merchants were more democratic in outlook and, secondly, as a general rule, politically inactive. Through an analysis of the epigraphic material, in conjunction with the sparse literary evidence, it was possible to demonstrate that merchants in a variety of states, including Athens, Corinth, Megara, and Corcyra, could have a significant amount of influence on political decision making. With many Greek states recognizing that their economic well-being was at least partly dependent upon merchants, and that these merchants were united by a common set of needs, desires and interests, the Greek mercantile communities could have a significant amount of political influence. This political influence manifested itself in either an active or a passive manner: under normal circumstances the mercantile community should be seen as exerting a passive influence on the political decision making of the *polis*, whereas in times of crisis, or as the result of exceptional events or circumstances, it is possible to identify various groupings within the mercantile community temporarily uniting to become an active political force.

As part of that reassessment process this article is based on two key assumptions: firstly, that the members of the Greek mercantile community had a higher social standing and acceptance than has previously been credited and, secondly, that the mercantile community was comprised of men hailing from a wide range of social and economic backgrounds, rather than being dominated by one particular group as previously supposed. Therefore the men comprising what I have termed the "mercantile

---

[5] Woolmer 2007

community" include rich, poor, and moderately affluent and more equal numbers of citizens, metics, and foreigners than has previously been assumed. This revision of the social standing and the level of assimilation of inter-regional merchants into Greek society present an opportunity to re-examine the roles that have, or indeed have not, been attributed to merchants on account of their occupation. This paper will therefore focus on the paradox that has arisen in regards to the relationship between merchants and the spread of political news and intelligence.

As a result of the new model that I am proposing for the affluence and composition of the mercantile community, it is now possible to demonstrate that merchants were far more prominent in intelligence gathering on behalf of the *polis*. This paper has been divided into three main sections; the first will examine the previous problems with merchants as disseminators of news and intelligence, the second will explore the various solutions I offer to these problems, whilst the third will discuss the sparse literary evidence which point to the regular use of intelligence gathered by the mercantile community.[6]

I. The Problems

Although it is generally accepted that there was a connection between merchants and the dissemination of news and information—for example, Lycurgus credits Rhodian merchants with playing an integral part in the dissemination of news and information throughout Rhodes—scholarly disagreement has arisen in regards to the volume and type of information that the mercantile community could effectively transmit.[7] Clearly the mercantile community, like all occupational groups, had a distinct set of interests and concerns about which they might transmit information, but which might not necessarily be of interest to anyone other than merchants. Examples of this type of narrow interest information include news of crop

---

[6] Intelligence gathering, according to Gerolymatos, can be divided into two main ways of collection, either overt or covert (1986, 12-13). Spying, for example, is a covert means of gathering intelligence whereas the incidental data collected by diplomats or merchants whilst visiting other states can be seen as overt. Therefore the use of the term "intelligence" in this paper envisages the type of *overt* espionage that any foreign visitor to a city could collect with a fair amount of ease, either consciously or unconsciously, on the condition that they had freedom of movement within the *polis*. My use of the term does not, therefore, include more *covert* types of espionage that have traditionally been associated with spies, secret agents, or, less frequently, scouts.

[7] Lycurg. *Leoc.* 18.

failures, high prices for commodities in other *poleis*, sailing or weather conditions, piratical activity, or the opening and exploitation of new trade routes. Although Starr goes too far with his assumption that merchants were the foremost disseminators of all types of news and information, including new ideas, technologies and techniques, Lewis' and Mossé's view that merchants only relayed political information when it was directly relevant to themselves, is similarly flawed.[8] Mossé concludes her article examining the links between trade and politics with the statement,

> "If the world of the emporium remained marginal in relation to the city during the second half of the fourth century to which the speeches of Demosthenes belong, it is surely because 'trade and politics' belonged to two mutually impenetrable domains."[9]

This is an opinion shared by Lewis, who similarly separates merchants from the political life of the *polis*. Lewis' downplaying of the importance of merchants within the 'official channels' for the collection and collation of intelligence reports is founded upon the traditional perception that the mercantile community was a fringe group comprised primarily of metics and foreigners. She therefore states, "There was to a large extent separation between the world of the respectable citizen and the world of the *emporion*."[10]

In order to consolidate her position, Lewis identifies four major concerns that Greek society had with news that had been transmitted outside of official channels, namely the identity of the bearer, the social class of the bearer, the nature of the account (i.e. was the account first or second hand), and the potential motivation of the bearer.[11] Clearly each of these concerns would, in relation to merchant messengers, be exacerbated if we accept the traditionally negative perceptions of the social status, affluence and ethnicity of the mercantile community. Thus, for example, the identity of a foreign inter-regional merchant would be hard to verify, which would in turn immediately call into question his credibility as a reliable source of intelligence.

The perceived poverty of the mercantile community would also have raised concerns in regards to a merchant's motivation for disseminating information. In general, it was believed that men of low affluence were far more likely to transmit news or intelligence because of financial incentives

---

[8] Starr 1974, 22-24; Lewis 1996; Mossé 1983.
[9] Mossé 1983, 63.
[10] Lewis 1996, 119.
[11] Lewis 1996, 77-93.

rather than altruistic motives. For example, in Aristophanes'' *Wealth*, there are conflicting ideas about the relationship between virtue and wealth. All the main characters are poor and as such view wealth as the just rewards for upright and respected citizens, thereby suggesting that in a perfect world only the most worthy and honest would become wealthy.[12] However, when the character Penia—a personification of the abstract concept of poverty—enters, she argues that poverty breeds in men virtues such as hardiness and industry, both of which help improve their character. Penia continues her argument by suggesting that it is in fact destitution (or excessive wealth) that creates the ills of society; however her opponents disagree, instead proposing that poverty corrupts a man's character and leads him to immoral behaviour.[13] Similarly Plato can be found theorising on the link between extreme poverty, or indeed wealth, and the corruption of one's character. Plato proposed that, on the one hand, poverty brought about degeneracy due to the occupations, the living conditions, and the social position a man was forced to endure when poor, while wealth, on the other hand, bred idleness and overindulgence.[14]

With archaic and classical Greek morality suggesting that social class and honesty were intrinsically linked, it was possible to justify the downplaying of mercantile participation within official channels for the collection and transmission of news and intelligence. If we move away from the traditional models for the composition of the mercantile community, this position is no longer tenable.

II. The Solutions

So what solutions can be offered to these problems, and how does the reinterpretation of the composition and social perception of the mercantile community affect their acceptability as sources of information? Having demonstrated that the mercantile community comprised men with various degrees of affluence and from different ethnic groups, including large numbers of citizens, it is now possible to overcome many of the hindrances identified by Lewis, thus greatly increasing the suitability of merchants as disseminators of official intelligence.[15]

In relation to the establishment of identity it is now possible to suggest that members of the mercantile community were far from hampered by

---

[12] Ar. *Plut.* 88-90, 386-9, 489-97.

[13] Ar. *Plut.* 52-34, 557-61.

[14] Pl. *Resp.* 422A, 590B.

[15] Woolmer 2007.

their occupation. With the prevalence of inter-regional business relations, and the associated friendship that went with them, merchants were in an advantageous position when it came to establishing their identity. Furthermore, the frequent use of symbola and letters of introduction gave evidence that the bearer was who he claimed to be.[16] The positioning of the mercantile community as an occupational group who was an integrated part of Greek society, rather than a self-contained fringe group, means that their visibility to other citizens was not diminished, and as a result merchants must be considered as just as identifiable as anyone else. Furthermore, the private business links and the bestowal of the public title *proxenos* serve to undermine Mossé's conclusion that the world of the emporium, in Athens at least, was a marginal one that was distinguished sharply from the world of citizens and politics.[17] The existence of *proxenoi,* who were in many cases charged with safeguarding the interests of *emporoi* and *nauklēroi*, also had the unexpected outcome of creating a further group of men who could vouch for the identity and reputation of a mercantile messenger. In Athens, any foreign merchant wishing to offer a report to the *boule* would require a citizen to speak on their behalf, and in all probability this would be a *proxenos*. By raising the information in a public arena, a citizen would be offering his own personal guarantee on the reliability of the information being disseminated.[18] Furthermore, there are a number of inscriptions that record the granting to certain trusted *proxenoi* of access to a city or state when it was at war.[19] Although both Xenophon and Aeneas Tacticus suggest that foreign commercial operatives should be prohibited from entering a city facing a siege, the

---

[16] Herman 2002, 58-69.

[17] Mossé 1983, 53-63.

[18] In addition to vouching for the reliability of information provided by foreign merchants, there are also significant number instances when commercial *proxenoi* are believed to have undertaken espionage on behalf of their patron city. Although I disagree with his ultimate conclusion, that over time the institution of *proxenia* became primarily concerned with the creation of secret agents, Gerolymatos' study of the use of *proxenoi* as spies is comprehensive, and I would refer the reader who requires additional detail to his work, Gerolymatos 1986.

[19] This is a clause found in the *proxeny* decrees of a wide variety of Greek states, including the Boeotians when honouring Nuba of Carthage, Cnidians who honour Iphiades of Abydos (*Syll.*[3] 187), the Rhodians of Lindos when honouring Aeginetan of Naucratis (*Syll.*[3] 110), and the Olbiopolitans who honour Chareigenes of Mesembri (*Syll.*[3] 219), whilst similar privileges were granted by Paerisades to a citizen of the Euxine Piraeus (*Syll.*[3] 217).

granting of unrestricted access, even at such times, highlights the huge trust some merchants could attain.[20]

The next concern of the Greeks, when assessing the reliability of their sources of information, was the social class and reputation of the disseminator. Clearly reputation played a considerable role in the everyday life of the Greeks, and it has been proposed that access to different types of information was an important way that the status of a stranger could be identified.[21] As a result of this conceptual link between access to information and social status, the personal reputation of the individual disseminating information could have a direct influence on the credibility of the information itself. Many of the Greek historians, including Herodotus, Thucydides, and Xenophon stress the credibility of their sources in order to prove the accuracy of their information. As a result of this need to prove truthfulness, Herodotus can be found recording that his sources were "distinguished men."[22] Furthermore, all three historians were keen to emphasise the "official" nature of their sources, with Thucydides stating that he "did not think it right to take my account of the war on the first witness I chanced upon."[23] Although there are a number of ways this statement can be interpreted, the most logical seems to be the one put forward by Hornblower, who argues that it is the by-product of social snobbery.[24] Thucydides can therefore be seen as trying to demonstrate that he did not garner his information from just anybody, but instead consulted upper class or more knowledgeable informants. Gomme has understood this passage as an attempt by Thucydides to contrast his methods of research, i.e. correlating and analysing a number of accounts, with that of Herodotus, whom he saw as in general accepting the first report he was given.[25] From such passages it is possible to identify that, amongst the historians, it was a commonly held belief that aristocrats or witnesses of high status were more likely to give reliable accounts.

The historians' belief that upper-class individuals were more reliable sources of information can be seen as a reflection of Greek society in general. Lewis observes that lower status informants are only identified in the Greek sources by toponym; for example the Histiaean who informed

---

[20] Aen. Tact. 29.12. Although Aen. Tact. alludes to a conspiracy that utilises the freedom of movement offered to merchants, he frustratingly provides no details. Xen. *Eq. mag.* 4.7.

[21] Lewis 1996, 19-20.

[22] Hdt. 9.16 (Theander), 2.3 (Priestly information), 2.28 (scribe of Saïs).

[23] Thuc. 1.21.

[24] See Lewis 1996, 177 n. 57.

[25] Gomme and Dover 1970, 141.

Xerxes of the Greek fleet's departure from Artemisium, recorded by Herodotus, or the Cretan who reports to Agesilaus in Xenophons' *Hellenica*.[26] With the rise of a social structure under which status followed wealth, rather than wealth following status, the idea that affluence and honesty were somehow linked began to be eroded.[27] During the classical period this revision process was still ongoing, and therefore, although the links between wealth and credibility were diminishing, it is still possible to identify poor litigants who feel it necessary to defend their moral character purely because of their low level of affluence.[28] On the basis of my suggested revision of the composition of the mercantile community to include men with a broad spectrum of affluence rather than merely the poor or destitute, it is again possible to eliminate some of the barriers previously thought to have limited the importance of merchants within the infrastructure of information exchange. If we now accept that a considerable proportion of the mercantile community was either moderately affluent or wealthy, then the social standing of these men would, following Lewis' argument, have greater credibility as bearers of news or intelligence.

The hypothesis that the Greeks drew a clear distinction between first-hand accounts and hearsay or rumour is one that we have already seen in relation to the historians. In the same way that historians could point to their use of eyewitness accounts and testimonies as a way of providing evidence that the details they provide were accurate and truthful, messengers could also establish the reliability of their reports if they could demonstrate that they, or their source, had witnessed the events first hand. For example, Xenophon records that Dercylidas was charged with carrying the news of the Spartan victory at Nemea to the allies in Asia Minor because he was actually present at the battle.[29] Although not a merchant, the example of Dercylidas highlights the importance placed upon firsthand accounts or eyewitness testimonies.

The pre-eminence of firsthand accounts again places merchants in an advantageous position, as they, or their associates, were frequently in a position to witness the major political events they reported. Although the information they collected could be distorted by the efforts of the people they observed, as can be seen in the case of a group of Athenian envoys in

---

[26] Lewis 1996, 86; Hdt. 8.23; Xen. *Hell.* 7.5.10.

[27] For a fuller discussion of the transformation from a social structure in which wealth followed social status to a system wherein social status followed wealth see Tandy 2000, 135-8.

[28] Lewis 1996, 88.

[29] Xen., *Hell.* 4.3.1-2.

416 BC, merchants could at least claim to be disseminating eyewitness reports.[30]

The final concern that has been voiced over the usefulness of merchants as sources of intelligence is their motivation for disseminating any information they acquired. Previous studies have concluded that merchants were rarely interested in disseminating any incidental intelligence they might acquire whilst abroad, due to the fact that the mercantile community was considered to be divorced from the interests of the *polis*. However, an examination of the evidence refutes this assessment and instead points towards merchants having a keen interest in local and foreign politics.[31] Xenophon, in the *Memorabilia,* states that *emporoi* took their place amongst other occupational groupings in the Athenian assembly, and suggests that they were in fact both politically interested and active.[32] Additionally, Thucydides describes the wealthy democrats of Corcyra as being men who dwelt in and around the harbour district, and Knorringa has reasonably suggested that these men were, in all probability, wealthy merchants.[33] Further evidence can also be found in the *Periplus Maris Erythraei*, which demonstrates that at least some elements of the mercantile community had an interest in politics both at home and abroad.[34] By correlating the information provided by the author of this work it is possible to create an almost complete political map of the ancient regions the work embraces.[35]

---

[30] Thuc. 6.6.3, 6.46.3-5, 6.8.1-3. In the case of Egesta, Athens dispatched a group of diplomatic envoys in order to ascertain the economic strength of the city and thus determine if it was worth supporting. The Egestans deceived the Athenians by publicly displaying, in a lavish manner, what little wealth they possessed, thereby suggesting a greater affluence than was the case in reality.

[31] Lewis 1996, 32.

[32] Xen. *Mem.* 3.7.6.

[33] Thuc. 1.25, 1.30, 1.38. Knorringa 1961, 59.

[34] Although the *Periplus Maris Erythraei* falls outside of the period discussed in the rest of this paper, it is the personal account of an Egyptian-Greek merchant, written sometime between AD 40 and AD 70, and is thus of importance. The text is complete and provides unrivalled insights into the lives of merchants sailing the trade routes between Egypt and Africa and between Egypt and India. From the account it is possible to identify the social and economic interactions of inter-regional merchants, and, more importantly for this paper, the type of incidental intelligence a merchant might acquire whilst abroad.

[35] Within the account, the author details for each of the regions he has traversed the type of ruling body, the extent of each country, and the general reaction to and treatment of foreign visitors. For example, in Africa the author examines the region of Berenice on the southern border of Roman Egypt, recording that this was where

With the evidence now being interpreted to indicate that citizens were an integral part of the mercantile community within many *poleis*, it becomes justifiable to theorise that the mercantile community might disseminate information for more altruistic motives. For a citizen, the transmission of information that could be of significant importance to the *polis* would be considered a civic duty. Just as citizens might fear being called unpatriotic if they voted against a popular decision in the assembly,[36] the same was true if they were found to have knowledge that could have been of benefit to the *polis*, but which they failed to communicate.[37] Although it is unlikely that any charges would be brought against a citizen who failed to share information that may have prevented damage or loss to the state, the likelihood is that such men would be branded traitors and thus shunned by peers. Secrecy and lack of communication were therefore seen as unnatural, and the citizen should, by definition, be willing to share any information he had at his disposal. What these examples begin to demonstrate is that merchants were an integral part of *polis* politics and, as a consequence, were concerned with disseminating any significant political news or intelligence, irrespective of whether it was of direct relevance to trading operations.

III. Mercantile Intelligence Gatherers

Although there is a scarcity of evidence which explicitly depicts merchants as spies, it is possible to identify that Greek inter-regional

---

the barbarian lands begin and that the region was recorded as being populated by a series of tribes ruled by local chieftains (*PME*, 2.1.7-10).

[36] See for example Thuc. 6.24.4, 3.42.5, 15.25.1, 15.33ff.

[37] For example, both Sparta and Crete encouraged the sharing of information amongst citizens through the promotion of the *sussition* (shared mess), membership of which was compulsory for citizens (Arist. *Pol.* 1271a26-37). The *sussition* provided the opportunity not only to share food, but also to hear conversation and information that reinforced the *polis* ethics. Additionally, the *sussition* provided a forum in which politics and foreign news could be heard and then debated. Therefore, citizen merchants who had travelled abroad could use the *sussition* as a platform from which they could impress their peers with the intelligence they had acquired in the course of their travels. As the sharing of relevant news and information was an expected part of the experience, and as the dissemination of valuable intelligence could raise the social and political standing and reputation of an individual, it is something that citizens would partake in willingly. Sparta: Plut. *Lyc.* 12.4, Xen. *Lac.* 5.5-6. Crete: Ephorus *FGrH* 70 F149 (= Strabo 10.4.16); Dosiadas *FGrH* 458 F2 (= Ath. 143d).

[37] Price (2003) 30-35.

merchants had a number of traits that made them ideal intelligence gathers. Firstly, with trade networks spanning from Britain in the west and possibly as far as India in the east, Greek merchants had an unrivalled opportunity to cross international borders. Secondly, due to the nature of Greek sailing techniques (i.e. hugging the coastal waters), it was a common sight to see foreign merchants sailing just off shore; thus, they rarely aroused suspicion. Thirdly, as already demonstrated, the author of the *Periplus Maris Erythaei* clearly indicates that merchants could be expected to know the type of ruling body, the extent of the country, and the reaction to foreign visitors in each of the regions they traversed. Fourthly, Xenophon advocates the consultation of inter-regional merchants prior to a siege in order to gauge the attitude and morale of an enemy city. Xenophon's justification for the employment of merchants as scouts is that, as a general rule, they were universally welcome because of the commodities they carried.[38] This use of merchants as a way of gathering intelligence is also alluded to by Aeneas Tacticus who warns that, although trade could bring in food and resources vital to a city facing a siege, it also presented merchants with an opportunity to collect intelligence.[39]

Fifthly, maritime merchants were in a unique position to evaluate the military strength of a *polis*, in particular its naval capabilities. With only a few *poleis* being in the same fortunate position as Athens and Corinth of having separate commercial and military ports, most cities were forced into using their only sizeable harbour to undertake both these functions. As a direct consequence of this, a visiting merchant could easily observe the build-up of military power or the readying of a fleet for a major naval offensive. The Rhodians, for example, during the time of their naval supremacy, were so security conscious that the death penalty was inflicted upon anyone convicted of spying, or even trespassing, in the naval dockyards.[40] This was also a particular concern for Aeneas Tacticus, who warns that any city facing a siege should be aware of the security risks posed by the type of intelligence that could be gathered by visiting merchants. He therefore proposes that, in order to minimise the opportunity for visiting merchants to gather intelligence, a state should introduce strict restrictions on the locations where mercantile vessels were

---

[38] Xen. *Eq. mag.* 4.7.
[39] Aen. Tact. 28.4-7. This was also a concern of Nicarchus who, in Aristophanes' *Acharnians* (912-926), threatens to denounce a Theban merchant as he was found to be importing candle wicks that could be used to set fire to the dockyards.
[40] Strabo 14.2.5.

permitted to moor.[41] Furthermore, he suggests that the city's revenue officials should examine carefully any commodities entering the *polis*, either by land or sea, in order to ensure, firstly, that nothing illegal is smuggled in, and, secondly, that no known spies are attempting to disguise themselves as merchants.[42]

Despite a number of the military tacticians suggesting that merchants *could* be used as spies, there are no surviving direct examples of this actually occurring, our closest account being the fictitious merchant in Sophocles' *Philoctetes*.[43] In the play, a merchant, Emporos, warns Neoptolemus of the Greek fleet sailing towards Troy, even listing the strength and number of vessels in the armada:

"With no great company I am homeward bound on my trader's voyage from Ilium to Peparethus with its cluster-laden vines, but when I heard that the sailors [550] were all of your crew, I resolved not to continue my voyage in silence, without first giving you my news and getting the due reward. You know nothing, I suspect, of your own affairs: the new designs the Greeks [555] have regarding you, and not only designs, but deeds in progress and no longer postponed."[44]

Although this example belongs to the realm of fiction, it does serve to demonstrate the ease with which merchants and espionage could be linked.

Richmond, in his article *Spies in Ancient Greece*, points to the importance of markets and trade centres as places of refuge for the would-be spy.[45] Firstly, on account of the large concentration of other transient elements, these centres offered ideal cover for any foreigner who wished to remain undetected. Furthermore, the agora and emporium were places where information was exchanged regularly, and, thus, rumours and news could easily be obtained without attracting undue attention. This hypothesis would appear to be borne out by the cases of Anaxinus, the

---

[41] Richmond points to the German invasion of Denmark and Norway in 1940 to demonstrate the usefulness of merchant vessels for making covert landings. Richmond 1998, 16 n. 33.

[42] Aen. Tact. 29, 2.5.

[43] Soph. *Phil.* 551-2.

[44] Soph. *Phil.* 551-5: πλέων γὰρ ὡς ναύκληρος οὐ πολλῷ στόλῳ ἀπ' Ἰλίου πρὸς οἶκον ἐς τὴν εὔβοτρυν Πεπάρηθον, ὡς ἤκουσα τοὺς ναύτας ὅτι σοὶ πάντες εἶεν συννεναυστοληκότες, ἔδοξέ μοι μὴ σῖγα, πρὶν φράσαιμί σοι, τὸν πλοῦν ποεῖσθαι, προστυχόντι τῶν ἴσων. οὐδὲν σύ που κάτοισθα τῶν σαυτοῦ πέρι, ἃ τοῖσιν Ἀργείοισιν ἀμφὶ σοῦ νέα βουλεύματ' ἐστί, κοὐ μόνον βουλεύματα, ἀλλ' ἔργα δρώμεν', οὐκέτ' ἐξαργούμενα.

[45] Richmond 1998, 6.

envoy of the Queen of Macedon, and Antiphon, a previous guest friend of Demosthenes, both of whom were charged with espionage having been discovered operating in the Piraeus.[46] Furthermore, Plutarch records that professional spies often disguised themselves as merchants in order to blend into the commercial community and thus remain invisible.[47] Although these examples do not demonstrate merchants undertaking espionage themselves, they are illustrative of how the occupation of merchant could provide the perfect cover for the would-be spy.[48] The ease with which information could be exchanged and collected in the harbours, agoras, and emporiums of the Greek states again implies that merchants were in an ideal position to garner intelligence and that commercial activities and information gathering often went hand in hand.

This theory is lent support by the actions of the Spartans during the early years of the Peloponnesian War. Thucydides, in his account for the year 430/29, records that from the very outset of war the Spartans had been capturing all Athenian and allied traders who sailed around the Peloponnese and had thrown them into pits. Furthermore, he claims that "Indeed, at the beginning of the war the Spartans killed as enemies all whom they captured on the sea, whether allies of Athens or neutrals."[49] One way of interpreting this passage is to suggest that the Spartans were so fearful of the political and military intelligence that could be collected by merchants that they were willing to execute both friend and foe in order to prevent the dissemination of sensitive information. This interpretation is supported by the actions of Alcibiades, who attempts to prevent the news of his expedition reaching his enemies by seizing mercantile vessels.[50] Similarly, the actions of an anonymous trader who tipped off the Peloponnesians on Abydus that the Athenians planned to slip by them, and the Sinopean merchants who reported Xenophon's intent to found a colony if provisions were not found for his men can also be interpreted in this way.[51]

Finally, although the historians of Philip and Alexander leave us in the dark about both men's intelligence gathering whilst preparing for the invasion of Persia, Richmond suggests we can gain an insight through an examination of Caesar's strategies prior to the invasion of Britain, as the

---

[46] Dem. 18.133; Ath. 2.66d.
[47] Plut. *Pel.* 14.2.
[48] Russell 1999, 105-106.
[49] Thuc. 2.67.4.
[50] Plut. *Alc.* 28, Xen. *Hell.* 1.1.15.
[51] Thuc. 8.102.2, Xen. *An.* 5.6.19.

Roman general was faced with many of the same problems.[52] When Julius Caesar first began to formulate his plans to invade the little-known island of Britain, he recognised the importance of acquiring intelligence pertaining to the region's political make-up, social infrastructures, topography, and military strength. Caesar informs his reader in the *Gallic Wars* that his first option was to summon merchants from all over the Mediterranean in order to try to determine the size of the island, the name of the indigenous people, the local customs, the local methods of warfare, and the location of deep-water harbours able to cope with the large number of vessels required to transport his troops.[53] Although Caesar records that he was unable to obtain any of this information due to the obscurity of Britain as a destination, clearly the expectation was that, under normal circumstances, merchants would have knowledge pertaining to all these things. The Britons, it is interesting to note, seem to have been more successful at obtaining intelligence from their mercantile community than the Romans. Caesar records that it is a group of merchants that warns the Britons of his planned invasion; this therefore eliminated the advantage of surprise he hoped to obtain and forced him to engage a fully prepared army.

Returning to Alexander, who was known for recognising the importance of accurate information,[54] it is hard to believe he would have achieved so many military victories if he had consistently ignored, or failed to obtain, up-to-date intelligence. It is therefore not too fanciful to suggest that he utilised the reports and accounts of merchants who had travelled the interior of the Persian empire, in a similar manner to Caesar, in order to gain the detailed intelligence vital to a successful campaign.[55]

Conclusions

From the scant evidence recorded by the Greek military analysts, and from the inferred parallels with Caesar's invasion of Britain, Richmond draws the conclusion that, "any Greek commander worth his salt will send

---

[52] Richmond 1998, 4-5.

[53] Caes. *B. Gall.* 4.21.

[54] Plutarch demonstrates Alexander's keen interest in up-to-date intelligence when he records that, as a child, Alexander questioned the Persian envoys about the lengths of roads and the topography of the route to the centre of the Great King's empire. Plut. *Alex.* 5.2.

[55] Starr also considers it highly probable that both Alexander and Philip used merchants as sources of information in their preparations for the invasion of Persia (Starr 1974, 22-4).

out scouts (*kataskopoi*) and question merchants, captives, prisoners, deserters and the like...,"[56] and it is hard to disagree with his hypothesis. The more positive picture of the social perception and standing of Greek merchants constructed by my previous research enables us to remove some of the main objections to the theory that merchants were useful conduits for the gathering and dissemination of intelligence. Despite there being no surviving sources which records explicitly the use of inter-regional merchants as credible sources of intelligence, the frequency with which the military analysts advise on how to employ counter-measures to protect the city against information gathering by members of the mercantile community implies that merchants were a recognised part of the espionage networks of the Greek *poleis*. The ability of inter-regional merchants to move unhindered across political boundaries without arousing suspicion, combined with their freedom of movement once in foreign states, gave merchants the ideal opportunity to act as spies or information gatherers on behalf of their *polis*.

Bibliography

Gerolymatos, A. *Espionage and Treason: A Study of Proxenia in Political and Military Intelligence Gathering in Classical Greece*. Amsterdam: Gieben, 1986.

Gomme, A. W., Andrews, A., and Dover, K. J. *A Historical Commentary on Thucydides*. Oxford: Clarendon Press, 1970.

Garnsey, P., Hopkins, K., and Whittaker C. R. (eds.) *Trade in the Ancient Economy*. Berkeley: University of California Press, 1983.

Herman, G. *Ritualised Friendship and the Greek City*. Cambridge: Cambridge University Press, 2002.

Horden, P and Purcell, N. *The Corrupting Sea; a Study of Mediterranean History*. Oxford: Blackwell Publishers, 2000.

Lewis, S. *News and Society in the Ancient World*. Chapel Hill (North Carolina): University of North Carolina Press, 1996.

Mossé, C. "The World of the Emporium in the Private Speeches of Demosthenes." In *Trade in the Ancient Economy*, edited by P. Garnsey, K. Hopkins and C.R. Whittaker, 53-63, Berkeley: University of California Press, 1983.

Price, D. "Cloak and Trowel; Should Archaeologists Double as Spies?" *Archaeology Magazine*, 56 (5) 2003: 30-35.

---

[56] Russell 1999, 54-55.

Reed, C. M. *Maritime Traders in the Ancient Greek World*. Cambridge: Cambridge University Press, 2003.

Richmond, J. A. "Spies in Ancient Greece." *G&R* 2nd Series 45(1) (1998): 1-18.

Russel, F. *Information Gathering in Classical Greece*. Ann Arbor: University of Michigan Press, 1999.

Starr, C. G. *Political Intelligence in Classical Greece*. Leiden: Mnemosyne Supplement 31, 1974.

Woolmer, M. A. *The Athenian Mercantile Community; a Reappraisal of the Social, Political and Legal Status of Inter-Regional Merchants During the Fourth-Century*. Unpublished PhD. Thesis, Cardiff University, 2007.

CHAPTER FIVE

HOW TO BECOME A RENOWNED GENERAL WITHOUT WINNING BATTLES: THE CASE OF CONON

LUCA ASMONTI

In his seminal paper on the "Rules of war in classical Greece,"[1] Josiah Ober analysed how the steady growth of the Athenian fleet in the decades after Salamis and, consequently, the growing political weight of the "masses" serving as rowers brought about a veritable revolution in the Greek customs of fighting. Traditionally, Greek vs. Greek conflicts had been pretty codified affairs. The fighting essentially consisted in the clash—or clashes—between two deployments of hoplite infantrymen. War was not supposed to affect non-combatants, and it had to be carried out during the usual summer campaign season, in respect of the prescribed periods of truce. A series of rituals unmistakably indicated the onset and conclusion of fighting, as well as victory and defeat.[2] The development of Athens into a maritime empire, whose wealth lay in accumulated liquidity,[3] was to be "fatal" to this code of military practice, as most clearly exposed in the conclusive chapters of the first book of Thucydides' *Histories*. On the eve of the conflict against Sparta, Pericles outlined to his fellow-citizens a revolutionary strategy, by the employment of which the *polis* would make the most of its strengths: the fleet, the liquidity coming from the allies, and the democratic constitution.[4] Most notably, unlike Sparta, Athens could afford to sustain a prolonged conflict:[5] what the Athenians had to do, therefore, was not simply to overcome the enemy on

---

[1] Now in Ober 1996, 53-71.
[2] Ober 1996, 56.
[3] Thuc. I.141.5.
[4] Financial conditions of the two contestants: Thuc. I.141.3-5. Superiority of the Athenian constitution: Thuc. I.14.6-8 The art of seamanship: Thuc. I.142.5-9.
[5] Thuc. I.141.6; see Ober 1996, 65.

the battlefield, but to exhaust progressively their resources and undermine the social-political basis of their power by means of protracted transmarine warfare. This was to revolutionise the role of *strategoi*, the generals at the head of the Athenian military. As Ober puts it:

> "It was the beginning of truly sophisticated long-term strategic analysis. Rather than worrying about the tactical problem of how to win a particular battle, Pericles thought trough the interplay of a variety of forces—military, financial, political, and psychological—over the course of a war that he knew would take several years at least [...]. He had in essence invented grand strategy."[6]

As we shall try to demonstrate here, the career of Conon (ca. 444 — 390 BC), the Athenian general veteran of the war against Sparta, who ten years after the disaster of Aegospotami would defeat the Spartan fleet at Cnidus, in many respects epitomises the growing importance of the *interplay* of forces cited by Ober in shaping the career of a successful military leader, especially as concerned the *behind-the-battlefields* duties of his office. In the brief space of these pages we cannot offer an exhaustive survey of the deeds of our man; rather, what we want to do here is to offer some hints to stimulate debate over the changing role of military leaders in the Aegean realm between the end of the fifth and the beginning of the fourth centuries BC.

Conon is usually remembered by ancient sources as the protagonist of the supposed revival of Athenian imperialism in the early years of the fourth century. After defeating the Spartans at Cnidus, Conon and his mentor Pharnabazus cruised the Aegean, expelling the Spartan garrisons from the islands and towns and promising independence and freedom to the "allies" of Lacedaemon. Thence the general triumphantly returned to Athens and completed the reconstruction of the Long Walls of the Piraeus, the greatest symbol of the maritime ambition of the *polis*..[7] For ancient sources,[8] his career was, indeed, encapsulated in those two highly symbolic achievements: destroying the Spartan fleet and rebuilding the Long Walls.

This attitude has inevitably affected our knowledge of the previous

---

[6] Ober 1996, 66.

[7] Battle of Cnidus: Xen *.Hell.* IV.3.11-12; Diod. XIV.83.5-84.4. Diplomatic activity in the aftermath of the battle: Xen. *Hell.* IV.8.2; Diod. XIV.83.3-4. The Long Walls rebuilt: Xen. *Hell.* IV.8.9.

[8] Dem. XX.68-69, XXII.72, XXIV.180; Isoc. IV.142, XII.97-105; Lyc. *Leoc.* 51; Din. I.75; see Nouhaud 1982, 335.

phases of his activity, which have been often read solely in the light of the battle of Cnidus and its outcome. For instance, it is often taken for granted that, as soon as Conon set sail to Cyprus after the disaster of Aegospotami, his only concern was how to restore the Athenian *arche* which had just been destroyed by the Spartan triremes, as envisaged in a eulogistic passage of Isocrates:

> "Who does not know about Conon, first among the Greeks for his very many glorious deeds, that when his own city had met with ill-fortune, he chose out of all the world Evagoras and came to him, believing that for himself he would provide the most secure asylum and for his country the most speedy assistance. And indeed Conon, although he had been successful in many previous ventures, in no one of them, it is believed, had he planned more wisely than in this; for the result of his visit to Cyprus was that he both conferred and received most benefits. In the first place, no sooner had Evagoras and Conon met one another than they esteemed each other more highly than those who before had been their intimate friends. Again, they not only were in complete harmony all their lives regarding all other matters, but also in matters relating to our own city they held to the same opinion. For when they beheld Athens under the domination of the Spartans and the victim of a great reversal of fortune, they were filled with grief and indignation, both acting fittingly [...]. And while they were deliberating how they might free Athens from her misfortunes, the Spartans themselves soon furnished the opportunity."[9]

The approach of most modern scholars is not too different from that of Isocrates; Conon was the victor of the battle of Cnidus, one of the most important naval engagements in the history of ancient Greece, so we can take for granted that, by the time he was appointed at the head of the Persian fleet, he was a skilled and above all successful general. There is therefore no need at all to investigate what Isocrates means by Conon's "many previous successful ventures." Yet that would be anything but a frivolous exercise, and one which would help to clarify what made a good and reliable *strategos* in the eyes of the Athenian *demos* or in those of a Persian satrap.

At the time of the end of the Peloponnesian War (spring 404), Conon was the commander in chief, or *strategos autokrator*, of the Athenian forces in the Aegean. He had taken over the office from the disgraced

---

[9] Isoc. IX.53.54. Conon at Cyprus: Isoc. IX.62-63; Plut. *Artax.* XXI.1; Iustin. VI.1.7.

Alcibiades in the spring of 406, following the defeat of Notium.[10] Being appointed *strategos autokrator* was possibly the highest responsibility that the Athenian state could entrust to an individual; it should therefore be assumed that Conon's profile was absolutely outstanding. M. Ostwald, for one, has no doubt that Conon was "an experienced soldier", who was kept "out of political trouble throughout a life devoted to the service of his country" by his "genius and good fortune".[11] We have no reason to doubt Conon's loyalty to Athens, but in what did his "genius" and "military experience" consist?

Prior to his appointment in 407/406, Conon had in all likelihood already served as *strategos* for two terms. In the winter or 414/413, he was dispatched to Naupactus, the Athenian naval outpost in the Peloponnese, at the head of a fleet of twenty triremes. Thucydides is our only source on these events, but he does not go any farther than saying that Conon *herche Naupaktou* and that at some time he had to set sail to Plerumnion to ask for reinforcements from his colleague Demosthenes, possibly after losing two ships in an engagement against the Corinthian fleet.[12] Three years later, soon after the overthrow of the Four Hundred, Conon was appointed to his second strategy, and was sent again to Naupactus. During this second tenure, he was also dispatched to Corcyra, where *stasis* had broken out between the local democratic faction, supported by Athens, and the pro-Spartans. The operation, however, was only partially successful.[13]

After the mission to Corcyra, we do not hear of Conon until his third appointment to the *strategia*, in 407/406.[14] Although Conon was soon to take over the supreme command of the fleet after the battle of Notium, we are very badly informed about his activity. From the narratives of Diodorus and Xenophon, we might gather that he had been at the siege of Andros from the fall of 407 to the moment he was called to take over the command of the fleet at Samos, but we do not know whether the town

---

[10] Battle of Notium: Xen. *Hell.* I.5.10-15; Diod. XIII.71.1-4; see Kagan 1987, 310; Lazenby 2004, 220-224. Appointment of Conon: Xen. *Hell.* I.5.16-18; Diod. XIII.74.1. Chronology: Kagan 1987, 312.

[11] Ostwald 1986, 428-432.

[12] Conon's first term in Naupactus: Thuc. VII.19.5, 31.4-5; see Barbieri 1955, 9. The Athenian naval outpost of Naupactus: Thuc. II.69.1, 80.1, I.103.3, see Badian 1990, 365, Hornblower 1991, 160-161. Thuc. II.9.4 cites the 'Messenians in Naupactus' among the Athenian *symmachoi* at the outbreak of the Peloponnesian War.

[13] Conon's second term in Naupactus and the mission to Corcyra: Diod. XIII.48.6-8.

[14] The board of *strategoi* for 407/406: Xen. *Hell.* I.5.16-18; Diod. XIII.74.1-2. Date of the *archeresiai*: Kagan 1987, 286.

capitulated before his departure.[15]

This is what Conon had so far achieved when he was entrusted with the supreme command of the Athenian fleet in the Aegean. These were the deeds which, as Ostwald put it, made Conon appear "a worthy successor of Alcibiades."[16] Given his three terms as *strategos*, Conon could be surely considered an above-averagely experienced general, but was that enough to make him the most suitable candidate for the job? Did the two terms spent at Naupactus and the siege of Andros really represent an outstanding resume? Most notably, Conon does not appear to have been involved in any major—and successful—battle.

In his book *Imperatores Victi*, Nathan Rosenstein argues that in late-republic Rome military defeats had virtually "no effect" on aristocratic competition, for defeated generals were granted a sort of immunity from the public's hostility, deriving from a widespread consensus, shared by both the political elite and the electoral body, on the basic principles of the Roman republican mentality, namely the role of divine intervention in human affairs—war above all—the cult of military discipline, and the acknowledged superiority of the aristocratic ethos.[17] This was not the case in classical Athens, where "successful war leaders enjoyed great influence in the political arena, but those whose operations failed regularly paid a heavy price."

Rosenstein corroborates his assumptions by citing the evidence on the cases of prosecution against *strategoi*,[18] most of which were actually connected with military failure; such perspective, however, can easily be found somewhat simplistic. For if the career of a strategos was to be judged exclusively on the number of victories, Conon's military career would surely have been much less impressive than that of Alcibiades, or of the other admirals, the likes of Thrasybulus and Thrasyllus, whose names were linked to the great naval victories of Cynossema, Abydus, Cyzicus, and Chios (410-408 BC).[19]

After the defeat at Notium and a quite slow-witted action against the

---

[15] See Kagan 1987, 323-324.

[16] See also Hatzfeld 1951, 293.

[17] Rosenstein 1990, 50-53 (mutual assistance among members of republican elites), 54-91 (divine intervention in war mechanics), 92-113 (discipline and bravery), 114-152 (aristocratic ethos). On the 'vulnerability' of Athenian *strategoi*, see also Pritchett 1974, 20; Sinclair 1988, 146-152. Evidence on *eisangeliai* against generals: Hansen 1975, 59-65, 69-120.

[18] Rosenstein 1990, 9, 166; see also Pritchett 1974, 20; Harris 1989, 264-265.

[19] Cynossema: Thuc. VIII.104.1-106.1. Cyzicus: Xen. *Hell.* I.1.14-22. Chios: Xen. *Hell.* I.1.1-7; Diod. XIII.45.1-47.2.

town of Cyme, in fact an ally of Athens,[20] the citizens dismissed Alcibiades and appointed a new board of generals, Conon, as we said, being at its head.[21] In a political perspective, this reshuffle has generally been read in terms of factional strife: Alcibiades had fallen into disgrace, drowning his associates with him, This eventually led to the dismissal of Theramenes, Thrasybulus, and Adeimantus,[22] as well as to the appointment of generals who were more acceptable to the groups hostile to Alcibiades, chiefly the so-called moderates. It would, however, be advisable not to confine our notion of "political factors" determining the appointment of senior officers to the bargaining among members of the elite, and take into consideration other, possibly more relevant, political issues. As for the board appointed after Notium, for instance, we should also wonder whether having been appointed outside Athens, by a gathering of soldiers, probably including non-Athenians, through a process which Thucydides interestingly defined as a *metabole*, viz. something quite close to *stasis*,[23] may have contributed to undermine the legitimacy of the role enjoyed by the likes of Thrasybulus and Alcibiades at Samos once their row of victories came to an end, whereas the career of Conon, however less spectacular, seems to have developed completely within the frame of democratic institutions.

Leaving aside generic references to Conon's aptitude as a naval commander, like Ostwald's or Hatzfeld's, the military issues at stake in the aftermath of Alcibiades' dismissal have been, as far as I know, slightly overlooked. My impression is that, from an exclusively military point of view, the appointment of Conon to the supreme naval command might be seen as a demonstration that Athenian *strategoi* were judged and selected by taking into account a wider range of skills than just strategic expertise and the ratio of victories to losses.

Providing effective training and adequate maintenance for the troops, administering sensibly the resources of the fleet, and acting as the

---

[20] The facts of Cyme: Diod. XIII.73.6; Corn. Nep. VII.2.

[21] The dismissal of Alcibiades: Xen. *Hell.* I.5.16; Lys. XXI.7; Corn. Nep. VIII.3; Plut. *Alc.* 36.3, *Lys.* V.2; Diod. XIII.74.1. It is not completely clear whether Alcibiades was simply not confirmed in the board at the *archeresiai* for 406/405, or rather he was indicted and removed directly after the facts of Notium and an extraordinary session of *archeresiai* had therefore to be held, as asserted in Busolt 1904, 1578. For a comprehensive analysis of the evidence, see Kagan 1987, 322-323.

[22] See Ostwald 1986, 430-431; Kagan 1987, 325-326; Buck 1998, 20-21, 46.

[23] The Samian *metabole*: Thuc. VIII.75.2, 76.1. Meaning of *metabole* in Thucydides: Price 2001, 313-315.

diplomatic representative of the *polis* were all duties which a *strategos* was supposed to perform efficiently. For the commander of the base of Samos, these "behind-the-battlefield duties" were, I think, as relevant as delivering successful battle-plans, especially in the aftermath of Notium. In order to understand why, it might be particularly interesting to discuss the degree of authority which the commanders at Samos were eventually granted, and the urgencies they had to face.

As I said, my impression is that Conon took over the command at Samos with the rank of *strategos autokrator*, or plenipotentiary commander. This is implied by the available evidence. For we learn from Diodorus that when the *ekklesia* elected Alcibiades to the board of *strategoi* in 407, he was granted "supreme power" (*strategon katastesanes autokratoras*) on both land and sea, and when he was dismissed, he had to give up his armaments as well as his *arche*, that is, I think, the plenipotentiary authority which he had been entrusted with, to Conon.[24]

From our sources, especially if one has in mind the grandiose scene of Alcibiades landing at the Piraeus described by Xenophon,[25] the grant of plenipotentiary (*autokrator*) powers appears as a personal reward for the *polis*' prodigal son; I am rather inclined to think that the very office of head of the fleet at Samos may have implied the grant of plenipotentiary power, principally by reason of the political, diplomatic and administrative responsibilities which it entailed.

The Athenian *demos* could decide to grant *autokrator* authority to a general, or a group of generals, who were to face a particularly delicate mission, especially when operating far away from Athens. The first known case of officials granted such authority is that of the three generals of the infamous Sicilian expedition of 415, who were given a freer-than-usual hand, particularly as concerned the recruitment of troops and the management of diplomatic relations with foreign states in the course of the campaign..[26] These two issues were, indeed, matters of primary concern for the commander at Samos, more than ever in the aftermath of Notium. On this account, it is interesting to observe that, from what we are told by our literary sources, one would assume that conducting large-scale military operations was hardly Conon's main task when he settled in Samos. Rather, the new commander seems to have been mainly concerned with the rationalisation and reorganisation of a fleet which had been badly affected by the recent defeats and by the haemorrhage of sailors, attracted

---

[24] Diod. XIII.69.3, 74.1-2.

[25] Xen. *Hell.* I.4.16-21; Plut. *Alc.* XXXII.1

[26] Generals of the Sicilian of expedition: Thuc. VI.8.1-3, 25.1-26.1, IG I³ 93, see Gomme, Andrewes and Dover 1970, 223-230, Hamel 1998, 201.

by the higher pay which the Spartans were now able to grant thanks to Persia's financial support.[27]

That was possibly not the first time that Conon had to deal with such organisational duties; indeed, he may have been entrusted with very similar responsibilities during his terms in charge of the base of Naupactus. Thucydides, as we have seen, simply says that in 414/413 Conon *herche Naupaktou*, without specifying his actual rank. Most scholars think that the appointment represented Conon's first *strategia*, as I do; but the debate is still open, or at least has been kept so by B. Jordan, according to whom Conon in 414/413 was not a *strategos*, but one of those *archontes*, or "governors", whom he thinks the Athenians used to appoint "in some of the subject states and in other strategic points."[28] Jordan suggests that this *archonship* was in fact an independent magistracy from *strategia*. At least in the case of Naupactus, this seems to clash with the available evidence. Besides Conon, Thucydides mentions the activity of at least three other *strategoi* operating at Naupactus: Phormio (430/429), Nicostratus, and Demosthenes (427/426).[29] Whereas the latter's mission is generally described as "to sail around Peloponnesus", with no other explicit connections with Naupactus than withdrawing there in a situation of emergency, Phormio and Nicostratus seem to be considered the Athenian generals officially in charge of governing the base of Naupactus. The former in particular seems to be described as the officer who actually supervised the settlement of the base.

My impression is that the political, diplomatic and organisational duties which Jordan thinks were entrusted to the *archontes* could be taken over by *strategoi*. Nevertheless, he is quite right to emphasise the growing importance of a sensible handling of political, diplomatic and financial factors in the Athenian-Spartan conflict. Naupactus, in particular, was surely one of those hotspots which needed to be entrusted to a *strategos* with wide extra-military responsibilities. For the commander at Naupactus—say, the *strategos* serving as *archon* of Naupactus—was at the head of a large fleet deployed very close to the enemy's heartland, which had to be trained and maintained. Furthermore, the commander at Naupactus had to entertain diplomatic relations with the Athenian allies in the area, like the Messenians in Naupactus, or to favour the instalment of Athenian-friendly regimes in the various towns of the region, as Conon

---

[27] Xen. *Hell.* I.5.20; Diod. XIII.76.2, 77.1.
[28] Jordan 1970, 233.
[29] Phormio: II.69.1; II.80.4, 81.1, 83.1, 90.2, 92.7, 102. 1; see Develin 1989, 119. Nicostratus: Thuc. III.72-75; see MacDowell 1965; Develin 1989, 124. Demosthenes: Thuc. III.91.1, 94-98.5, 102.3; IV.76-77.1.

would do in Corcyra.

On the basis of what can be read about Conon's early days at Samos, we may assume that in the aftermath of Notium, the priorities for whoever was to take over the command of the *polis'* Aegean forces, a job which may have implied *autokrator* authority, were to reorganise the fleet to fit a smaller budget and to revitalise diplomatic relations with the neighbouring states, in order both to find sources of funding and to undermine the political ascendancy of the Lysander-Cyrus partnership in the area.[30] Conon, who in his two previous *strategiai* had served as *archon* at Naupactus, had the suitable experience in naval base-management and diplomatic relations to take over the job. By the time of his appointment as the substitute of Alcibiades, thus, his reputation as a military *genius* possibly lay mainly on what he had achieved outside the battlefield. This pattern of skills would also prove crucial in the following phases of his career.

Among the Aegean allies of Athens with whom Conon had to entertain diplomatic relations, one of the most prominent was surely Evagoras, the ambitious king of Salamis of Cyprus, who since his coronation in ca. 415 appears to have supported in various ways the Athenian fleet in the Aegean by providing money and foodstuff for the crews and possibly serving as a mediator with the satrap Tissaphernes.[31] His efforts were eventually rewarded with the grant of Athenian citizenship.[32]

It was Evagoras who, after the disaster of Aegospotami, offered his hospitality to Conon. In Salamis the Athenian lived as an *idiotes*, as Isocrates puts it, a private citizen, looking after his personal interests. Our knowledge of ancient Salamis owes a great deal to the work of the great Swedish archaeologist E. Gjerstad, director of the Swedish expedition in Cyprus between the 1920s and 1930s. As his excavations have documented, the reign of Evagoras coincided with a period of great expansion of the town's naval infrastructures. In Gjerstad's opinion, this naval expansion is the sign that Evagoras, since the earliest phases of his reign, was already planning to undertake a large-scale naval campaign against the Great King, as he would in fact do in the late-390s and early-380s.[33]

Later on, this thesis was thoroughly reviewed by E. Costa Jr. The scholar firstly observed that Gjerstad's reconstruction is, in fact, in contrast with the available literary evidence, where there is no sign of

---

[30] Xen. *Hell.* I.5.1-4.
[31] Starr 1974, 46-47.
[32] IG I^3 113; Andoc. II.20; Isoc. IX. 54.
[33] Isoc. IX.47; see Gjerstad 1948, 490-491.

Evagoras aiming to challenge the authority of the Great King at this early stage of his reign. Costa therefore concludes that those naval preparations were indeed concerned with the development of Salamis into an important hub for Mediterranean trading while, militarily, a more likely target for Evagoras was to expand his ascendancy over the other Cypriot kingdoms, to attain which, the support—or, at least, the neutrality—of Artaxerxes was absolutely necessary.[34]

It is generally assumed that Conon rewarded Evagoras' hospitality by co-operating with him in his ambitious plans for Salamis. According to E. Raptou, for instance, the arrival of an experienced Greek admiral at Salamis coincided with the implementation of an internationally more ambitious policy on the side of Evagoras, waiting for the right occasion to "reject" the Great King's authority.[35] In the latter respect, my position is possibly closer to Costa's than Raptou's, at least until any piece of evidence comes out, suggesting that, say, in the very late years of the fifth century, the Salaminian King did conduct some anti-Persian operations, eventually employing Conon as his admiral. Indeed, the impression we gather from some sources, like Lysia's oration *On the Property of Aristophanes*,[36] is that Conon conducted a fairly pacific and maybe sedentary life in Salamis, looking after his family and his assets. This, however, is in no contradiction with the notion of Conon co-operating with Evagoras in the naval developments, both commercial and military, of Salamis. For he may have employed the experience gained at Naupactus and Samos to supervise the preparation and the Salaminian fleet and other naval infrastructures.

He may have taken over a similar task when Pharnabazus, the satrap of Caria, appointed him at the head of the Persian fleet, in the winter of 398, as we gather from Diodorus.[37] S. Hornblower has observed that this date contrasts with the information provided by other authors, which would lead one to think that the Athenian was entrusted the command of the Persian fleet at a later time, in 397/6. These authors are Philochorus, who mentions Conon leaving Cyprus to join Pharnabazus in the year of the Athenian archon Suniades of Acharnae (indeed, 397/6); Isocrates, stating in the *Panegyricus* that the "Rhodian War" lasted three years (397-394), and finally Xenophon, mentioning the trip of a Syracusan shipowner called Herodas, who in 396 fled from Phoenicia to the Peloponnesus to inform the Spartans that the Great King and Tissaphernes were preparing

---

[34] See Costa 1974, 40-44.
[35] Raptou 1999, 252.
[36] Lys. XIX.34-36.
[37] Diod. XIV.39.1-4.

an expedition, "but whither it was bound, he said he did not know."[38] This contradiction, however, is possibly only apparent. For whereas the sources cited by Hornblower all clearly refer to the actual beginning of military operations, Diodorus is also concerned with the preceding phase of preparations, during which Pharnabazus already seems to have been employing Conon as his advisor:

> "Pharnabazus, after the truce had been made with the Lacedaemonians, went back to the King and won him over to the plan of preparing a fleet and appointing Conon the Athenian as its admiral; for Conon was experienced in the encounters of war and especially in combat with the present enemy, and although he excelled in warfare, he was at the time in Cyprus at the court of Evagoras the king. After the King had been persuaded, Pharnabazus took five hundred talents of silver and prepared to fit out a naval force. Sailing across to Cyprus, he ordered the kings there to make ready a hundred triremes and then, after discussions with Conon about the command of the fleet, he appointed him supreme commander at sea, giving indications in the name of the King of great hopes Conon might entertain."[39]

This is a crucial point, implying that Pharnabazus had hired Conon not only to lead the Persian fleet in battle, but also to oversee the preparation of galleys and crews for the forthcoming campaigns and, possibly, to carry out an overall reorganisation of the Persian navy in order to sustain a naval conflict against Sparta and its Aegean allies. This process, if I interpret correctly the reference to Conon's experience of war against Sparta, was to be inspired precisely by the "grand strategy" which Athens and Sparta had developed in the conflict of 431-404.

In the spring or early summer of 397, after having supervised preparations in Cyprus and Cilicia,[40] Conon moved his forces to Caunus, where the headquarters of the Persian fleet had been set up.[41] The assault against the forces at Caunus, carried out by the Spartan navarch Pharax at the head of one hundred and twenty triremes in the late summer or early fall of 397/396, marked the beginning of hostilities. These would last until the summer of 394.[42] It is noteworthy that, leaving aside Cnidus, our evidence records Conon undertaking only one other major naval operation

---

[38] Philoc. *FGrHist* 328 F 144/5; Isoc. IV.142; Xen. *Hell.* III.4.1.

[39] Diod. XIV.39.1-2.

[40] Diod. XIV.39.3-4.

[41] Xen. *Hell.* III.2.12.

[42] Blockade of Caunus: Xen. *Hell.* III.2.12-14; Diod. XIV.39.4-6. Chronology: De Sanctis 1983, 70-71.

in this lapse of time, namely the occupation of the Spartan base of Rhodes, in the late spring to early summer of 396.[43] Apart from that operation, we interestingly find him occupied with a very diverse range of dealings, like masterminding a democratic *coup* in Rhodes, sedating a revolt of his Cypriot crews and discussing the budget and provisions of his fleet with king Artaxerxes and the satrap Tithraustes.[44]

In a recent book, Kimberley Kagan has observed that

"War is the central subject of every ancient work of history, and battle is its highlight. Battles change the outcome of wars and of history; they test men's character, offering even ordinary individuals the opportunity to achieve glory or dishonour."[45]

Battles are surely the highlight of wars, but wars are not made up of battles only. This is particularly true for the Peloponnesian War, during which the contestants developed a new kind of warfare, based on protracted transmarine fighting and on the boycott of the enemy's social, economical and political system, which would also characterise the Aegean conflicts of the early decades of the fourth century, including the war of Pharnabazus against Sparta.

War had become more expensive and exhausting. Naval commanders were now requested to govern large bases, often for very prolonged periods and far away from home, in which the presence of foreign mercenaries was constantly growing. For a naval commander, therefore, knowing how to manage his own forces became almost as crucial as knowing how to face the enemy. The crews had to be kept disciplined and regularly paid to avoid desertions. To attain this, establishing good terms with foreign states was often essential. The successful career of Conon demonstrates unequivocally the crucial importance of these factors.

Bibliography

Badian, E. "Athens, the Locrians and Naupactus." *CQ* 40 (1990): 364-369.

Barbieri, G. *Conone.* Rome: Signorelli, 1955.

Buck, R. *Thrasybulus and the Athenian Democracy. The Life of an Athenian Statesman.* Stuttgart: Franz Steiner Verlag, 1998.

---

[43] Diod. XIV.79.6-8; Paus. VI.7.6.

[44] Democratic *coup* in Rhodes: *Hell. Ox.* XV.1-3. Meeting with Artaxerxes and Tithraustes: *Hell. Ox.* XIX.1-3; Diod. XIV.81.4-6. Revolt of the Cypriot crews: *Hell. Ox.* XX.1-6

[45] Kagan 2006, 1.

Busolt, G. *Griechische Geschichte bis zur Schlacht bei Chaeroneia*, Vol. 3.2. Gotha: F.A. Perthes, 1904.

Costa Jr., E. "Evagoras I and the Persians, ca. 411 to 391 B.C." *Historia* 23 (1974): 40-56.

de Sanctis, G. *Scritti minori, nuovamente editi da A. Ferrabino e S. Accame*, Vol. 5. Rome: Edizioni di storia e letteratura, 1983.

Develin, R. *Athenian Officials, 684-321 B.C.* Cambridge: Cambridge University Press, 1989.

Gjerstad, E. *The Swedish Cyprus Expedition. Vol. 4. Pt. 2, The Cyprogeometric, Cypro-archaic and Cypro-classical periods.* Stockholm: The Swedish Cyprus Expedition, 1948.

Gomme, A., Andrewes, A., and Dover, K. J. *A Historical Commentary on Thucydides*, Vol. IV. Oxford: Oxford University Press, 1970.

Hamel, D. *Athenian Generals. Military Authority in the Classical Period.* Leiden: Brill, 1998.

Hansen, M. H. *Eisangelia. The Sovereignty of the People's Court in Athens in the Fourth Century BC and the Impeachment of Generals and Politicians.* Odense: Odense Universitetsforlag, 1975.

Hatzfeld, J. *Alcibiade, étude sur l'histoire d'Athènes à la fin du Ve siècle.* Paris: Presses universitaires de France, 1951.

Hornblower, S. *A Commentary on Thucydides*, Vol. 1. Oxford: Oxford University Press, 1991.

Jordan, B. "A note on the Athenian strategia." *TAPA* 101 (1970): 229-239.

Kagan, D. *The Fall of the Athenian Empire*. Ithaca, NY and London: Cornell University Press, 1987.

Kagan, K. *The Eye of Command*. Ann Arbor: University of Michigan Press, 2006.

Lazenby, J.F. *The Peloponnesian War. A Military Study*. London: Routledge, 2004.

MacDowell, D. "Nikostratos." *CQ* 15 (1965): 41-51.

Nouhaud, M. *L'utilisation de l'histoire par les orateurs attiques*. Paris: Les belles lettres, 1982.

Ober, J. *The Athenian Revolution. Essays on Ancient Greek Democracy and Political Theory*. Princeton: Princeton University Press, 1996.

Ostwald, M. *From Popular Sovereignty to the Sovereignty of Law: Law, Society and Politics in Fifth-Century Athens*. Berkeley, Los Angeles and London: University of California Press, 1986.

Price, J. *Thucydides and Internal War*. Cambridge: Cambridge University Press, 2001.

Pritchett, W. K. *The Greek State at War*, vol. 2. Berkeley, Los Angeles and Oxford: University of California Press, 1974.

Raptou, E. *Athènes et Chypre à l'époque perse (VIe-IVe s. av. J.-C.): histoire et données archéologiques.* Lyon: Maison de l'Orient Méditerranéen, 1999.

Rosenstein, N. *Imperatores Victi. Military Defeat and Aristocratic Competition in the Mid and Late Republic.* Berkeley, Los Angeles and Oxford: University of California Press, 1990.

Sinclair, R. K. *Democracy and Participation in Athens.* Cambridge: Cambridge University Press, 1988.

Starr, C. *Political Intelligence in Classical Greece.* Leiden: Brill, 1974.

CHAPTER SIX

MILITARY ETHICS IN THE WRITING OF HISTORY: THUCYDIDES AND DIODORUS ON DELIUM

SONYA NEVIN

Thucydides provided a full and vivid account of this campaign of the Peloponnesian War, which included the fortification of a sanctuary and the grisly use of bodies as a strategic bargaining tool (Thuc. 4.89-4.101). The later historian Diodorus Siculus followed him over the territory of the Delium campaign (Diod. Sic. 12.69-70). He wrote his own account, clearly drawing on the earlier version, but also making conspicuous omissions and additions. In *his* account, Diodorus consciously omitted all the ethically charged aspects of the incident—the very aspects that formed the main component of Thucydides' version of events. In this paper I will consider what motives might be behind the differences in these accounts and what role military ethics had, in both the writing of history and in the conduct of war in Classical Greece.

The Delium campaign took place in 424 BC. After some seven years of maritime campaigns, under pressure from Spartan invasions, the Athenians decided upon a radical change in strategy and voted to strike out by land. Thucydides records how they marched into Boeotian territory and made a fortified base for themselves in the sanctuary of Apollo at Delium ("Ἀπόλλωνος ἱερόν" Thuc. 4.76.4). Very soon afterwards they were soundly beaten in a battle nearby, and a number of troops fled back to the relative safety of Delium (Thuc. 4.96.6-8).

Thucydides covers the initial fortifying of the sanctuary in some detail. He reports:

> A ditch was dug all round the temple and its precincts; the earth thrown up from the digging was made to form a rampart in which stakes were fixed; vine wood was cut from the temple grounds and thrown in together with stones and bricks from the houses nearby which they demolished. So

they did everything they could to raise the level of the fortifications. (Trans. Warner)

τάφον μὲν κύκλῳ περὶ τὸ ἱερὸν καὶ τὸν νεὼν ἔσκαπτον, ἐκ δὲ τοῦ ὀρύγματος ἀνέβαλλον ἀντὶ τείχους τὸν χοῦν, καὶ σταυροὺς παρακαταπηγνύντες ἄμπελον κόπτοντες τὴν περὶ τὸ ἱερὸν ἐσέβαλλον καὶ λίθους ἅμα καὶ πλίνθον ἐκ τῶν οἰκοπέδων τῶν ἐγγὺς καθαιροῦντες, καὶ παντὶ τρόπῳ ἐμετεώριζον τὸ ἔρυμα. (Thuc. 4.90.2)

The detail of the description makes it very clear that the Athenians' activities encompassed the sacred area. That Thucydides was very deliberate in alluding to the use of the sacred area is well illustrated by comparison with the account by Diodorus. His account of the Delium campaign contains much that has been drawn from Thucydides. However, where Thucydides refers to the site as, "Delium, the temple of Apollo" (Thuc. 4.89.4), with its sacred precinct, vines and holy water, Diodorus calls it simply "Delium" (Diod. Sic. 12.69.1). Where Thucydides details the incursions upon the sacred ground, Diodorus reports only that the Athenians "threw a wall about it" (Diod. Sic. 12.69.2). Thucydides' attention to the cutting of sacred vines from the *temenos* is particularly significant as it recalls to the reader's mind the recent massacre on Corcyra (Thuc. 3.70). There, only a book earlier, accusations of a similar offence had escalated into an all-out bloodbath, unrestrained by any standards of normal morality and heavily criticised by an appalled Thucydides.

This ominous evocation of the potential problems of using sacred land is missing from the start of Diodorus' account, along with the moral undertones of the allusion. Any implicit or explicit criticism is likewise diminished by the absence of any focus on the sacred nature of the space involved.

The bulk of the Thucydidean narrative then recounts not so much the battle itself, but the siege that followed—or rather a dispute that took place during the siege (Thuc. 4.97-100). The Athenians accuse the Boeotians of holding on to the bodies of those who have fallen in the recent battle—an obscene taboo by normal Greek standards. The Boeotians in turn, respond by saying that the bodies will not be restored until the Athenians have vacated the sanctuary. What is more, they add, the Athenians' sacrilege is far worse as they are occupying a sacred site and using its holy water for secular purposes.[1] For more than two weeks

---

[1] A genuine concern. See Parker 1983, 149-152 and 162 and Guettel Cole 1988, 161.

this dispute went on with neither side claiming to be innocent of impiety, but rather that the other side was the more guilty.[2]

In many ways the discussion of what the Athenians did at Delium stands both in and outside the ongoing debate about the "rules" or "norms" of Greek warfare. Whenever, or indeed if one believes that such rules existed for some areas of conflict, there is no doubt that conventions to safeguard religious sites had been known since Homeric times, even if the occasional flouting of those conventions was as old as their existence. The Achaeans may have taken Chryseis from the sanctuary of Apollo, but their action is characterised as a fault and they soon recognised the error of their ways, thus beginning the Iliad.[3] Traditions surrounding the end of the Trojan War recount more lapses in religious observance, but once again actions against sanctuaries are presented as offences and condemned, as indicated in this example from the early sixth century:

> Much better for the Acheans if
> they'd punished Aias' sacrilege
> with death: when they were sailing home
> past Aegae, they'd have had a gentler sea. (Trans. Campbell)

> ἦ μάν κ' Ἀχαίοισ' ἦς πόλυ βέλτερον
> αἰ τὸν θεοβλ]άβεντα κατέκτανον.
> οὕτω κε π]αρπλέοντες Αἴγαις
> πραυτέρα]ς ἔτυχον θαλάσσας. (Alcaeus 298.4-7. P.Oxy.2303).

Josiah Ober has argued that conventions for hoplite warfare arose in the seventh century, and he has placed the idea that, "Hostilities against certain persons and in certain places are inappropriate," as point three on a sliding scale of Greek ethical priorities.[4] While Peter Krentz disputes many of Ober's views on the conduct of war, he too argues that "Some customs—the ones in which the gods took an interest—certainly go back to Homer."[5] The protection of sanctuaries and their staff would certainly count as a custom "in which the gods took an interest". Like

---

[2] Orwin 1994, 91-96.

[3] "Which of the gods was it that made them quarrel? It was Apollo…who started the feud because he was furious with Agamemnon for not respecting his priest Chryses." *Il.* 1.9. It is of note also that when Chryses offers ransom, "all the other Greeks shouted in agreement. They wanted to see the priest respected." *Il.* 1.21 (trans. Rieu).

[4] Ober 1996, 56.

[5] Krentz 2002, 24.

van Wees, Krentz regards the formal hoplite agon as a Classical, not
Archaic development, but he still appears to believe that any
corresponding guidelines for the agon were pre-dated by religiously
orientated restrictions.[6]

In the seventh century, Greek communities began using sanctuaries
to house their treasuries.[7] This was the monumentalisation of the much
older practice of making dedications, and it would be a very strange
development indeed if no conventions existed to protect sacred sites. It
seems more likely that the practice of building treasuries grew out of the
security that was already offered to both the sites themselves and to the
wealth of votive offerings they contained. In the fourth century, it was
thought that those in (what we would call) the Archaic period had
customs which demanded respect for sacred sites, even if these customs
might be breached. Aeschines provides one such example with his
comments about the First Sacred War in the sixth century, which was
said to have been started in order to end the sacrilegious attacks on the
sanctuary and its pilgrims (Aeschin. 3.107-8). The historical reality of
this war is by no means certain,[8] but the tradition alluding to it relies on
the fourth century belief that any such conventions went back many
generations. Krentz has observed that "claims made in the second half
of the fifth century… do not prove that customs were really old,"[9] but in
this instance the claim is perhaps more plausible.

For a fifth century perspective on the antiquity of protection for
sacred sites we can turn to Herodotus, who clearly believed that warfare
in the sixth century had acknowledged certain restrictions. His account
of the end of Cleomenes makes this clear (Hdt. 6.75-84). Once the king
is dead, all the Greeks agree that his madness and demise were caused
by his sacrilegious behaviour while on campaign. They are only said to
disagree on which particular act of sacrilege was the worst and therefore
the cause of his divine punishment. Each community predictably
chooses the event that was perpetrated against themselves. The
Athenians cite the sacred grove cut down at Eleusis, the Argives recall
their sacred grove, burnt down along with the soldiers hiding inside.
Others blame the bribing of the Pythia—not an act of physical
aggression, but apparently seen as a comparably sacrilegious act.
Modern scholars studying the life of Cleomenes have generally

---

[6] Krentz 2002, 24 n. 9. For van Wees on the development of hoplite war see van
Wees 2000, 155-156.
[7] Morgan 1990, 5; Osborne 1996, 89-90 and 214; Price 1999, 60.
[8] Davies 1994, 192-206; Howe 2003, 129-146; Morgan 1990, 135 and 144-145.
[9] Krentz 2002, 24.

concluded that he was not quite the villain that Herodotus paints, but nonetheless the story's construction hinges on the acceptance that Greeks of the pre-Classical era expected respect to be shown for religious sites even in times of war.[10]

The belief that sanctuaries should be inviolate during war appears to have been a long-established tradition by the time of the Classical era, but what more can we know about it? When we say that the Greeks expected respectful treatment of their sanctuaries, what did they believe constituted "respect" or its breach? The specifics of this custom are far from clear, and the clarification of this issue is complicated, as is so often the case, by the nature of the sources. Ancient historians rarely engage in such blunt activity as labelling one action "good" or another "bad." Even when they do, modern readers may still find themselves guessing at what aspect of the action makes it reprehensible or otherwise.

This paper will address these issues, considering how ancient authors dealt with military ethics as a subject and how this affects our analysis of ancient military protocols. Much modern scholarship on the subject has assessed the "rules of war," by summarising accounts of ethically sensitive incidents.[11] This paper will suggest that a more qualitative approach is required, with due regard for the impact of historiographical considerations. The incidents that authors chose to relate may not reflect historical reality in quite as direct a manner as we might like. Our interpretation of such narratives as influenced by individual historiographical motivations must surely affect both our interpretation of events that is offered by the historian and the frequency with which religiously sensitive incidents seem to appear. Did ancient authors record every occasion on which a sanctuary was violated during warfare and, if not, how subjective were their choices?

It is significant that Thucydides depicts both sides as acknowledging the concept of rules of war at Delium. The Boeotians talk of the "norms of the Greeks" ("τὰ νόμιμα τῶν Ἑλλήνων" Thuc. 4.97.2) which require armies to keep off their enemies' temples. And the Athenians, too, talk of "Greek law" ("τὸν δὲ νόμον τοῖς Ἕλλησιν εἶναι" Thuc. 4.98.1) although they argue that this same "Greek law" demands that those who control a piece of land also control the temples there.[12] The Athenians also refer to "ancestral

---

[10] On the hostility towards Cleomenes in Herodotus' sources see Cartledge 2002, 124; Evans 1991, 72—but not Scott 2005, 293: "It is hard to think there was smoke without fire."

[11] Pritchett 1991, 160-168; Garlan 1972, 36-38; Ducrey 1999, 295-300.

[12] On the concepts of *nomos* and *nomimos* see Ostwald 1986, especially 100-101.

custom" ("τὰ πάτρια" Thuc. 4.98.8), when they claim the return of their dead. Clearly, there is a working concept of rules of war, but those rules appear so ambiguous as to invite disputes of this nature. It is plausible that any rules or customs relating to these issues might be vague—they are certainly unwritten—but it appears that part of Thucydides' theme in this debate is to demonstrate the way both sides cynically exploit that vagueness.

Both sides offer a series of excuses for their actions, creating a pair of speeches that are curiously desultory. The traditional scholarly reaction to these speeches was condemnation of the Thebans.[13] Over time, however, there has been a growing realisation that Thucydides makes the claims of both armies appear flawed. Jordan has called the Athenian speech "Pure sophistry and special pleading, mixed with evasions, falsehoods and irrelevant legalisms."[14]

Both he and Orwin have discussed the "self-contradictory" nature of the speeches, drawing the conclusion that the reader is guided to regard them as flawed.[15] This sophistry is of course not Thucydides' own narratorial comment, but that of the competing forces, who are unusually referred to only as "the Athenians" or "the Boeotians".[16] Thucydides has gone to great lengths to reconstruct a pair of speeches that he could not have personally heard.[17] The use of religious terms to argue in defence of deeply unreligious behaviour recalls to the reader's mind (to the discredit of the speechmakers) Thucydides' strong criticism of the carnage on Corcyra, where "To fit in with the change of events, words too had to change their usual meanings" ("τὴν εἰωθυῖαν ἀξίωσιν τῶν ὀνομάτων ἐς τὰ ἔργα ἀντήλλαξαν τῇ δικαιώσει" Thuc. 3.82.4, trans. Warner).

Donald Lateiner has demonstrated how the use of recurring motifs within his work enabled Thucydides to control his accounts in order to express the extremity of dire situations. In particular, he has illustrated the manner in which references to heralds and to corpses act "as indicators of

---

[13] E.g. Grote 1872, 394; Gomme 1956, 570-571; Pritchett 1985, 191-2. Bury 1955, 444 claims that "the conduct of the Boeotians was a greater departure from recognised custom", although he concedes that the Athenian response was little more than a "quibble".

[14] Jordan 1986, 130. For a similar view see Eatough 1971, 244: "the Athenian reply is implausible, often irrelevant, and full of the worst kind of sophistry, with a cynical use of religious sentiment to further military ends."

[15] Orwin 1994, 91-96; Jordan 1986, 129-130.

[16] Orwin 1994, 91.

[17] By this time Thucydides would have departed for his ill-fated campaign in the North.

societal values, and as a kind of punctuation or structuring device."[18] Heralds appear at pivotal or significant moments indicating a changing situation, while the neglect or abuse of corpses acts as an indicator of great social crisis. The recurrence of these motifs throughout the text provides a link between the extreme events which both identifies their extremity and provides implicit criticism.

Both heralds and corpses feature heavily in the Delium dispute. Their appearance draws the attention of the reader to the great social significance of the event. That there should be a pair of speeches at all is a signal of its importance. Such pairs only appear in Thucydides at critical moments of shifting attitudes.[19] Lateiner has demonstrated how through the debate at "Delium between heralds and about corpses, Thucydides describes in a specific incident the trivialization of politics and the diminution of religious and moral values caused by the Peloponnesian War."[20]

The flawed nature of the arguments, the evocation of the situation on Corcyra, and the use of the herald/corpse motif all indicate that Thucydides turned the events at Delium into a lesson on war and morality that was part of the wider meaning of his work. That Socrates felt able to mention his participation at Delium in his defence speech years later indicates that some Athenians, at least, remembered the events there in a less negative way than Thucydides (Pl. *Ap.* 17e).[21] Thucydides' account, however, suggests that the behaviour of both sides was reprehensible, and expresses deep concern about the moral degradation caused by the war. The appearance of Euripides' *Supplicants* not long after the campaign suggests that Thucydides was not alone in this concern.[22]

Given the importance ascribed to these events by Thucydides, it is curious that Diodorus should have chosen to omit those very features that were so important to Thucydides. The heralds, the corpses, the sacred water, the dispute—none of these have any place in Diodorus' account. By comparison, the event loses all moral significance in his version, and the campaign is just another stepping stone in the course of the war.

Why would an author who knew his Thucydides well decide to discount the very features that make this incident distinctive? Diodorus has something of a reputation as a cut-and-paste historian—more of a compiler

---

[18] Lateiner 1977, 97.

[19] Cogan 1981, 7.

[20] Lateiner 1977, 103.

[21] Alcibiades also recalls Socrates presence on the campaign. (Pl. *Symp.* 221a-c).

[22] The connection between Delium and the production was noted as long ago as 1890 by Giles 95 and 98. See more recently Bowie 1997, 45-56, esp. 48-49.

than an independent editor. But why did he cut but not paste those principal features? It is not enough to say that it was done in the interests of brevity. Some additional elements appear that he clearly took from elsewhere. But the non-Thucydidean features that he includes have no moral element, concerned as they are with the Thebans' use of the spoils (Diod. Sic. 12.70.5).

It could be suggested that the reason for these differences is that Diodorus used the historian Ephorus for this section. It is unfortunate that the relevant section of Ephorus has not survived in an independent form, so we are unable to know if he included any detail on the sanctuary or the dispute. The use of Ephorus remains a strong possibility, although the comments in Diodorus (12.70.3) that the Thebans defeated the Athenians because of their superior bodily strength seem uncharacteristically anti-Athenian, perhaps indicating a Boeotian or pro-Boeotian source, not as Bury suggested a historical reality brought about by "laborious athletic training" on the part of the Thebans.[23]

Despite the differences that do appear, even a cursory look at the similarities reveals enough correlation to suggest the influence of the Thucydidean account. The plan, the protagonists, and the place are all the same, as are the numbers said to be involved and the mistake that leads to this unwanted battle.[24] Both writers present the Athenians as an ill-equipped force who, as both writers remind us, had left Athens in a hurry, intending to build a fort, not fight a pitched battle. Both observe that the Athenians were forced to fight whilst still arranging their troops and, once the battle has been fought, both notice the grim detail that only the onset of night ended the slaughter of defeated troops.[25] The Boeotian attack on Delium also appears in Diodorus, only without reference to the dispute or the sacred dimension (Diod. Sic. 12.70.6).

It cannot, however, be assumed *a priori* that Diodorus took Thucydides as his main source for Delium, because it cannot be securely demonstrated.[26] On the other hand, we *can* be sure that Diodorus had a

---

[23] Bury 1955, 443.

[24] Thuc. 4.89-91, Diod. Sic. 12.69.1-2. It was intended that the Boeotians should be distracted by pre-arranged revolutions in several of their cities, but these did not happen, leaving the full Boeotian force free to deal with the Athenian force under Hippocrates.

[25] Arranging their troops: Thuc. 4.96.1, Diod. Sic. 12.670.1. The post battle pursuit: Thuc. 4.96.8, Diod. Sic. 12.70.4

[26] Gomme 1956, 568 believed that Diodorus drew on Thucydides, saying that "Diodorus' account follows Thucydides in its arrangement, with few errors and less confusion than is usual with him." Toher 2001, 180-2 has also argued in

degree of knowledge of Thucydides because of explicit references that he makes to him.[27] He refers to the earlier writer on several occasions, one of which is, in fact, close to the Delium section.[28] We even know that Diodorus considered Thucydides a reliable historian, as he refers to his reputation for accuracy (Diod. Sic. 1.37.4). So it is certainly possible that Diodorus worked directly from Thucydides. Furthermore, it might be said that any primary use of Ephorus is tantamount to an *indirect* use of Thucydides. It is thought that Ephorus "depended extensively on Thucydides for the fifth century BC."[29] Therefore, it is not safe to say that whatever was in Thucydides was in Ephorus; but it is reasonable to say that while Thucydides was *probably* available to Diodorus, the Thucydidean tradition *definitely* was.

It can be assumed for the moment that Diodorus was fully cognizant of the contents of Thucydides account, but it is still worth dwelling a while longer on the possibility that he was working primarily with Ephorus. It has been demonstrated that there are many occasions when Diodorus modified, or intruded into, sections of Ephorus. Diodorus had a moral programme that he wished to expound. Where his primary source exemplified this programme, he was ready to include it unaltered. Where his primary source failed to express this programme, he readily added ethical observations or incidents included in other works. This process of selection and editing enabled him to form the moral and ethical theme that runs through the work.[30]

Diodorus differed from Ephorus in his readiness to include examples of negative behaviour as warnings. The dispute at Delium might certainly have fallen into that category. So even if Ephorus had chosen to omit this aspect of the campaign, it may nonetheless have appeared in the pages of Diodorus. Either Diodorus was not motivated enough to retain the ethical

---

favour of the primary use of Thucydides, while Huxley 1991, 320-321 prefers the use of Ephorus.

[27] E.g. Diod. Sic. 13.40.3, 13.54.5, 13.60.6, 13.80.5.

[28] Diod. Sic. 1.37.4: Xenophon's and Thucydides' reputation for accuracy. 12.37.2: reference to Thucydides' choice of material, starting and end point. 14.84.7: the end point of Thucydides.

[29] Hornblower 1995, 57.

[30] On Diodorus and Ephorus see Sacks 1990, 35. For a similar treatment of Polybius see Sacks 1990, 141 and Eckstein 1995, 225-229 and 232. See also Drews 1962, especially 385-386. Even Stylianou 1998, 49, n. 139, so critical of Diodorus' abilities, accepts that Diodorus used more than one source as well as making his own contributions, although Stylianou differs from Drews and Sacks in his interpretation of the extent and significance of this (Stylianou 1998, 49-139).

features of the Thucydidean account, or, using the Ephoran account, he felt no motivation to include additional Thucydidean elements.

Toher has argued that Thucydides was the main source for Diodorus' account and that, on the basis of the chariots that appear in Diodorus but not in Thucydides, the additional material comes not from Ephorus, but from Euripides.[31] If this is the case, then Diodorus took the chariots from Euripides, but ignored the ethical aspects of his version as well as that of Thucydides. The principle point is that, whoever his main source and the source of his additional material, Diodorus knew the Thucydidean narrative—and yet the incident made distinctive by Thucydides for its ethical dimension was not retold by Diodorus in those terms.

Finally, it must be added that even if we leave Ephorus and Thucydides aside for a moment, the omission of the ethical dimension cannot be said to have been caused by ignorance. Diodorus himself refers to Delium as a temple elsewhere in his work when he recounts an incident that occured there some two hundred years later (Diod. Sic. 29.1-3).[32]

The omission of the ethical factors of the events at Delium should not encourage us to think that Diodorus had no place for moralising in his work. Diodorus *did* have an interest in morality *and* in the ethics of warfare.[33] However, those incidents in Thucydides that receive the most thorough and pathos-filled descriptions are frequently dismissed by Diodorus in a few brief lines or phrases. Such is the case with the Athenian plague, the fall of Plataea, the civil war on Corcyra, and the fall of Melos. These incidents are Thucydides' seminal events in terms of morality and the conduct of war, receiving extensive treatment in his work. Diodorus does not follow him down this route, preferring to draw his conclusions about the evils of war on other occasions. Table 6-1 illustrates this divergence.

---

[31] Toher 2001, 180-182 discusses the relationship between Diodorus' Delium narrative and the events of Euripides' *Supplicants*, highlighting the appearance of chariots in both, but failing to address the other elements that appear in Diodorus but not in Thucydides, i.e. the Thebans' subsequent use of spoils from the campaign (Diod. Sic. 12.70.5).

[32] Diodorus does not offer his own opinion on this occasion, but he does include the criticism of others. In this respct his interpretation of the later incident differs significantly from his treatment of the earlier campaign. He could have edited those elements out entirely had he chosen to, but clearly Diodorus did have space for moral factors when the situation suited him.

[33] In a clear example, he attributed the Macedonian conquest of Greece to the sacrilege committed during the Sacred War of the 350s when Delphi was plundered (Diod. Sic. 16.64). See also Sacks 1990, esp. 42-44, as well as Hau in this volume, on the moral themes of Diodorus.

Further insights into the variable use of ethically sensitive incidents are obtained when we consider the reasons behind another divergence between the two writers. The infamous Sicilian expedition of the Athenians is one of Thucydides' principal events in terms of reflection on war. The suffering of the Athenians, the extent of their moral collapse, and the cruelty inflicted upon them in their helplessness, all receive a full and harrowing treatment. Rarely is disaster more complete than as it appears in this account (Thuc. 6.1-7.87, especially 7.72-87). As in the case of the Delium campaign, what we see in Diodorus is a very different version. This time Diodorus does not omit all the ethical factors of the events, but the moral issues that receive emphasis are very different to those in Thucydides.

From Diodorus we do hear briefly of the suffering of the Athenians, and we are left with no doubt that great numbers of them died (Diod. Sic. 13.11.5 and 13.33.1). But the principal factor in his version is the debate of the Sicilians as they consider and then decide upon the fate of their Athenian captives. This is dealt with in a massive fourteen chapters, an unprecedented length in Diodorus (Diod. Sic. 13.19.4-13.32.6). This can be compared with only one chapter in Thucydides, in which the decision is reported without reference to the decision making process (Thuc. 7.86.1).

Despite the apparently specific focus of the speech upon the fate of the Athenians, the arguments contained within that speech appeal to the most fundamental moral themes of the entire *Bibliotheke*. Throughout the work, Diodorus himself seeks to demonstrate the principle that whilst clemency and moderation can maintain an empire, cruelty and harshness towards one's subjects will inevitably bring that empire crashing down.[34] Those speechmakers whom Diodorus presents as keen to destroy the Athenians make no bones about the link between this punishment and the Athenians' merciless imperialism. "This is what they have brought upon themselves", they essentially argue, in keeping with the recurrent theme of the *Bibliotheke* (Diod. Sic. 13.29.4-31.3).

Given this perspective on the Athenians, it is perhaps surprising that there was less comment earlier in the *Bibliotheke* on the fall of Melos. It is significant for our purposes that, in fact, this incident *did not* go without comment, but that that comment was deliberately delayed. Diodorus waited until this later stage, the judging of the Athenians' harshness, before making those comments. It is only in the speeches of the Sicilians that the cruelty of the Melians' fate is condemned (Diod. Sic. 13.30.6).

---

[34] Sacks 1990, 42-44.

The effect is to make absolutely clear the link between Athenian harshness and the beginning of the end of their empire.

There is perhaps another reason why this moral conclusion should be placed within the context of the Sicilian debate. The careers of Diodorus and Thucydides were separated not only by several hundred years, but also by geography. Diodorus is, after all, Diodorus of Sicily, born and reared a long way from the home of Thucydides the Athenian. As a Sicilian, Diodorus was understandably more concerned by the Sicilian role in the campaign.[35] There is also the Sicilian reputation to be considered—a factor that is even mentioned in his version of the speeches:

> "If we put them to death we shall merely be indulging our anger, sating a fruitless passion, whereas if we put them under guard, we shall have the gratitude of the men we succoured and the approbation of all other peoples. Yes, some will answer, but there are Greeks who have executed their prisoners. What of it? If praise accrues to them for that deed, let us nevertheless imitate those who have paid heed to their reputation." (Trans. Oldfather).

> ἀνελόντες μὲν γὰρ αὐτοὺς τῷ θυμῷ μόνον χαριούμεθα, τὴν ἄκαρπον ἐπιθυμίαν ἐκπληροῦντες, φυλάξαντες δὲ παρὰ μὲν τῶν εὖ παθόντων τὴν χάριν ἕξομεν παρὰ δὲ τῶν ἄλλων ἁπάντων τὴν εὐδοξίαν. Ναί, ἀλλά τινες τῶν Ἑλλήνων ἀπέσφαξαν τοὺς αἰχμαλώτους. Τί οὖν; εἰ μὲν αὐτοῖς ἐκ ταύτης τῆς πράξεως ἔπαινοι τυγχάνουσι, μιμησώμεθα τοὺς τῆς δόξης πεφροντικότας. (Diod. Sic. 13.25.4-26.1).

The incident was far too notorious to be omitted entirely, but by rejecting any significant focus upon the suffering of the Athenians Diodorus managed to ameliorate the horror of the story. He concentrated upon the Sicilian perspective, presenting them less as the perpetrators of an atrocity than as the agents of inevitability.

So, here we see a twofold explanation of Diodorus' account of the Sicilian expedition of the Athenians. His interpretation of events gave him scope to express the disaster as part of his moral vision of history, where harshness and cruelty soon fail in their attempts at empire. It also gave him leave to draw on a range of Sicilian sources and to explore a localised interest, in what might be called *his* history, i.e. the history of the

---

[35] Bosworth 1992 has suggested that similar issues of "memory and partiality" created the differences between Thucydides' account of the fist Sicilian expedition in 427 BC and those of Philistus and Diodorus. See esp. 53-55.

Sicilians.[36] The manner in which he did this went a long way towards recovering the historic reputation of the island.

Could the same be said of the Delium campaign? Hardly, because for the Sicilian historian, the Delium campaign had neither of these factors of interest. Taking place on the Greek mainland, fought between Athens and Boeotia, this campaign had none of the local flavour that made the Sicilian campaign so significant to him. The power dynamic of the situation was also different. Although Athens was an increasingly harsh imperial power at this point, the Boeotians with whom they fought were not part of their empire. To say that it was a match between equals would be arguable, but this certainly was not the oppressor/oppressed dynamic that so interested Diodorus. As the Delium incident failed to fulfil either of these criteria, Diodorus was willing to cut it down to its bare essentials, omitting in the manner that we have seen all the ethical factors that mattered to Thucydides so much. For Thucydides, the Delium incident contained features that corresponded to his own major concerns, namely an example of how the Athenians and other Greeks gradually allowed the Peloponnesian War to erode their sense of propriety and their ethical standards, military or otherwise.[37]

Thus, the very different purposes of these historians led to a completely different presentation of the same ethically sensitive incidents. This must always have been the case. A purely quantitative approach to the analysis of the ancient historians' presentation of ethically sensitive incidents does not provide sufficient understanding of them. A more qualitative appreciation is better suited to deal with the nuances of each situation.

It then becomes tempting to ask: was the example of Hellenic moral decline *all* that motivated Thucydides to produce such a lengthy account of Delium? At this point it is worth taking a look at how the account of this campaign fits into the structure of the *History* as a whole. I am not the first to point out how the Delium narrative is broken up by the appearance of Brasidas.[38] The Athenian plan is introduced, but then interrupted by news that at "about this time of the summer Brasidas was on his way to the Thracian area with seventeen hundred hoplites." "Βρασίδας δὲ κατὰ τὸν αὐτὸν χρόνον τοῦ θέρους πορευόμενος ἑπτακοσίοις καὶ χιλίοις ὁπλίταις ἐς τὰ ἐπὶ Θράκης." (Thuc. 4.78.1, trans. Warner). For eleven chapters we hear how Brasidas gathers pace, going from success to success. Then the *History* turns back to Boeotia, for the battle and siege at Delium. Then it returns

---

[36] On his use of the Sicilian Timaeus see Pearson 1986.

[37] Gomme 1956, 571; Lateiner 1977, 103. See also Creed 1973, 230.

[38] Dewald 2005, 97; Hornblower 1996, 256-257; see also Rawlings 1981, 50-54.

once more to Brasidas, whose success is such that only about a month after the Battle of Delium was fought, he and his Peloponnesians take Amphipolis. That, of course, was the event that ended the military career of none other than our author, Thucydides. Table 6-2 clarifies the sequence of Thucydides' narrative.

Through this use of juxtaposition Thucydides suggests criticism of the decisions and actions that led to the disaster at Delium, and, by implication, this provides a defence for his failure in the North. The arrangement keeps the threat to Athenian resources in the North constantly in the reader's mind throughout the developing situation in Delium, suggesting that the Athenians would have been better off concentrating their efforts on that threat, rather than getting entangled in a shameful mess in Boeotia. Only after the loss of Amphipolis do the Athenians seem to realise how significant this aspect of the war is, and Thucydides reminds us that this realisation comes all too late, after "the Athenians had just been defeated in Boeotia." "τῶν Ἀθηναίων ἐν τοῖς Βοιωτοῖς νεωστὶ πεπληγμένων." (Thuc. 4.108.5, trans. Warner).

It has often been said how little his personal involvement influenced Thucydides' account of Amphipolis.[39] To a certain extent this is very true; he certainly does not blow his own trumpet, nor does he explicitly bemoan his misfortunes. It is, of course, somewhat problematic to infer motivation, but can we be sure that his lack of success there did not influence his extended presentation of the debacle at Delium, the disaster that contributed to his downfall? I would argue that we cannot. Personal interest may well have a role here after all. The loss of Amphipolis was a serious blow to the Athenian war effort.[40] When dealing with this campaign, it is important to bear in mind "the crucial importance of the city of Amphipolis [and] the cost to Athens in establishing it".[41] Thucydides acknowledges the economic and strategic problems that its fall caused: "the city was useful to them for the importation of timber for shipbuilding and for the revenue it produced." "ἡ πόλις ἦν αὐτοῖς ὠφέλιμος ξύλων τε ναυπηγησίμων πομπῇ καὶ χρημάτων προσόδῳ" (Thuc. 4.108.1, trans. Warner), but then minimises these same problems by stating that the belief of the allies who subsequently revolted, that Athens was weakened, was mistaken (Thuc. 4.108.4).

---

[39] E.g. Gomme 1956, 578 and 584.

[40] Attica was not able to provide Athens with the wood that was needed to maintain a fleet, Borza 1987, 34. See also Knight 1970, 154 on the threat posed to the Athenian grain supply.

[41] Pouncey 1980, 4. See also Borza 1987, 49 and Kallet-Marx 1993, 176 on the importance of Amphipolis to Athens.

In fact the Athenians *were* weakened, and were left in the undesirable position of having to deal directly with the sometimes hostile kings of Macedon for the procurement of the timber that was so essential to them.[42] They did manage to secure timber through these means, but this was a more unreliable method than dealing with their own colony and did nothing to restore the loss of revenue "from gold and silver mines" that the fall of Amphipolis represented.[43] The fall of Amphipolis was a serious blow, and Athens was never able to recover this valuable city.[44] Sparta's growing control over the resources that Athens relied on was what eventually brought about the Spartan victory.

Even though Thucydides does acknowledge the importance of the loss of this city, he does so briefly, in a way that minimises its immediate and long-term implications. The focus on the allies' reaction rather than on the economic implications distracts the reader from the seriousness of the situation as a whole. This refocusing is re-enforced by the manner in which Thucydides claims that the allies were mistaken. He does this by offering a rare analysis, in the format that Gribble has characterised as "narrator-authorised and thus 'correct' analysis".[45] Far from presenting the fall of Amphipolis as the disaster it was, Thucydides leads the reader into a positive interpretation of the situation it created:

> We go into the ring full of the perception of the disaster the fall of Amphipolis represents for Athens, and come out of it with a renewed perception of her strength. Thus the passage starts with the panicky reaction at Athens, and finishes with the beginning of Athenian counter-measures …[and]…renewed appreciation of her future resilience.[46]

When Thucydides discusses the decision of the allies to defect after the fall of Amphipolis, he refers back to the defeat at Delium as a contributory

---

[42] Borza 1987, 39 and 43-44.

[43] Kallet-Marx 1993, 176. Already in 425 BC Athens was struggling financially and needed to dramatically increase tribute (M-L 69 (66)). Although it was not tribute paying, the loss of Amphipolis compounded this growing problem. See Gomme 1956, 580 and 581 and Knight 1970, 161: "The Athenians were forced to over-reach themselves militarily and financially" so that defeat was perhaps inevitable.

[44] Borza 1987, 44 n. 48: "Even though Amphipolis was technically ceded to Athens by the Peace of Nicias…the city renounced her relationship with Athens and over the next sixty years resisted every Athenian attempt to force her back into the fold."

[45] Gribble 1998, 58.

[46] Gribble 1998, 60.

explanation (Thuc. 4.108.5). This may of course have been a genuine factor in their revolt, but nonetheless it is significant that Thucydides as narrator directly intrudes into the narrative at this stage to remind the reader that factors un-related to Amphipolis were to blame. It should also be remembered that Thucydides refers to doubts about the loyalty of the allies in this area as early as 4.82, anticipating the problems Athens would have if Brasidas were successful. The Athenians took some steps at this time, but as the reader already knows, "the Athenians were already preparing for their offensive on land against Boeotia which led to the battle of Delium and they can have had very few troops to spare."[47] Even at this stage in the narrative Thucydides is suggesting to the reader that the Athenians had their priorities wrong. We might accept that there are "no grounds for suspecting his narrative contains any falsehood or distortion of the facts," but there is certainly a manipulation of emphasis.[48] As Westlake has noted:

> "Judgements which less discerning readers imagine to be their own are in fact those of Thucydides and have been unobtrusively put into their minds by his selection and arrangement of material, by implied approval and implied criticism, by contrast at one point and emphasis at another, [and] he uses subtle methods of this kind very extensively to influence the verdict of his readers on the actions of those concerned in the events leading to the loss of Amphipolis.[49]

The meticulous treatment of the fall of Amphipolis shows how careful Thucydides was to control its presentation. It is plausible that his extended narrative of Delium is part of this presentation, contributing to the minimisation of the seriousness of the loss of Amphipolis.

By the end of book four, the reader is aware that two disasters had befallen Athens before the negotiation of peace. By providing an extensive account of Delium and by minimalising the seriousness of the loss of Amphipolis in the manner Gribble has outlined, the Delium campaign appears as the more striking of the two, though Amphipolis was arguably the more significant set-back. By focusing on Delium, Thucydides both distracts from the loss of Amphipolis and tries to excuse it. Had a different outcome resulted from the Amphipolis campaign, we would perhaps have heard less about Delium. The Delium campaign's importance to the moral theme of the *History* has already been discussed, but perhaps its

---

[47] Westlake 1969, 128.
[48] Westlake 1969, 124.
[49] Westlake 1969, 125.

importance for Thucydides' personal reputation should also be considered. An understandable concern for his reader's perception of his activities may have affected, if not motivated, the entire presentation of the Delium campaign. This should, in turn, affect how we as modern scholars view its importance in the study of military ethics. To take Delium as an incident in isolation is to badly decontextualise it. While it is presented to us as unusual and shocking, its presence in the text may be little more than a literary ruse to distract from the author's own personal failing.

So, to conclude, what exactly do we have here with the narratives of the Delium campaign and that of the 415 BC Sicilian expedition? We have two authors narrating the same two incidents, and in both cases offering very different treatments. It is my suggestion that Diodorus' omissions in the case of Delium were a direct response to Thucydides' use of controversial incidents as a structuring device and as an expression of declining Greek morality. Diodorus recognised that Thucydides' treatment encompassed features of military ethics and moralising and chose to do something distinct from this.

The manner in which ancient Greek historians dealt with ethical concerns and the details of atrocities seems to have been significantly affected by the individual moral programme of each writer. Issues such as who won which battle might be recorded with a fair degree of consensus and regularity, just as the fundamentals of major battles are rarely disputed, and there is often a uniformity regarding their presentation; but when it comes to what happened *after* these battles, events such as pursuit, the recovery of bodies or interaction with non-combatants and sanctuaries, these things seem to have been considered significant for the *interpretive purpose* of the author rather than for their own intrinsic worth as historical information. The Delium campaign was significant to Thucydides because it involved states in which he was particularly interested, and because it exemplified certain themes that were fundamental to his work in its entirety. It also enabled him to ameliorate the negative impression created by his own military failure in that same year. For Diodorus this was quite simply not the case. He chose not to omit it entirely, but he focused his ethical reflections elsewhere. He saved them for a situation that involved the people about whom *he* was concerned, shaping them to express his vision of morality in the scheme of history.

Thucydides' account makes it very clear that there were customs, "νομοί", of war in Classical Greece, and he must have expected his readers to recognise them. These customs appear to have been relatively unspecific, as might be expected if they grew—as they must have done— out of practice rather than legislation, but they existed nonetheless.

Ambiguous custom, or flouted custom, is still to be distinguished from no custom at all. Thucydides' narrative, supported by Euripides' reaction as evidenced by the *Supplicants*, suggests that the events at the sanctuary of Apollo at Delium were unusual and appalling. This must be regarded as a valid point of view, but closer analysis of both his motivations and other contemporary factors should make us hesitant to accept this as the definitive point of view. The incident appears to be so distinctive because it is shaped within the narrative to act as an example of general moral decline. Thucydides' decision to use Delium for this purpose may also have been motivated by the author's need to redeem his own personal reputation. These factors have perhaps led us to perceive this incident as more significant than it might otherwise have seemed. That others felt less strongly about it is suggested by Diodorus' relative indifference and Plato's willingness to depict Alcibiades discussing his part in it in the *Symposium* and Socrates referring to it as part of his defence. This is not to suggest that the events at Delium were entirely unproblematic in religious terms, but perhaps popular attitudes to events of this kind were more robust than has been assumed. Thucydides' near monopoly on the interpretation of this particular incident should not be confused with a general contemporary interpretation. The decision to occupy the sanctuary was approved by popular vote, after all. The events of the Delium campaign remain exceptional, but this may reflect historiographical tendencies rather than contemporary military practice.

It has often been said that history is written by the victors. With these incidents that is not quite the case, but they certainly demonstrate that the history of events beyond the battlefield required the assistance of a writer with particular motivations in order to make it on to the page. The material is selected to an even greater degree than we are used to facing. When we try to discern the parameters of behaviour in warfare, it is worth remembering that there is no such thing as an ethically neutral version of the writing of history.

Tables

	Thucydides	Diodorus
Athenian Plague	2.47-55, detailed account, which describes the collapse of Athenian morality.	12.45-46, 12.50 and 58, the plague hinders the war effort, no comment on its moral impact.
Fall of Plataea	2.1-9, an unsuccessful attack on Plataea, 180 Theban prisoners executed. 2.71-78, siege. 3.51-68, Plataea destroyed.	12.42, Theban prisoners returned unharmed. 12.56, brief account of destruction of the city.
***Stasis* on Corcyra**	3.69-85, lengthy account, full of horrors and Thucydides' explicit condemnation of events.	12.57, brief account, with few atrocities and no authorial comment.
Fall of Melos	See esp. 5.84-114, an unprecedented and extensive debate on the fate of the conquered.	12.80.5, in one sentence, records the fall, executions and enslavement.

Table 6-1. Differences in Thucydides and Diodorus' accounts of various events.

3.13	**Mytilene advises Sparta to attack Athens through its resources.**
4.70	**Brasidas interrupts Athens at Megara while in the region to recruit for Thracian campaign.**
4.76	Athenians plan "to seize Delium, the temple of Apollo in the territory of Tanagra".
4.78	**"About the same time...Brasidas was on his way to the Thracian area with 1,700 hoplites."**
4.78-88	**Brasidas campaigns successfully in the North, winning peoples over with his clemency and upright character.**
4.89-101	Athenian defeat and involvement in impiety at Delium.
4.102-116	**"The same winter" Brasidas captures Amphipolis. Thucydides names himself as the general involved (4.106.3).**
4.108	The Athenians realise the value of Amphipolis. Their allies in the area revolt partly because the Athenians had just been defeated in Boeotia.

Table 6-2. The entries in bold refer to the narrative of Brasidas, the lighter to that of the Athenians.

Bibliography

Borza, E. N. "Timber and Politics in the Ancient World: Macedon and the Greeks." *PAPS* 131 (1) (1987): 32-52.

Bosworth, B. "Athens' First Intervention in Sicily: Thucydides and the Sicilian Tradition." *CQ* 42 (1) (1992): 46-55.

Bowie, A. M. "Tragic Filters for History: Euripides' *Supplices* and Sophocles' *Philoctetes*." In *Greek Tragedy and the Historian*, edited by C. Pelling: 39-63. Oxford: Clarendon Press, 1997.

Bury, J. B. *A History of Greece to the Death of Alexander the Great. 3rd ed. revised by R. Meiggs.* London: Macmillan & Co, 1955.

Cartledge, P. *Sparta and Lakonia. A Regional History 1300-362 BC.* London and New York: Routledge, 1979/2002.

Cogan, M. *The Human Thing: The Speeches and Principles of Thucydides' History.* Chicago and London: University of Chicago Press, 1981.

Creed, J. L. "Moral Values in the Age of Thucydides." *CQ* 23 (2) (1973): 213-231.

Davies, J. K. The Tradition about the First Sacred War. In *Greek Historiography*, edited by S. Hornblower, 193-213. Oxford: Clarendon Press, 1994.

Dewald, C. *Thucydides' War Narrative. A Structural Study.* Berkeley, Los Angeles, London: University of California Press, 2005.

Drews, R. "Diodorus and his Sources." *AJP* 83 (4) (1962): 383-392.

Ducrey, P. *Le Traitement des Prisonniers de Guerre dans la Grece Antique des Origines à la Conquête Romaine.* Paris: E. de Boccard, 1999.

Eatough, G. "The Use of Osios and Kindred Words in Thucydides." *AJP* 92 (2) (1971): 238-251.

Eckstein, A. M. *Moral Vision in the Histories of Polybius.* Berkeley and London: University of California Press, 1995.

Evans, J.A.S. *Herodotus: Explorer of the Past.* Princeton: Princeton University Press, 1991.

Garlan, Y. *La Guerre dans L'Antiquite.* Paris: F. Nathan, 1972.

Giles, P. "Political Allusions in the Supplices of Euripides." *CR* 4 (3) (1890): 95-98.

Gomme, A. W. *A Historical Commentary on Thucydides. Vol. 3. The Ten Years War. Books 4-5.24.* Oxford: Clarendon Press, 1956.

Gribble, D. "Narrator Interventions in Thucydides." *JHS* 118 (1998): 41-67.

Grote, G. *A History of Greece: From the Earliest Period to the Close of the Generation Contemporary with Alexander the Great. Vol. 6.* London, J. Murray, 1872.

Guettel Cole, S. "The Uses of Water in Greek Sanctuaries." In *Early Greek Cult Practice. Proceedings of the Fifth International Symposium at the Swedish Institute at Athens 26-29 June,* 1986, edited by R. Hagg, N. Marinatos and G.C. Nordquist, 161-165. Stockholm: Skrifter Utgivna av Svenska Institutet i Athen. Vol.38, 1988.

Hornblower, S. "The Fourth-Century and Hellenistic Reception of Thucydides." *JHS* 115 (1995): 47-68.

—. *A Commentary on Thucydides. Vol. 2. Books 4-5.24.* Oxford: Clarendon Press, 1996.

Howe, T. "Pastoralism, the Delphic Amphiktyony and the First Sacred War: the Creation of Apollo's Sacred Pastures." *Historia* 52 (2003): 129-146.

Huxley, G. "Boiotian Charioteers in Diodoros." *Philologus* 135 (2) (1991): 320-321.

Jordan, B. "Religion in Thucydides." *TAPA* 116 (1986):119-147.

Kallet-Marx, L. *Money, Expense, and Naval Power in Thucydides' History 1-5.24.* Berkeley, Los Angeles, Oxford: University of California Press, 1993.

Knight, D. W. "Thucydides and the War Strategy of Perikles." *Mnemosyne* 23 (1970): 150-161.

Krentz, P. "Fighting by the Rules: The Invention of the Hoplite Agon." *Hesperia* 71 (1) (2002): 23-39.

Lateiner, D. "Heralds and Corpses in Thucydides." *Classical World* 71 (1977): 97-106.

Morgan, C. *Athletes and Oracles. The Transformation of Olympia and Delphi in the Eighth Century BC.* Cambridge: Cambridge University Press, 1990.

Ober, J. *The Athenian Revolution: Essays in Ancient Greek Democracy and Political Theory.* Princeton: Princeton University Press, 1996.

Orwin, C. *The Humanity of Thucydides.* Princeton: Princeton University Press, 1994.

Osborne, R. *Greece in the Making 1200-479BC.* London and New York: Routledge, 1996.

Ostwald, M. *From Popular Sovereignty to the Sovereignty of Law: Law, Society and Politics in Fifth Century Athens.* Berkeley and London: University of California Press, 1986.

Parker, R. *Miasma. Pollution and Purification in Early Greek Religion.* Oxford: Clarendon Press, 1983.

Pearson, L. "The Speeches of Timaeus' History." *AJP* 107 (1986): 350-368.

Pouncey, P. *The Necessities of War: A Study of Thucydides' Pessimism*. New York, Guildford: Columbia University Press, 1980.

Price, S. *Religions of the Ancient Greeks*. Cambridge: Cambridge University Press, 1999.

Pritchett, W. K. *The Greek State at War. Part 4*. Berkeley, Los Angeles, London: University of California Press, 1985.

—. 1991. *The Greek State at War. Part 5*. Berkeley, Los Angeles, Oxford: University of California Press.

Rawlings, H.R. *The Structure of Thucydides' History*. Princeton: Princeton University Press, 1981.

Sacks, K. *Diodorus Siculus and the First Century BC*. Princeton: Princeton University Press, 1990.

Scott, L. *Historical Commentary on Herodotus Book 6, Mnemosyne Supplement 268*. Leiden and Boston: Brill, 2005.

Meiggs R. and Lewis, D. *A Selection of Greek Historical Inscriptions to the End of the Fifth Century BC*. Oxford: Clarendon Press, 1969, revised 1988.

Stylianou, P. J. *A Historical Commentary on Diodorus Siculus book 15*. Oxford: Clarendon Press, 1998.

Toher, M. "Diodoros on Delion and Euripides' Supplices." *CQ* 51 (1) (2001): 178-182.

van Wees, H. "The Development of the Hoplite Phalanx: Iconography and Reality in the 7th Century." In *War and Violence in Classical Greece*, edited by H. van Wees, 125-166. London: Duckworth and the Classical Press of Wales, 2000.

Westlake, H. D. "Thucydides and the Fall of Amphipolis." In *Essays on the Greek Historians and Greek History*, edited by H. D. Westlake. Manchester: Manchester University Press, 1969: 123-138. (First published as "Thucydides and the Fall of Amphipolis." in *Hermes* 90 (1962): 276-287.)

CHAPTER SEVEN

THE VICTOR AFTER THE VICTORY:
A NARRATIVE SET-PIECE IN GREEK
HISTORIOGRAPHY FROM HERODOTUS
TO DIODORUS OF SICILY[1]

LISA IRENE HAU

κάλλιόν ἐστι τοῦ νικᾶν τὸ τὴν νίκην ἐνεγκεῖν ἀνθρωπίνως.

"More glorious than being victorious is bearing victory with moderation."
—Diod. Sic. 13.19.5

All the works of Greek historiography are essentially concerned with the same theme, namely war (and, with a slight variation, negotiation to avoid war). This naturally means that they deal with many of the same situations. There is a distinction, however, between situations that are customarily treated in great detail (such as battles, war-councils, and arrivals of new commanders) and other, equally common, situations which are usually not mentioned or are commonly passed over summarily (such as declarations of war and the treatment of wounded men after battle). One situation often painted in minute detail is that of a victorious commander and his handling of the immediate aftermath of his victory.

Before we turn to the characteristics of this "set-piece" of the victor after the victory, it will be helpful to define what I mean by set-piece. To that end, the narratological distinction between "scene" and "summary" is

---

[1] I would like to thank Ed Bragg for single-handedly arranging the conference at which this paper was originally presented, and also the audience at that conference, who offered helpful comments. I would also like to thank Lene Rubinstein, Hans van Wees, Judith Owen, and Elizabeth Macaulay-Lewis for reading through drafts of this paper and suggesting several improvements.

useful.[2] The classic definition of the two was offered by Genette: a summary is when the narrative moves faster than the story (i.e. the events narrated), i.e. when a long story is compressed into a short narrative; a scene is when the narrative is "real-time", i.e. when the narrative moves as slowly as the story.[3] For the purpose of discussing ancient Greek historiography, I propose to define the two in more detail. A scene in Greek historiography usually involves interaction between two or more characters, it often gives specific details of time and place, and it often includes direct (or indirect) speech. Direct speech is "real-time" by necessity, but the rest of the scene may move slightly faster than that. The summary can be defined as a narrative moving faster than a scene, with no direct speech. The speed of a summary varies: sometimes several years, decades, or centuries are covered in a single paragraph; at other times, the narrative of a few days stretches over several pages.

A set-piece is a situation that occurs often in Greek historiography and is often turned into a narrative scene. One such set-piece is that of the victorious commander dealing with spoils and captives, the "victor after the victory set-piece".[4] This set-piece is interesting for both historical and literary reasons. It is interesting historically because the Greek historians are our most important source for the behaviour of victorious commanders in antiquity and for their contemporaries' reactions to it. It is interesting in terms of literature because the set-piece of the victor after the victory is found in every extant work of historiography from Herodotus to Diodorus of Sicily, sometimes in very elaborate form. Whether one reads the Greek historians as history or literature, it is interesting that this set-piece almost always carries a moral significance as the narrator invites the reader to evaluate morally the behaviour of the victor.

It is the purpose of this paper to pursue the victor after the victory set-piece in Greek historiography from Herodotus until Diodorus of Sicily, just before Greek and Roman historiography converge. I shall examine how both the form and the content of the set-piece change over time, but also how some *topoi* of the set-piece continue to appear in different

---

[2] Apart from scenes and summaries stand ethnographical, technical, programmatic, and moral digressions.

[3] Genette 1980, 93-95. For narratology used in the study of (ancient) historiography see Rood 1998, 9-14.

[4] There are many other set-pieces in Greek historiography. Some of the more common are "sea-battle", "land-battle", "the commander and his officers", "negotiation between ambassadors", and "negotiation between commanders".

authors from different time periods.[5] Finally, I shall see what conclusions may be drawn from this.

The first victor after the victory set-piece in extant Greek historiography is the scene between Cyrus of Persia and Croesus of Lydia in Herodotus 1.86-90.[6] The scene is set at 1.86.1, where Croesus is captured and led to Cyrus. At 86.2, we learn the victor's intentions for his important prisoner:

ὁ δὲ συννήσας πυρὴν μεγάλην ἀνεβίβασε ἐπ' αὐτὴν τὸν Κροῖσόν τε ἐν πέδῃσι δεδεμένον καὶ δὶς ἑπτὰ Λυδῶν παρ' αὐτὸν παῖδας, ἐν νόῳ ἔχων εἴτε δὴ ἀκροθίνια ταῦτα καταγιεῖν θεῶν ὅτεῳ δή, εἴτε καὶ εὐχὴν ἐπιτελέσαι θέλων, εἴτε καὶ πυθόμενος τὸν Κροῖσον εἶναι θεοσεβέα τοῦδε εἴνεκεν ἀνεβίβασε ἐπὶ τὴν πυρήν, βουλόμενος εἰδέναι εἴ τίς μιν δαιμόνων ῥύσεται τοῦ μὴ ζῶντα κατακαυθῆναι.

Cyrus had a large pyre built and had Croesus chained with fetters and mount it, and two times seven Lydian boys with him; either because he intended to dedicate these first-fruits to one of the gods, or because he wanted to fulfil a vow, or because he had heard that Croesus was god-fearing, and made him mount the pyre from a desire to find out if some divine power would snatch him away to prevent him from being burned alive. (Hdt. 1.86.2)[7]

The narrator does not explicitly condemn Cyrus' way of treating his prisoner, but the fact that he can only guess at Cyrus' motive distances both the narrator himself and the reader from the king's decision. By expressing lack of certainty about his protagonist's thoughts, the narrator conveys a sense of puzzlement to the reader: why would a victor want to do something like that? As the attention of the reader is turned to the strangeness of the victor's behaviour, it is a small step to think of the behaviour as wrong.[8]

---

[5] It could be argued that "set-piece" is just another word for a *topos*. However, I prefer to reserve the designation *topos* for the features within the set-piece that recur in a number of historiographical authors.

[6] The passage is usually discussed in the context of the story of Croesus with scant attention paid to its role in the story of Cyrus. For some thoughts on this aspect of the passage, see Harrison 2000, 42.

[7] All translations in this paper are my own.

[8] It may be argued that Herodotus' Cyrus is generally a positive character for whom the reader is meant to feel sympathy. However, in the narrative of Cyrus' death (Hdt. 1.204-214), the king clearly forms part of the pattern of powerful rulers turned overconfident which runs as a moralising thread through the *Histories*. His

As the flames begin to lick the pyre, Croesus thinks of his dramatically changed fortunes and calls out the name of Solon, who years earlier has told him not to count himself happy before his life has ended happily. Cyrus is intrigued, he asks Croesus to explain, and then:

καὶ τὸν Κῦρον ἀκούσαντα τῶν ἑρμηνέων τὰ Κροῖσος εἶπε, μεταγνόντα τε καὶ ἐννώσαντα ὅτι καὶ αὐτὸς ἄνθρωπος ἐὼν ἄλλον ἄνθρωπον, γενόμενον ἑωυτοῦ εὐδαιμονίῃ οὐκ ἐλάσσω, ζῶντα πυρὶ διδοίη, πρός τε τούτοισι δείσαντα τὴν τίσιν καὶ ἐπιλεξάμενον ὡς οὐδὲν εἴη τῶν ἐν ἀνθρώποισι ἀσφαλέως ἔχον, κελεύειν σβεννύναι τὴν ταχίστην τὸ καιόμενον πῦρ καὶ καταβιβάζειν Κροῖσόν τε καὶ τοὺς μετὰ Κροίσου.

When Cyrus had heard the explanation that Croesus gave, he changed his mind and realised that he himself was a human being and was about to burn alive another human being, who had been his equal in good fortune. And fearing the punishment for this action and considering that nothing is safe in human life, he ordered the burning fire put out as quickly as possible and told both Croesus and those with him to come down. (Hdt. 1.86.6).

It is worth noting that the narrator, who in 1.86.2 had to guess wildly in order to report Cyrus' motives for burning Croesus, now knows exactly what is going on in his protagonist's head when the latter changes his mind and decides to spare his prisoner. This change in focalization is indicative of the author's moral stance: as long as Cyrus is a "bad victor", Herodotus distances himself from him, but when he changes to a "good victor", Herodotus identifies with him.

What makes Cyrus change his mind is a sudden realisation of the similarity between himself and his defeated enemy, their shared humanity, emphasised by the repetition of the word ἄνθρωπος. This empathy is brought about by his sudden understanding of the changeable nature of human fortune: Croesus has once been as happy and successful as he himself is now, and he himself could one day end up like Croesus now. Thus, in this instance of the victor after the victory set-piece, Cyrus is transformed from a "bad victor" into a "good victor" by an understanding of the instability of human fortune. The fact that Cyrus is able to think about the changeability of fortune at the very moment when his success might seem most secure distinguishes him from most successful characters

---

initial impulse to burn Croesus alive alerts the reader to Cyrus' arrogant side and foreshadows the actions that will eventually lead to his death. See also n. 9.

in the *Histories*, where success usually fosters complacency and overconfidence, which is then punished by superhuman forces.[9]

In the end, however, it is not Cyrus who saves Croesus, but Apollo. Cyrus orders the flames put out, but they are already too strong. Croesus then prays to Apollo, and rain breaks from a clear sky and extinguishes the pyre. This makes Cyrus realise that "Croesus was dear to the gods and a good man" (εἴη ὁ Κροῖσος καὶ θεοφιλὴς καὶ ἀνὴρ ἀγαθός, Hdt. 87.2)—and the reader, of course, realises the same thing. This means, by implication, that Cyrus was wrong to want to burn Croesus. Thus, the divine intervention reinforces the moral evaluation which was hinted at by the narrator's uncertainty about Cyrus' motives for maltreating Croesus.

It is remarkable that Herodotus achieves all this without at any point *explicitly stating* that burning one's prisoners of war is wrong. This lack of explicitness is important because it stands in contrast to what we shall see in the later historiographers below.

My last point about the scene of Cyrus and Croesus has to do with what happens in the next chapter, 1.88. Here, Cyrus' newfound mildness in victory turns out to be *to his own advantage*. As Croesus watches the Persian soldiers plunder Sardis, he asks Cyrus what they are doing. Cyrus replies smugly, "they are plundering your city", and Croesus replies, "not my city, but yours" (Hdt. 1.88.3).[10] This makes Cyrus call a halt to the plundering, and when he then asks for Croesus' advice, he receives a detailed plan for the handling of war-booty, which he decides to follow and which works out perfectly.

A further two victor after the victory scenes are found in Herodotus, both taking place between the victor and one other character. One is 3.14-15, the scene between the victorious Cambyses and the captured Psammenitus. It shows Cambyses as the bad victor and constitutes the first piece in the gradual characterisation of this king as mad and impious. The other is 9.78-79 between the victorious Pausanias and one of his allied commanders, Lampon. It shows Pausanias as the good and moderate

---

[9] Most obviously Croesus (1.26-56, esp. 32-34), Polycrates (3.39-43 and 3.120-125), Darius (4.83-142), and Xerxes (books 7-8), but there are others. The fact that Cyrus is different means that he is potentially able to navigate a life without grave misfortunes. This potential is fulfilled when he takes Croesus as his advisor, but it is ruined when he finally succumbs to the human weakness of overconfidence, forgets that he is a human being, and plunges himself into disaster (1.204-214).

[10] 1.88.3: οὔτε πόλιν τὴν ἐμὴν οὔτε χρήματα τὰ ἐμὰ διαρπάζει· οὐδὲν γὰρ ἐμοὶ ἔτι τούτων μέτα· ἀλλὰ φέρουσί τε καὶ ἄγουσι τὰ σά, "they are plundering neither my city, nor my possessions: for nothing among those things is still mine. No, they are carrying off and plundering *your* possessions."

victor, who lectures Lampon on the dishonour and moral wrongness of maltreating the corpse of a fallen enemy. The fact that the defeated towards whom the victor can choose to show moderation or immoderation is dead rather than a captive makes the scene unique in the Greek historiography of our period.[11]

In Thucydides, even though many battles are won during the course of *The Peloponnesian War*, we do not find many victor after the victory scenes. Mostly, the victor's behaviour towards the defeated—which is generally harsh—is dealt with in a few lines of summary narrative.[12] There are two exceptions: the Spartan embassy to Athens at 4.17-20 and the Mytilene Debate at 3.36-50.[13] For now, we shall concentrate on the Mytilene Debate.[14]

Here, the victor is the Athenian people, who (Thuc. 3.36) decide to execute all the men of defeated Mytilene and sell the women and children as slaves. The narrator, like the narrator of Herodotus, does not explicitly condemn the decision of the victor, but his description of the decision shows his disapproval:

...καὶ ὑπὸ ὀργῆς ἔδοξεν αὐτοῖς οὐ τοὺς παρόντας μόνον ἀποκτεῖναι, ἀλλὰ καὶ τοὺς ἅπαντας Μυτιληναίους ὅσοι ἡβῶσι, παῖδας δὲ καὶ γυναῖκας ἀνδραποδίσαι,...

... and in anger they decided to kill not only those present, but also all the Mytilenians who were of military age and to enslave the women and children... (Thuc. 3.36.2)

The information that the decision was made *in anger* immediately signals that it was likely to be a wrong decision.[15] Moreover, "not only...but also" turns the attention of the reader to an escalation in extreme behaviour. It

---

[11] —but has an obvious forerunner in Achilles' treatment of Hector's body in the *Iliad*.

[12] The victors are usually the Athenians: over Hestiaea 1.114, Torone 5.3, Scione 5.32, and Melos 5.116. Victors in *stasis* fall into a different category.

[13] It is tempting also to class the Melian Dialogue in this category even though the Athenians at the time of the dialogue are not yet victorious over Melos. This fact is easily forgotten when one reads the dialogue, but when it is remembered, it only makes the Athenian behaviour even more shockingly arrogant. Thus, the dialogue fills the same function as a victor after the victory set-piece, namely moralising on success-induced arrogance which will lead to a fall.

[14] Good and detailed discussions of the Mytilene Debate can be found in de Romilly 1963, Macleod 1978, Williams 1998, and Stahl 2003.

[15] See de Romilly 1963, 158 and Hornblower 1996 *ad loc*.

was bad enough that the Athenians decided to kill those Mytilenians who were present in Athens (this group consisted partly of ambassadors there to present the case of their countrymen (Thuc. 3.28.1), partly of suppliants raised from the altars by Paches and promised that their lives would be spared (Thuc. 3.28.2), and should thus have been sacrosanct), but it was even worse that they decided to massacre the common people who had had no part in Mytilene's decision to revolt.

The very next day, however, the Athenians themselves realise that their decision is overly harsh (…ὠμὸν τὸ βούλευμα καὶ μέγα ἐγνῶσθαι, πόλιν ὅλην διαφθεῖραι μᾶλλον ἢ οὐ τοὺς αἰτίους, Thuc. 3.36.4). They put the decision to the vote again, and much narrative space is taken up by the two speeches delivered, one for sticking to the previous decision by Cleon, one for relenting and sparing the non-implicated Mytilenians by Diodotus. The debate is narrowly won by Diodotus.

Interestingly, this speech, which after all is an exhortation to mildness and moderation, does not contain a single reference to either the changeability of fortune or to common humanity, the two things that transformed Cyrus from a bad to a good victor. Furthermore, Diodotus says explicitly that he does *not* want the Athenians to act from justice (Thuc. 3.44.1), from pity, or from mildness (μήτε οἴκτῳ πλέον νείμαντες μήτ' ἐπιεικείᾳ, Thuc. 3.48.1). Instead he claims that it is in the victor's own interest (χρησίμως, Thuc. 3.44.4; ξυμφορώτερον, Thuc. 3.47.5) to treat the defeated mildly because this will foster loyalty and encourage others to consider surrender instead of holding out till the bitter end. This is significant because, in contrast with the narrative of Croesus and Cyrus where the mildness of the victor turns out inadvertently to be to his own advantage, the victor's own advantage is here used as a conscious motive for treating the defeated with mildness.

In terms of the moral message to the reader, the speech carries a double meaning. On the one hand, Diodotus' arguments about the victor's own interest are fairly convincing. On the other, his repeated stressing of the Athenians' disregard for justice, pity, and mildness actually has the effect of focusing the reader's mind rather firmly on these qualities.[16] This

---

[16] The narrator does not tell us whether this was Diodotus' intention with the speech; if so, this puts the speech in the same category of subversive speeches as Nicias' second speech before the Sicilian Expedition. Modern commentators, however, tend to regard the speech as delivered in earnest (de Romilly 1963, Macleod 1978, Williams 1998), and some claim to see in it Thucydides' own point of view (de Romilly 1963, 156-171; Stahl 2003, 119). As far as I know, only Kagan 1975 and Manuwald 1979 have argued that the speech is subversive. Connor 1984, 79-91 gives a good analysis of the persuasiveness of the speech.

encourages the reader to evaluate the Athenians negatively in spite of their transformation in practice from "bad victor" to "good victor". In this way, the moralising is even more subtle than in Herodotus. The narrator does not comment at all; the speech is left to make its own impression.

Continuing to the next generation of historiographers and Xenophon's *Hellenica*, we find no examples of the "bad victor" being transformed into the "good victor". What we do find are examples of the bad victor being brought to suffer in return.[17] The most interesting example is 4.5.6-9 where Agesilaus, king of Sparta, has won an important victory (in the Corinthian War) over a coalition of Corinthians and Thebans. When some Boeotian envoys arrive to ask for peace terms, Agesilaus ignores them and pointedly keeps admiring his spoils—thus acting, the narrator declares, with great arrogance (μάλα μεγαλοφρόνως).[18] In other words, this is an instance of the victor abusing his victory even if the abuse is less serious than Cyrus burning Croesus or the Athenians executing all of the Mytilenians.[19] Just like Cyrus, Agesilaus is interrupted in his arrogance—not by one of his captives, however, but by a messenger:

ἔτι δὲ καθημένου Ἀγησιλάου καὶ ἐοικότος ἀγαλλομένῳ τοῖς πεπραγμένοις, ἱππεύς τις προσήλαυνε καὶ μάλα ἰσχυρῶς ἰδρῶντι τῷ ἵππῳ. ὑπὸ πολλῶν δὲ ἐρωτώμενος ὅ τι ἀγγέλλοι, οὐδενὶ ἀπεκρίνατο, ἀλλ' ἐπειδὴ ἐγγὺς ἦν τοῦ Ἀγησιλάου, καθαλόμενος ἀπὸ τοῦ ἵππου καὶ προσδραμὼν αὐτῷ μάλα σκυθρωπὸς ὢν λέγει τὸ τῆς ἐν Λεχαίῳ μόρας πάθος.

While Agesilaus was still sitting down looking like a man exulting in what he had accomplished, a horseman was driving his sweating and foaming horse towards him. Asked by many what his message was, he answered no one, but when he was near Agesilaus, he jumped off his horse, ran up to him with doom written on his face, and told him of the disaster that had befallen the regiment at Lechaeum. (Xen. *Hel.* 4.5.7)

---

[17] Most obviously (apart from the passage discussed here) at Xen. *Hel.* 2.1.31-32 where the former victor is now a captive.

[18] μεγαλοφρόνως can be either positive or negative. In its positive sense, however, it usually means "generously", and as there is nothing generous about Agesilaus' conduct here, the adverb is most easily taken in its negative sense.

[19] Many scholars have claimed that Xenophon is uncritical of Agesilaus and blind to his unpleasant side (e.g. Cawkwell 1979, 38-39). However, newer scholarship has become increasingly aware that Xenophon could be critical of Agesilaus (e.g. Anderson 1974, 166-169; Gray 1989; Tuplin 1993, 69; Dillery 1995). One of the negative character traits Xenophon noticed in him was apparently arrogance.

This image of the arrogant and self-satisfied commander being approached by a distraught messenger from the destroyed army is striking. Even though, just as in Herodotus and Thucydides, the narrator does not explicitly state that Agesilaus was wrong to treat the Boeotian envoys so arrogantly, the dramatic details of the foaming horse, the messenger's refusal to talk to anyone but the commander, and his serious looks when he delivers the message all amount to the message that, as Croesus learned, "nothing is safe in human life". This is essentially the same moral which we have seen in Herodotus: fortune is changeable, all human beings are weak in the face of it, and this common human fate should make a victor treat the defeated with mildness and moderation. The moralising is still subtle. The narrator does not make his point explicitly, but trusts in the juxtaposition of Agesilaus' arrogance and his army's defeat to carry the message.[20] The moral point gains in sharpness from the subsequent narrative of the disaster suffered by the Lechaeum regiment (Xen. *Hel.* 4.5.11-18), which turns out also to have been caused by overconfidence induced by success.[21]

An interestingly difficult question is whether Agesilaus is being punished for his arrogance by divine powers (as the Spartans as a people are punished by divine powers for occupying the Theban Cadmea, Xen. *Hel.* 5.4.1), or whether he is simply unlucky. Xenophon leaves the answer to this question much more open than do some later historians as we shall see below.

---

[20] For a detailed analysis of this passage reaching much the same conclusion see Gray 1989, 157-160. Higgins 1977, 111-112 and Tuplin 1993, 71 also comment on its dramatic impact. Breitenbach 1950, 41 is talking about *explicit* moralising when he picks the scene as an example of the lack of moralising in Xenophon. Soulis 1972, 40-41, who ridicules the passage, misses the point entirely.

[21] Xenophon has been blamed (by e.g. Schwartz 1889, 189 and Soulis 1972, 40) for not relating the facts of the disaster at Lechaeum until after Agesilaus has received the news of it, or even mentioning it before this scene. The delaying of this information, however, heightens both the dramatic and the moral point. The fact that the news of the disaster now come as much as a shock to the reader as it does to Agesilaus adds an emotional impact to the didactic scene: the reader is meant not just to know, but to *feel* that his fortune can change at any moment. (Cf. Rood 1991, 286 on the Thucydidean narrative technique he terms "temporal misplacement": "Events are often narrated not in their chronological order, but where they best allow us to understand their psychological effect on contemporaries.")

The *Hellenica* also contains scenes of the good victor who knows how to handle his victory with moderation.[22] One example is Agesilaus after another victory:

ἐπεὶ δ' ἡ μὲν νίκη Ἀγησιλάου ἐγεγένητο, τετρωμένος δ' αὐτὸς προσενήνεκτο πρὸς τὴν φάλαγγα, προσελάσαντές τινες τῶν ἱππέων λέγουσιν αὐτῷ ὅτι τῶν πολεμίων ὡς ὀγδοήκοντα σὺν ὅπλοις ὑπὸ τῷ νεῷ εἰσι, καὶ ἠρώτων τί χρὴ ποιεῖν. ὁ δέ, καίπερ πολλὰ τραύματα ἔχων, ὅμως οὐκ ἐπελάθετο τοῦ θείου, ἀλλ' ἐάν τε ἀπιέναι ᾗ βούλοιντο ἐκέλευε καὶ ἀδικεῖν οὐκ εἴα. τότε μὲν οὖν, καὶ γὰρ ἦν ἤδη ὀψέ, δειπνοποιησάμενοι ἐκοιμήθησαν.

When the victory had fallen to Agesilaus and he himself, wounded, had been carried to the phalanx, some of the horsemen rode up and told him that about eighty of the enemy, with their arms, had taken refuge in the temple, and they asked him what they should do. And he, although he had received numerous wounds, nevertheless did not disregard the god, but ordered them to allow the people in the temple to go away to whatever place they wanted, and not to allow them to commit any crimes. Then (for it was already late), they had their evening meal and went to sleep (Xen. *Hel.* 4.3.20).

This shows a positive side of Agesilaus: his piety, which makes him respect the gods even in victory and even when in pain. Again, the narrator does not explicitly tell the reader what to think of this behaviour, but he stresses the unexpectedness of it by the adverbs καίπερ and ὅμως and by the negation: "Agesilaus did *not* disregard the god…" We understand that he *could have* disregarded the god; we may even be meant to expect him to do so and be impressed when it turns out that he does not.

After Xenophon, we are faced with a gap in our material as no substantial part of any historiographical work is extant from the next 200 years. The gap is partly filled by the thousands of so-called fragments of otherwise lost historical works, which are in reality references to these historians or, at best, quotations from them in later writers. This state of affairs makes it hazardous to say anything about the development of the victor after the victory set-piece in these centuries: any didactic point may have been added by the later author, who may have put his own twist or interpretation on the events which he found narrated in his source.[23]

---

[22] Xen. *Hel.* 3.1.24-28, 7.2.16.
[23] I hope to discuss these problems and their impact on our understanding of the moralising of the fragmentary historians more fully elsewhere; such in-depth

Nevertheless, there are some indications that the set-piece did occur in at least a few of the now fragmentary historians.

One such indication is Plutarch's *Nicias* 28.1-4, the narrative of the debate in the Syracusan assembly about the Athenians captured at the Asinarus River in 413 BC. When the Syracusans have decided to make the day of the capture into a national holiday, to set free the captured slaves and allies, but to throw the Athenians into the quarries and to execute their generals, the Syracusan statesman Hermocrates protests, saying that "more glorious than being victorious is handling victory with honour" (ὅτι τοῦ νικᾶν κρεῖττόν ἐστι τὸ καλῶς χρῆσθαι τῇ νίκῃ), but he is shouted down. Then Gylippus, the Spartan commander, asks to be allowed to take the Athenian generals back to Sparta alive, and the narrator digresses to explain why the Syracusans had never liked Gylippus and how corrupt he would later turn out to be, prefacing this with the source indication "as Timaeus says" (ὡς δὲ Τίμαιός φησι). After the digression, Plutarch gives two different versions of how the Athenian generals died, with source indications: Philistus and Thucydides say that they were executed, but Timaeus claims that Hermocrates managed to send them word of the assembly's decision while the meeting was still going on, and that they killed themselves. The two references to Timaeus (who lived ca. 350-260 BC, in the first half of the "gap" between Xenophon and Polybius), have earned the passage a place in Jacoby's collection of Timaeus fragments (*FGrH* 566 F101) despite the fact that Plutarch mentions two other sources and is likely to have used even more.[24] However, the one sentence which is crucial to a didactic interpretation of the passage, Hermocrates' dictum about handling victory with honour, occurs in a very similar form in a passage from Diodorus of Sicily, which is almost certainly based on Timaeus: "*more glorious than being victorious is bearing victory with moderation*" (κάλλιόν ἐστι τοῦ νικᾶν τὸ τὴν νίκην ἐνεγκεῖν ἀνθρωπίνως,[25] Diod. Sic. 13.19.5). The two expressions are so similar that they are likely to derive from the same

---

discussion is not the purpose of this article. For good discussions of how to work with fragments see the classic article by Brunt 1980, and the more recent restatement of the problem by Schepens 1997.

[24] On Plutarch's use of sources see Russell 1973 and Pelling 1995.

[25] The adverb ἀνθρωπίνως is sometimes translated "humanely", which is of course tempting, but which misses the point of the Greek slightly. "Inhumanely" is synonymous with "beastly" and as such understands a comparison with animals in respect of brutality. ἀνθρωπίνως, on the other hand, is the opposite of ὑπὲρ ἄνθρωπον, which means "too arrogantly for a mere mortal"—that is, the envisioned comparison is with gods, not with animals. Thus, it can be translated "as a man should" or "moderately".

source, and it therefore seems more than likely that this phrase, at least, was in Timaeus' narrative of the Syracusan assembly, however it otherwise differed from the Plutarchan and Diodorean narratives.[26] We can then hypothesise on fairly safe grounds that Timaeus narrated the assembly as a victor after the victory scene of the "bad victor" variation.

We cannot know if any of the *topoi* identified in the victor after the victory scenes of the Classical historians were present in Timaeus' version of the set-piece, but it seems that his message was the same: the victor should not abuse his prisoners, but treat them humanely. Considering the honour-related connotations of the terms καλῶς and κάλλιον, it seems likely that he recommended such humane behaviour on the grounds of the victor's honour and the impact it would have on his reputation; but we cannot know if this excluded any argument from the victor's own advantage or from fellow-feeling on the basis of the changeability of fortune.

One other fragment from this period seems to point to an original victor after the victory scene. This is found in yet another passage from Plutarch (Plu. *Pericl.* 18 = Duris *FGrH* 76 F67). Here, Plutarch criticises the historian Duris of Samos (ca. 340-260 BC) for "making a tragedy out of" (ἐπιτραγῳδεῖ) the Athenian capture of Samos under Pericles. Plutarch goes on to summarise Duris' version of events (which he professes not to believe):[27] the Samian trierarchs and marines were sent to Miletus where they were tied to planks and left in the marketplace for ten days before they were executed by having their heads bashed in with clubs; finally their bodies were thrown out unburied. A narrative of such events will have provided Duris with the perfect opportunity for a victor after the victory scene, and Plutarch's accusation of tragedy-writing certainly points to a narrative rich in dramatic and pathetic detail. Unfortunately, we cannot know exactly how this was realised, nor be certain that the narrative carried a didactic message.

Thus, the set-piece of the victor after the victory seems to have stayed part of the genre of historiography in the interval between Xenophon and Polybius, but because of the lack of material it is impossible to know how it developed during this time. All we can say for certain is that in

---

[26] I intend to discuss this fragment more fully elsewhere. For a good summary of the discussion about how much of the Plutarch passage is from Timaeus see Stylianou 1998, 58-61.

[27] Landucci Gattinoni 1997, 229-233 argues for an acceptance of Duris' version. It is also accepted by Pédech 1989, 379. *Contra* Jacoby 1926b, 116-117 and Kebric 1977, 79.

Polybius' *Histories* the set-piece is thriving, and it has changed significantly since Xenophon.

In Polybius, the victor after the victory set-piece diversifies. It now comprises not only scenes between the victorious commander and his prisoners of war (e.g. Plb. 8.20.9-12, 10.17.6-15, 10.18, 10.19, 29.20), some of which are accompanied by very explicit moralizing by the narrator, but also summaries of a victor's devastation of his enemy's land (e.g. Plb. 4.62, 5.8.3-12.8) or negotiations with ambassadors from the defeated (e.g. Plb. 1.31.5-7 with 1.35.1-3), both followed by detailed and explicit moralising. In addition, we find short summaries of the collection of spoils from a captured city, followed by either a long discussion of the advisability of transferring precious objects to one's own city from the defeated enemy (Plb. 9.10) or a detailed explanation of how the Romans usually distribute their war booty (Plb. 10.16.1-17.5).

This brief list showcases neatly the most important difference between the Polybian victor after the victory set-piece and the one found in the Classical historians: the explicitness of the message. Gone is the subtlety and ambiguity of Herodotus, Thucydides, and Xenophon; the Polybian narrator states his messages directly, and often the didactic lecturing (moral or practical) takes up more space than the narrative of events itself. Thus, Polybius is the first extant historiographer to produce a theoretical passage on how to behave as a victor, 5.10.9-12.8, occasioned by Philip V's destruction of the colonnades and votive statues of Thermus during the Social War.[28] Here, the narrator extols the behaviour of Antigonus Doson towards the defeated Spartans and of Philip II towards the defeated Athenians because they did not κακῶς ποιεῖν (Plb. 5.9.9), but acted considerately and moderately (τῇ δ' εὐγνωμοσύνῃ καὶ μετριότητι, Plb. 5.10.2) thereby showing mildness and nobility (πραότητος καὶ καλοκαγαθίας, Plb. 5.10.3). Interestingly, such behaviour is recommended not just because it is morally good (Plb. 9.6-7), but also because it is more advantageous for the victor than terror tactics (Plb. 5.9.10, 5.10.4).[29]

The inclusion of such explicit narrator lectures means that there is little need for the more subtly didactic victor after the victory scene. Nevertheless, such scenes exist and are often among Polybius' most vivid passages. One example, showing the victor treating the defeated with

---

[28] I have discussed this passage in more detail elsewhere (Hau 2006) and shall here only touch on its relevance for the victor's treatment of defeated persons, leaving aside any discussion of destruction of land or buildings.

[29] On Polybius' attitude to terror tactics, see Hau 2006.

mildness for his own benefit is 10.17.6-16. Here, Scipio the Elder has conquered New Carthage and collects the inhabitants of the captured city in the marketplace. He then releases the citizens with their families, tells the artisans that they are for the present slaves of Rome, and uses the most fit of the remaining prisoners to replenish the crews on his ships. The two latter groups he promises freedom if they show loyalty and eagerness. Polybius goes into great detail describing the practicalities of these dispositions and their advantages for Scipio, but also explicitly and vividly notes the gratitude of the released citizens and the loyalty of the acquired slaves. Finally, he concludes:

τοῦτον δὲ χειρίσας τὸν τρόπον τὰ κατὰ τοὺς αἰχμαλώτους μεγάλην μὲν εὔνοιαν καὶ πίστιν ἐνειργάσατο τοῖς πολιτικοῖς καὶ πρὸς αὑτὸν καὶ πρὸς τὰ κοινὰ πράγματα, μεγάλην δὲ προθυμίαν τοῖς χειροτέχναις διὰ τὴν ἐλπίδα τῆς ἐλευθερίας.

By this treatment of the captives he inspired the citizens with great loyalty and fidelity, both towards himself and towards the common cause, and the artisans with great readiness to serve because of their hope for freedom (Plb. 10.17.15).

The idea that treating defeated enemies with moderation is to the advantage of the victor is nothing new. We saw it in Herodotus, where Croesus became the advisor of Cyrus, and in Thucydides it formed the main thrust of Diodotus' speech. The difference here is in the victor's intention (as narrated by the historian). In Herodotus, Cyrus had not planned for his actions to be for his own advantage, it was a by-product of changing his behaviour for the better. In Thucydides, the speech advocated acting for one's own advantage, but its continuous stressing of the neglect of morality turned the reader's attention to the immorality of the Athenians. In Polybius, by contrast, the elder Scipio is doing what he knows is best for himself, and this just happens to be the same thing that is best for his prisoners. Thus, the theme of the victor's advantage, which was important in the theoretical 5.9-12 provoked by Philip at Thermus, is equally important in some victor after the victory scenes (another example is Plb 1.31.57 with 1.35.1-3).

This does not mean, however, that self-interest is the only reason given by Polybius for bearing victory with moderation. Witness the famous scene where Scipio the Younger and Polybius himself, as a character in his own *Histories*, watch the burning of Carthage:

καὶ ἐπιστρέψας ἐξ αὐτῆς καὶ λαβόμενός μου τῆς δεξιᾶς "ὦ Πολύβιε,"
ἔφη "καλὸν μέν, ἀλλ' οὐκ οἶδ' ὅπως ἐγὼ δέδια καὶ προορῶμαι μή ποτέ
τις ἄλλος τοῦτο τὸ παράγγελμα δώσει περὶ τῆς ἡμετέρας πατρίδος·"
ταύτης δὲ δύναμιν πραγματικωτέραν καὶ νουνεχεστέραν οὐ ῥᾴδιον εἰπεῖν·
τὸ γὰρ ἐν τοῖς μεγίστοις κατορθώμασι καὶ ταῖς τῶν ἐχθρῶν συμφοραῖς
ἔννοιαν λαμβάνειν τῶν οἰκείων πραγμάτων καὶ τῆς ἐναντίας περιστάσεως
καὶ καθόλου πρόχειρον ἔχειν ἐν ταῖς ἐπιτυχίαις τὴν τῆς τύχης
ἐπισφάλειαν ἀνδρός ἐστι μεγάλου καὶ τελείου καὶ συλλήβδην ἀξίου
μνήμης.

He turned away from it (i.e. the burning city) towards me, grasped me by
the hand and said, "Polybius, this is a glorious moment, but somehow I
fear and foresee that some day someone else will give this same order with
regards to my country." It is difficult to mention a more statesmanlike and
perceptive ability than this: in the moment of greatest victory and of
catastrophe for the enemy to have thought for one's own fate and the
opposite situation and, to put it briefly, to keep in mind in success the
instability of fortune—that is a characteristic of a great man and one
worthy of remembrance (Plb. 38.21).

The moral message is familiar, though stated much more clearly than we
have seen in the earlier historians. It propounds the same awareness of the
changeability of fortune that we saw already in Herodotus, and the reader
is no doubt meant to understand that this awareness creates a fellow-
feeling with other human beings—exactly the feeling that made Cyrus
desist from burning Croesus. The same message is found in Plb. 29.20, the
speech of Aemilius Paullus delivered in the Senate after his defeat of
Perseus.

It is interesting to note that—as far as can be seen from the
fragmentary text—the *actions* of Scipio which lead up to the scene at the
burning city and the narrator's praise reflect no awareness of common
humanity. He has given the order to burn Carthage to the ground, and now
he is watching his order being executed. To a Greek reader, the destruction
of an entire city must surely have seemed as terrible in the time of
Polybius as it did in the time of Thucydides when the Athenians changed
their minds about Mytilene. Polybius, however, was a close friend of
Scipio the Younger, and he clearly wants his readers to see Scipio as a
sympathetic character. Therefore, he includes Scipio's speech to show that
Scipio was completely aware of the changeability of fortune and of the
common weakness of human beings, in other words, that Scipio was *not*
an arrogant victor. In this way, Polybius manages to turn what would

traditionally have been a set-piece of the "bad victor" into a set-piece of the "good victor".[30]

And this brings us back to the third reason for displaying moderation towards the defeated in Polybius: the victor's honour. Neither Scipio nor Aemilius states this as a motivation in their speech as given by Polybius. However, from the narrator's enthusiastic praise of Scipio (ἀνδρός ἐστι μεγάλου καὶ τελείου καὶ συλλήβδην ἀξίου μνήμης) it seems clear that the reader is meant to regard his conduct as eminently honourable.

The fourth and final reason for bearing victory (or any other success) with moderation in Polybius is that the opposite tends to lead to disaster. This is seen, for instance, in the case of M. Atilius Regulus (Plb. 1.31.57 with 1.35.1-3), who wins a victory over the Carthaginians in the First Punic War and treats the ambassadors sent to him to discuss peace with such arrogance that they depart in anger. Soon after, he is defeated in battle and captured by the very people he has offended. The narrator concludes:

Ἐν ᾧ καιρῷ πολλά τις ἂν ὀρθῶς ἐπισημαινόμενος εὕροι πρὸς ἐπανόρθωσιν τοῦ τῶν ἀνθρώπων βίου συντελεσθέντα. καὶ γὰρ τὸ διαπιστεῖν τῇ τύχῃ, καὶ μάλιστα κατὰ τὰς εὐπραγίας, ἐναργέστατον ἐφάνη πᾶσιν τότε διὰ τῶν Μάρκου συμπτωμάτων.

In this situation one who reasons correctly can find many events which can contribute to the better conduct of human life. For to distrust fortune, and especially in success, was through Marcus' misfortunes clearly shown to all to be advisable (Plb. 1.35.1-2).

Polybius never explicitly says that such disasters happen to the arrogant by divine design (though *tykhe* can in the *Histories* be a justly punishing power, see e.g. 15.20.4-6 and 23.10), but the sheer regularity with which those who abuse success are soon brought to suffering makes it seem like a law of nature.

Thus, in Polybius, a good man is supposed to act with moderation in victory for a combination of reasons: because it is to his own advantage; because the knowledge that fortune is changeable makes him feel connected with those who at the moment suffer misfortune; because it is honourable; and because he will suffer if he does not.

---

[30] I am not implying that Polybius approved of the destruction of Carthage, only that he wanted to represent Scipio in as good a light as possible. For my discussion of this problem, arguing that Polybius disapproved of the destruction of Carthage, see Hau 2006.

After Polybius, we are again faced with a gap in extant material of roughly a hundred years. Again, however, a passage from Plutarch commonly considered a "fragment" of an earlier historian seems to indicate that victor after the victory scenes stayed a staple set-piece of historiography throughout the period. This is Plu. *Marc.* 20.11 (= Posidonius *FGrH* 87 F43), which consists of a scene between M. Claudius Marcellus and a certain Nicias, the only pro-Roman citizen of Engyion, which Marcellus has just conquered. Nicias supplicates Marcellus and begs for the lives and freedom of his fellow-citizens, and Marcellus not only grants the request, but gives Nicias land and other gifts besides. Plutarch rounds off the episode by stating that he has found it in Posidonius (ταῦτα μὲν οὖν Ποσειδώνιος ὁ φιλόσοφος ἱστόρησε), a Stoic philosopher and the most influential historian of his time (he lived ca. 135-51 BC). It is, of course, impossible to know what this scene looked like in Posidonius, but considering that Plutarch explicitly employs it as an example (παράδειγμα) of Roman kindness and humanity (εὐγνωμοσύνη and φιλανθρωπία) and that Posidonius is generally believed to have written history as a collection of moral examples to serve his Stoic philosophy,[31] it is likely that he also moralised explicitly on Marcellus' moderation.

After Posidonius, we arrive at the final author in this survey, Diodorus of Sicily. In Diodorus, victor after the victory scenes are even more numerous than in Polybius and show the same range. Apart from scenes between the victor and his captive(s) (e.g. Diod. Sic. 13.19.4-33.1, 14.105, 14.112, 16.87, 17.37.3-38.7, 19.11.4-7, 27.6, 32.23), there are scenes of the victor in the captured city or sanctuary (e.g. Diod. Sic. 13.90.1-5, 16.24.4-5, 32.24), between the victor and ambassadors from the defeated (e.g. Diod. Sic. 13.52-53, 23.12, 24.9.2-3), and of the victor being celebrated by his troops (e.g. Diod. Sic. 16.20.5-6). Very often these scenes are accompanied by explicit moralising of the kind also found in Polybius.[32] A typical example of such explicit didacticism is 17.38.4-6,

---

[31] Laffranque 1964, Malitz 1983, Kidd 1999 and 2003.

[32] The question how much of Diodorus' moralising can be said to have been originally composed by him and how much he took over from his sources is too vast to enter into here, and I hope to discuss it elsewhere. For our purposes suffice it to say that if one believes that Diodorus uncritically took over moralising passages from his sources without changing their moral point, it must mean that victor after the victory scenes were a standard set-piece in much of the Greek historiography which we have now lost. This strengthens my point that the set-piece was an integral part of the genre of Greek historiography, but makes it difficult to base arguments about the chronological development of the set-piece

which forms the conclusion to the long and detailed scene between Alexander the Great and the female relatives of Darius:

> καθόλου δ' ἔγωγε νομίζω πολλῶν καὶ καλῶν ἔργων ὑπ' 'Αλεξάνδρου συντετελεσμένων μηδὲν τούτων μεῖζον ὑπάρχειν μηδὲ μᾶλλον ἄξιον ἀναγραφῆς καὶ μνήμης ἱστορικῆς εἶναι. αἱ μὲν γὰρ τῶν πόλεων πολιορκίαι καὶ παρατάξεις καὶ τὰ ἄλλα τὰ κατὰ τὸν πόλεμον προτερήματα τὰ πλείονα διὰ τύχην ἢ δι' ἀρετὴν ἐπιτυγχάνεται, ὁ δ' ἐν ταῖς ἐξουσίαις εἰς τοὺς ἐπταικότας ἔλεος μεριζόμενος διὰ μόνης τῆς φρονήσεως γίνεται. οἱ πλεῖστοι γὰρ διὰ τὴν εὐτυχίαν ἐπαίρονται μὲν ταῖς εὐπραξίαις, ὑπερήφανοι δ' ἐν ταῖς εὐτυχίαις γινόμενοι τῆς ἀνθρωπίνης καὶ κοινῆς ἀσθενείας ἐπιλανθάνονται· διὸ καὶ τοὺς πλείστους ὁρᾶν ἔστι τὴν εὐτυχίαν ὥσπερ τι βαρὺ φορτίον φέρειν ἀδυνατοῦντας.

In short, I think that of the many glorious actions that Alexander performed, none was greater nor more worthy of recording and historical remembrance. For sieges of cities, battles, and the other victories won in war are usually accomplished through the agency of fortune or through bravery, but he who in success has any pity for those who are unfortunate is acting only from wisdom. For most people are elated in success because of their good fortune; they become arrogant in success and forget the common human weakness. Therefore, one can see that most people are unable to bear success just as if it were a heavy burden. (Diod. Sic. 17.38.4-7)

We encounter here several of the moral messages which recur in victor after the victory scenes throughout the *Bibiotheke*: the claim that most people become arrogant when victorious (or otherwise successful), the likening of success to a heavy burden,[33] and the thought that one should stay humble in success because of "the common human weakness" (τῆς ἀνθρωπίνης καὶ κοινῆς ἀσθενείας). This last expression is interesting. In the *Bibliotheke*, it has become a constantly used shorthand—with the variations ἡ ἀνθρωπίνη τύχη, ἡ κοινὴ ἀσθένεια and ἡ ἀνθρωπίνη ἀσθένεια[34]— for the idea that a victor should be aware of the changeability of fortune

---

on the text of Diodorus. For the two extremes in modern Diodorus scholarship see Sacks 1990 and Stylianou 1998. A reasonable middleground is found by Drews 1962, Hadley 1996, and Rubincam 1990 and 1998. See also the discussion of Nevin in this volume.

[33] Recurs at 13.30.1 and 23.15.1. The same simile used of peace occurs at 15.5.1.

[34] ἡ κοινὴ τύχη: Diod. Sic. 14.46.4, 18.67.4, 19.11.6. ἡ ἀνθρωπίνη τύχη: Diod. Sic. 23.12.1. ἡ ἀνθρωπίνη ἀτυχία: Diod. Sic 13.22.5. ἡ κοινὴ ἀσθένεια: Diod. Sic. 13.21.5, 17.38.6. ἡ ἀνθρωπίνη ἀσθένεια: Diod. Sic. 10.19.1, 13.24.5 and 6, 18.59.6, 26.1.2 and 3, 27.14.1.

and realise that both he and his victims are human beings, and so should not hurt them. This idea, as we have seen, goes all the way back to Herodotus and is also found in Polybius, but in no earlier historian is it as pervasive as in Diodorus.

The basic message to the reader is the same as the one presented by the earlier historians, namely that the victor should treat the defeated with moderation. There are three reasons for this. One is the "common human weakness" in the face of changeable fortune and the fellow-feeling which accrues from it. Another is the wonders such magnanimous conduct does for the victor's reputation, and, closely tied in with this, the victor's own general advantage. This is pointed out in 17.38.3 just before the passage quoted above: "not only was he praised by those whom he had treated well, but he also acquired great fame throughout all of his own army for the exceeding propriety of his conduct" (...οὐ μόνον ὑπὸ τῶν εὖ παϑόντων ἐπαίνων ἐτύγχανεν, ἀλλὰ καὶ παρὰ πᾶσι τοῖς συστρατευομένοις περιβόητον ἔσχε τὴν ὑπερβολὴν τῆς ἐπιεικείας) and is a recurring feature of the Diodorean victor after the victory set-piece.[35] Both of these reasons we have seen in earlier historians.

However, the third reason given in the *Bibliotheke* for treating the defeated with moderation is a reason which in earlier historiography was only implicit and ambiguous. This is the idea of the retribution suffered by the arrogant victor. We have seen hints of this in Xenophon and Polybius, but in Diodorus it becomes explicit. Witness the conclusion to 13.12, where the Roman consul M. Atilius Regulus has treated ambassadors from the defeated Carthaginians arrogantly (as we have seen that he does in Polybius, who was in all probability Diodorus' source for the episode).

ὁ μὲν οὖν ὕπατος οὔτε τὸ τῆς πατρίδος ἔϑος ἐν τοῖς τοιούτοις μιμησάμενος οὔτε τὴν ἐκ ϑεοῦ νέμεσιν εὐλαβηϑεὶς συντόμως τῆς ὑπερηφανίας ἀξίᾳ πειέπεσε τιμωρίᾳ.

"And so, as he had neither followed the customs of his country in such situations nor taken any thought for divine retribution, the consul soon encountered a punishment worthy of his arrogance" (Diod. Sic. 23.12).

Such divine punishment of the arrogant victor occurs often in the *Bibliotheke*, and much more unambiguously than in the earlier historians.[36]

---

[35] Cf. Diod. Sic. 11.26.1-3, 14.105, 17.37.3-38.7.
[36] Cf. Diod. Sic. 13.86, 14.70-74, 14.76.1, 19.103.5, 20.13.1-3, 24.9.2-3, 27.6.2.

So, what conclusions can be drawn from this brief survey? I hope to have shown that the victor after the victory set-piece is an important component of the genre of historiography from the time of Herodotus to the time of Diodorus. Moreover, it seems clear that the historians of these 400 years wanted to communicate the same basic message to their readers, namely that the defeated and the captured should be treated with moderation.

Perhaps more surprisingly, the rationale given for such moderate behaviour rests on the same assumptions: that the powerlessness of all human beings in the face of fortune should spark a fellow-feeling between them, that moderate behaviour is advantageous to the victor, that such behaviour increases his honour, and that arrogant and cruel behaviour will be punished, either by other human beings or by divine powers. All of these reasons are present in Herodotus, in Polybius, and in Diodorus. In Thucydides' Mytilene Debate only the victor's advantage is expressed, but the other reasons form part of the speech given by the Spartan ambassadors at Thuc. 4.17-20 when they sue for peace from Athens. In Xenophon, the idea of the punishment of the bad victor is predominant, but it is never clear whether the retribution is purely human or also divine. In the fragmentary historians, we cannot know what reasons were offered, but it seems reasonable to hypothesise on the basis of the citations in later authors that they were very similar to those found in the extant historians.

What changes, then, is not the message, but the form in which it is delivered. As we have seen, the moral didacticism becomes increasingly explicit throughout the period, culminating in the detailed moralising lectures offered by Polybius and Diodorus. In this, the victor after the victory set-piece follows the trend of other types of moralising in Greek historiography, which develops from subtle hints in Herodotus, Thucydides, and Xenophon, to explicit lecturing in Polybius and Diodorus.[37]

Why was the victor after the victory set-piece so popular? It is not enough to answer that the situation of a victorious commander who has to deal with spoils and captives occurred regularly in the wars chronicled by the ancient historians, for so did other situations like the treatment of wounded men after a battle, of which these authors tell us very little. Rather, it seems that the ancient historians deliberately chose situations, such as the "victor after the victory", which afforded scope for moral didacticism, and turned them into set-pieces. The narrative of such situations facilitate moralising by showing a historical character in a

---

[37] I hope to discuss the development of moralizing in Greek historiography generally elsewhere.

situation which affords the ultimate opportunity for displaying spectacular good or bad behaviour, much as the tragedians chose extreme situations in order to magnify good and bad human behaviour.

This does not mean that we should immediately disregard as unhistorical all the information that the Greek historians give about victorious commanders. The fact that something has been turned into a set-piece does not in itself make it untrue. These situations *did* occur frequently, and no doubt some commanders abused the defeated while others did not. It is even likely that some commanders—such as Philip V, who famously had an abbreviated version of Theopompus' *Philippica* made for his own reading[38]—were influenced in their actions by reading victor after the victory scenes in historiographical literature. Thus, historiography fulfils its role as both memorial and teacher, both literature and historical source.

Bibliography

Anderson, J. K. *Xenophon,* London: Duckworth, 1974.

Breitenbach, H. R. *Historiographische Anshauungsformen Xenophons,* Freiburg in der Schweiz: Paulusdruckerei, 1950.

Brunt, P. A. "On Historical Fragments and Epitomes" *CQ* 30 (1980): 447-494.

Cawkwell, G. L. "Introduction" in *Xenophon, a History of my Times.* Harmondsworth: Penguin Books, 1979.

Connor, W. R. *Thucydides.* Princeton, N.J: Princeton University Press, 1984.

Drews, R. "Diodorus and his sources." *AJP* 83 (1962): 383-392.

Eckstein, A. M. *Moral Vision in the Histories of Polybius.* Berkeley and London: University of California Press, 1995.

Edelstein, L. and Kidd, I. G. *Posidonius. The Fragments.* Cambridge: Cambridge University Press, 1972.

Genette, G. *Narrative Discourse,* Translated from *Discours du Récit,* Paris. Oxford: Blackwell, 1980/1972.

Gray, V. *The Character of Xenophon's Hellenica.* London: Duckworth, 1989.

Hadley, R. "Diodorus 18.6.1-3: a case of remodelled source materials." *AHB* 10 3-4 (1996): 131-147.

Harrison, T. *Divinity and History. The Religion of Herodotus,* Oxford: Clarendon Press, 2000.

---

[38] See Theopompus *FGrH* 115 T31.

Hau, L. I. "Diodoros of Sicily (32.2 and 4) and Polybios." *C&M* 57 (2006): 67-102.

Higgins, W. E. *Xenophon the Athenian.* Albany: State University of New York Press, 1977.

Hornblower, S. *Thucydides.* London: Duckworth, 1987.

—. *A Commentary on Thucydides I-II.* Oxford: Clarendon Press, 1991-1996.

Jacoby, F. *FGrH*, Berlin: Weidmann,1926-1955.

Kagan, D. "The Speeches in Thudydides" *YCS* 24 (1975): 71-94.

Kebric, R. B. *In The Shadow of Macedon: Duris of Samos*, Historia Einzelschriften, Wiesbaden: Steiner, 1977.

Kidd, I. G. *Posidonius. The Commentary I-II*, Cambridge: Cambridge University Press, 1988.

—. *Posidonius. The translation of the fragments*, Cambridge: Cambridge University Press, 1999.

—. "Posidonius (2)" in *OCD,* Oxford: Oxford University Press, 2003.

Laffranque, M. *Posidonius d'Apamée: essai de mise au point,* Paris: Presses Universitaires de France, 1964.

Landucci Gattinoni, F. L. *Duride di Samo*, Rome: "L'Erma" di Bretschneider, 1997.

Macleod, C. "Reason and Necessity: Thucydides 3.9-14, 37-48." *JHS* 98 (1978): 52-68. (Also in *The collected Essays of Colin Macleod,* Oxford: Clarendon Press, 1983, 88-102).

Malitz, J. *Die Historien des Posidonios*, München: Bech, 1983.

Manuwald, B. "Der Trug des Diodotus (zu Thoukydides 3.42-48)." *Hermes* 107 (1979): 407-422.

Pédech, P. *La Méthode Historique de Polybe*, Paris: Les Belles Lettres, 1964.

—. *Trois Historiens Méconnus: Théopompe, Duris, Phylarque,* Paris: Les Belles Lettres, 1989.

Pelling, C. "Plutarch's Adaptation of his Source-Material." In *Essays on Plutarch's Lives*, edited by B. Scardigli, 125-154. Oxford: Clarendon Press, 1995.

de Romilly, J. *Thucydides and Athenian Imperialism*, Oxford: Blackwell, 1963. (= translation of *Thucydide et l'Impérialisme Athénien.* Paris: Les Belles Lettres, 1947).

Rood, T. *Thucydides - Narrative and Explanation.* Oxford: Clarendon Press, 1991.

Rubincam, C. "Review of "The Greek Historians of the West: Timaeus and his Predecessors" *CPh* 85 (1990): 227-232.

—. "Did Diodorus Siculus take over cross-references from his sources?" *AJP* 119(1) (1998): 67-87.

Russell, D. A. *Plutarch,* London: Duckworth, 1973.

Sacks, K. *Diodorus Siculus and the First Century.* Princeton, N.J: Princeton University Press, 1990.

Schepens, G. "Jacoby's *FGrHist*: Problems, Methods, Prospects." In *Collecting Fragments/Fragmente sammeln,* edited by G. W. Most, 144-172. Göttingen: Vandenhoeck & Ruprecht, 1997.

Schwartz, E. "Quellenuntersuchungen zur griechischen Geschichte." *RhM* 44 (1889): 161-193.

Soulis, E. M. *Xenophon and Thucydides.* Athens. 1972.

Stahl, H.-P. *Thucydides: man's Place in History.* Swansea: The Classical Press of Wales, 2003. (Translated from: *Thucydides: die Stellung des Menschen im geschichtlichen Prozess,* Münster: Beck, 1966).

Stylianou, P. J. *A Historical Commentary on Diodorus Siculus book 15*, Oxford: Clarendon Press, 1998.

Tuplin, C. *The Failings of Empire, a reading of Xenophon's Hellenica 2.3.11-7.5.27,* Historia Einzelschriften, Stuttgart: F. Steiner, 1993.

Walbank, F. W. *A Historical Commentary on Polybius I-III*, Oxford: Clarendon Press, 1957-1979.

—. "Political Morality and the friends of Scipio." *JRS* 55 (1965): 1-16.

—. *Polybius,* Berkeley: University of California Press, 1972.

—. "Polybius between Greece and Rome." In *Polybe,* 3-38.Geneva: Fondation Hardt, 1974.

Williams, M. F. *Ethics in Thucydides. The Ancient Simplicity,* Lanham, Md: University Press of America, 1998.

CHAPTER EIGHT

"DO GLORIOUS BATTLES NO LONGER INSPIRE YOUR DREAMS?"[1]: MOMENTS OF COMPROMISE AND FANTASIES OF PEACE IN THE ILIAD[2]

LYNN KOZAK

When thinking about the *Iliad* it is easy to be consumed by war, by the blood of battles, by the fight for honour, and by the thirst for glory and fame. But there are pockets of peace to be found amidst the clashing of spears; moments where peace seems possible even when the destruction of Troy looms large in the audience's imagination. These narrative moments are spread throughout the epic, where women wash clothes and raise children rather than mourn their husbands and wait to be raped, and where men look after their farms and their families and feast with their friends, instead of watching them fall to the ground with their armour clattering around them. There are moments where the hope for the quiet life pushes through the fierce battle and asserts itself, however briefly, on the minds of warriors and in the hearts of their audience.

Oliver Taplin does a marvellous job of discussing how Book 18's description of the Shield of Achilles goes into great detail to glorify not war, but peace. He fits this seeming oddity into the larger context of the epic: "The *Iliad* is not only a poem of war, it is also a poem of peace. It is a tragic poem, and in it war prevails over peace, but that has been the

---

[1] The Klingon commander Koris, questioning if Worf is still a Klingon warrior though he has lived among humans, in the episode "Heart of Glory" from *Star Trek: The Next Generation*.

[2] This paper was given under the title "Reluctant Warriors" to a very patient, helpful, and responsive audience. Many thanks also to Edward Bragg for organising the conference, and this volume, as well as to Lisa Irene Hau and Elizabeth Macaulay-Lewis, for their useful editing and forgiving attitude. The text used throughout this paper is Allen 1931. All translations are my own.

tragic history of so much of mankind."[3] The goal of this paper is to take this thoughtful understanding of the poem and expand it to an exploration of how the theme of peace flows between narrative style, plot, and character construction in the *Iliad*, while also paying some particular attention to its role in the story and character of Hector. Disassembling the poem in this way will reveal the constant balancing act that the poem plays between war and peace, even in its characterisation of warrior-heroes.

As Taplin notes, but I would like to re-emphasize here, the narrative itself dwells on peace in surprising ways, and to a surprising extent, in a plot that at its heart focuses on battle. This is especially true in its similes. Similes are particularly poignant in reminding the audience of peace;[4] think of the many occasions where scenes of violence are mitigated through peaceful similes.[5] While the majority of the *Iliad*'s similes are of natural imagery, there are many that include human elements, ranging from the palatial to the bucolic. Menelaus' arrow wound, with the blood running down his leg, is compared to a prized pair of purple-coloured ivory horse cheek pieces (4.141-7). Death is often described with a flair for the ordinary: think of the death of Euphorbus, compared to a storm uprooting a carefully cultivated olive tree (17.50-60), or the death of Asius compared to the felling of a tree for ship timber (13.389-91), or the death of Simoeisius, compared to the felling of a poplar for chariot-wood (4.482-7). While these similes capture the violence of death in the image of the fallen tree, they also cloak that violence in the everyday, constructive human activities of farming and building. The armies themselves are also often linked with non-violent imagery, as in the series of similes used to describe the Achaians in Book 2. While the initial comparisons are to

---

[3] Taplin 1980, 17. Taplin makes this point early on in his paper: "My starting-point is that the shield is not the only place in Homer where we encounter peace and prosperity and people delighting in their lives…There will be three main sources. First the settled societies of the *Odyssey*…Secondly there is the peacetime world of many of the similes, especially in the *Iliad*. And lastly, Troy, at least Troy were it not for the war, as it was in the days of peace before the Achaians came" (Taplin 1980, 4). In this paper I focus solely on the *Iliad*, advocating an expansion of Taplin's latter two "sources," to include truces within the *Iliad*, as well as characters' individual fantasies and assertions about what peace might be.

[4] When I say "remind," I do not think that these similes distract from the battle at hand, but rather throw the violence into relief through contrast with the everyday activities of peacetime. For a discussion of the function of the Homeric simile, see Porter 1972, 11 n. 1.

[5] Bassett 1921, 137 defines the following category of similes as "Contrast of Political Conditions. Between war and peace: scarcely half a dozen similes are taken from war."

mountain forest fires (2.455f.), fowl (2.459-63), and leaves and flowers beginning to blossom (2.467f.), human and bucolic elements are slowly integrated into this new spring. When compared with insects swarming in the springtime, the season is defined by "milk wetting pails" (γλάγος ἄγγεα δεύει, 2.471), and the leaders are then compared to "men who are goatherds, among the wide flocks of goats" (ὥς τ'αἰπόλια πλατέ' αἰγῶν αἰπόλοι ἄνδρες, 2.474).[6] Perhaps the most striking simile to describe the armies comes in Book 11 when the two armies are grouped together,[7] compared to two lines of reapers, driving forward and cutting through fields of wheat or barley (11.67-9).[8]

The continuous reminder of peacetime activities, seeded throughout the poem in these similes, prepares us for the more immediate effects of war on the poem's characters. As Taplin says, these abstract references to a generalised peacetime come to represent, for the Trojans, Troy before the war, and so all that they have lost; the poem balances this in its treatment of the Achaians, frequently referring to all that they have left behind.

The strong pull of the home, possessions, and family on a warrior brings to mind Odysseus, who, according to the *Cypria*, feigned madness in order to avoid going on the expedition at all.[9] And even within the *Iliad*, there is Echepolus, who actually decided to stay home among his things, sending one of his mares to aid the war effort (23.296ff.)[10] But the Trojans' *epikouroi* and the Achaians have all left their often far-away

---

[6] This image invokes the common epithet "shepherd of men" (ποιμένι λαῶν).

[7] This confluence of the two armies represents a larger trend of an implicit equality between the armies, at least in their shared tragic situation: "For many of the Trojans and the Achaians on that day / were laid out prone in the dust beside one another." (πολλοὶ γὰρ Τρώων καὶ Ἀχαιῶν ἤματι κείνῳ/ πρηνέες ἐν κονίῃσι παρ' ἀλλήλοισι τέταντο. 4.543f.)

[8] Porter 1972, 13f.: analyses "similes which compare war to an agricultural or pastoral scene," including 20.495f., 5.499f., 13.588f., 16.638f., 21.257f.

[9] Procl., *Chrest.* 119-121.

[10] van Wees 1992, 171: "It has already been pointed out that, even if heroes like Achilles and the sons of Kastor choose war over a quiet life, many others "shudder" at the sight of weapons (*Od.* 14.225f.) and prefer to stay at home (23.295-9)." These two examples are extreme and not entirely useful. Even Achilles fantasises about his future peacetime married life (9.393ff.) and considers his standard peacetime obligation to care for his father (24.540f.) There is also no judgement passed on Echepolus for his wishing to stay at home and enjoy his wealth. The vast majority of warriors fight while still keeping an interest in their peacetime lives. Having said this, I would like to explore the tension between wealth and participation in war, particularly in the narratives of Homer and Thucydides, further in the future.

homes to come and join the fight. The poem includes descriptions of a wide spectrum of "what is left behind," often in characters' direct speech, but sometimes as narrative comment and contrast on a warriors' death: Achilles' many things in Phthia (9.364ff.), Sarpedon's wife and child (5.480f., 5.687f.), Pandarus' good chariot and horses (5.192ff.), and, perhaps most tragically of all, Iphidamus' wife, whom he had traded much for but whom he has yet to enjoy when he dies (11.240ff.). And then there is the case of Othryoneus, who fights just for Priam's promise of a wife, and dies (13.361-382); it is as though he fights for the very possibility of peacetime contentment.[11]

While most of the Achaians and the *epikouroi* fight under the constant reminder of what they have left behind, the Trojans leave nothing behind, but have already lost much, and have much still to lose. For them, the urgency of their situation is most famously depicted in Hector's return to the city in Book 6, where he visits Andromache and their small son Astyanax. Hector, because of the immediacy of his family and his role as the principal Trojan fighter, thus becomes the most important illustration of the conflict and balance between a character's wartime and peacetime personas. It is Hector who nostalgically waxes about the Troy that was[12] and what has been lost:

> Before people would speak about the city of Priam
> describing it as a place of so much gold, and so much bronze;

---

[11] Leaving behind wives and children and leaving behind property are interchangeable in the *Iliad* and are often lumped together by the characters themselves. Sarpedon mentions his wife and child in the next line after his possessions; the mention of Iphidamus' wife is immediately followed by the price that he paid for her. Briseis provides a precedent for this, as she clearly constitutes an intersection of "property" and "love" for Achilles (Achilles refers to her as a γέρας at 1.161, but ἄλοχον θυμερέα at 9.336). I am not sure that this concept is as foreign to modernity as we might presume: homesickness is surely based on a combination of longing for our homes and possessions along with our missed loved ones; it is simply all that is familiar to us, all that is our own. Think of Helen at 3.139f: "So speaking the goddess cast longing into her heart,/ for her previous husband, and for her city, and for her parents." (Ὣς εἰποῦσα θεὰ γλυκὺν ἵμερον ἔμβαλε θυμῷ/ ἀνδρός τε προτέρου καὶ ἄστεος ἠδὲ τοκήων) It is also worth considering here the dual meaning of φίλος, which can describe both one's possessions and one's loved ones, under the blanket of 'one's own'. Cf. *LSJ* entry I.2.c.; e.g. *Il.* 2.261, 3.31, 5.155, 9.555, 9.610, 19.209, 22.58, 22.408.

[12] Cf. Achilles' comments about Troy at 24.543-6; yet, his sympathy for Priam, based on what he has heard (ἀκούομεν, 22.543), does not hold the same weight, nor carry the same detail, as Hector's nostalgia for his own city.

but now the beautiful treasures have disappeared from our homes,
many belongings to Phrygia and lovely Meionia
have gone, being sold off, when great Zeus raged.

πρίν μὲν γὰρ Πριάμοιο πόλιν μέροπες ἄνθρωποι
πάντες μυθέσκοντο πολύχρυσον πολύχαλκον·
νῦν δὲ δὴ ἐξαπόλωλε δόμων κειμήλια καλά,
πολλὰ δὲ δὴ Φρυγίην καὶ Μηονίην ἐρατεινὴν
κτήματα περνάμεν' ἵκει, ἔπει μέγας ὠδύσατο Ζεύς.
(18.288-292)

For Hector, this nostalgia for the Troy that was is coupled with the
urgent necessity to defend the Troy that is, even if it means an ill-advised
attack on the invading Achaians. As Sarpedon scolds Hector:

But you have stood here and not even ordered the rest
of your people to stay and defend their wives… It is necessary for all these
things to remain a care for you, night and day…

τύνη δ' ἕστηκας, ἀτὰρ οὐδ' ἄλλοισι κελεύεις
λαοῖσιν μενέμεν καὶ ἀμυνέμεναι ὤρεσσι.
σοὶ δὲ χρὴ τάδε πάντα μέλειν νύκτάς τε καὶ ἦμαρ
(5.485f., 491)

Necessity does not only come upon those who defend their homes and
families; those who have left these behind still find themselves under
compulsion to fight (ἀνάγκη). When the battle-tide turns against the
Achaians, starting in Book 11 with Zeus' promise to give glory to Hector
once Agamemnon has withdrawn, the Achaians find themselves on the
defensive, and under the dreaded ἀνάγκη (14.178).[13] In Book 12, where the
Lapithai are fiercely guarding the Achaian wall against the Trojan siege, a
poignant simile illustrates this reversal, as Asius the Trojan says:

I never thought the fighting Achaians
would be able to hold our strength and our hands invincible.
But they, as wasps quick-bending in the middle, or as bees
might make their homes at the side of the rocky way, and will not
abandon the hollow house they have made, but stand up
to men who have come to destroy them, and fight for the sake of their
children

---

[13] E.g. 12.178, 14.128, 15.345, where the Achaians fight due to ἀνάγκη. See also
13.114, where Aias says: "now it is impossible for us to hold back from the battle"
(ἡμέας γ' οὔ πως ἔστι μεθιέμεναι πολέμοιο).

so these, though they are only two, are unwilling to give back from the
gates, until they have killed their men, or are taken.

οὐ γὰρ ἔγωγ' ἐφάμην ἥρωας Ἀχαιοὺς
σχήσειν ἡμέτερόν γε μένος καὶ χεῖρας ἀάπτους.
οἳ δ', ὥς τε σφῆκες μέσον αἰόλοι ἠὲ μέλισσαι
οἰκία ποιήσωνται ὁδῷ ἔπι παιπαλοέσσῃ,
οὐδ' ἀπολείπουσιν κοῖλον δόμον, ἀλλὰ μένοντες
ἄνδρας θηρητῆρας ἀμύνονται περὶ τέκνων,
ὣς οἵ γ' οὐκ ἐθέλουσι πυλάων καὶ δύ' ἐόντε
χάσσασθαι πρίν γ' ἠὲ κατακτάμεν ἠὲ ἁλῶναι.
(12.165-172)

By using a simile that creates the Lapithai, and thus the Achaians, as
parents resolute to guard their homes and their children, Asius' description
creates a parallel between the Achaians and the Trojans that depends not
on the larger contextual motivations for the war, but rather on the
immediate situation of offence and defence.[14] Once one is fighting for
one's life, the title of aggressor starts to lose its meaning; likewise when
one is on the attack, fighting to destroy the enemy's ships and shelters, the
title of besieged begins to fade.[15]

It is this truth, and the parallels that are constantly drawn between
killer and killed, that makes the idea of peace so appealing to both sides.
For an epic about war, there are a remarkable number of instances within
the narrative where peace is suggested, and even established, between both
individuals and armies; these are places where the peacetime scenes of
similes, and the peacetime lives of soldiers, become almost tangible.

The motivations of individuals in proposing an end to the fighting vary
greatly. Agamemnon proposes retreat to his army twice in earnest, not in

---

[14] This truth of war is also found in Thucydides; cf. Thuc. 7.77.4-5 where Nikias
insists to his Athenians, who have *invaded* Sicily, that "wherever you stand, you
are a city already...and in whatever place each man is forced to fight, winning it,
he will have a fatherland, and a fortress" (πόλις εὐθύς ἐστε ὅποι ἂν
καθέζησθε...ἕκαστος ἢ ἐν ᾧ ἂν ἀναγκασθῇ χωρίῳ μάχεσθαι, τοῦτο καὶ πατρίδα καὶ
τεῖχος κρατήσας ἕξειν).

[15] Ἀνάγκη as an external force that is capable of affecting either side in battle is
mirrored and balanced with χάρμη as an internal force, also mutable according to
circumstance. Caldwell (1919, 21) observes, "Χάρμη is not a constant thing. The
pain of a wound causes it to disappear. When the tide of battle turns and defeat
impends and the death-dealing arrows pour in thickly, all memory of the joy of
battle is lost and the fighters think longingly of home and family and peace (*Il.*
13.620-39, 13.721)."

the interest of peace, as much as in the fear of defeat, and due to the possibility of having been betrayed by Zeus.[16] Paris' offer to face Menelaus in single combat while the rest of the armies swear a truce is a direct response to Hector's scolding and seemingly stems from guilt. Hector's own proposal for single combat seems oddly detached from the larger conflict, and while at the behest of the gods, still seems mostly like an effort to gain personal glory. Glaukos and Diomedes famously find a reason for peace in the exchange of their genealogies; theirs is an individual peace rooted in a tradition that predates the war and will outlast the war. All of these are worth considering, but I want to look particularly at the army-wide truce in Book 3 and the individual truce between Aias and Hector in Book 7. Both of these cases have broader implications of peace for the Achaians and the Trojans that serve as a constant background for the individual motivations involved.

The oath between the armies in Book 3 represents the will of the people as much as the will of Paris and Menelaus; the narrative tells us this in a number of ways. Hector is the first to consider the Trojans as a whole, in his rebuke to Paris:

> (you are) a great pain to your father, and your city, and all the people
> a joy to your enemies, and a disgrace to you yourself...But really the
> Trojans are the cowards, or they would have already
> clothed you in mantle of stone, for the sake of these evils that you have
> done.

> πατρί τε σῷ μέγα πῆμα πόληΐ τε παντί τε δήμῳ,
> δυσμενέσιν μὲν χάρμα, κατηφείην δὲ σοὶ αὐτῷ;
> ἀλλὰ μάλα Τρῶες δειδήμονες· ἦ τέ κεν ἤδη
> λάϊνον ἕσσο χιτῶνα κακῶν ἕνεχ' ὅσσα ἔοργας.
> (3.50f., 3.56f.)

While Paris himself is perhaps too self-absorbed to directly acknowledge the effect of his actions on the Trojans, Menelaus certainly sees his role in the war and how it affects the people:

> I think now is the time to separate
> the Achaians and the Trojans, since you have suffered much evil
> for the sake of my quarrel with Alexandrus, because he began it.

> φρονέω δὲ διακρινθήμεναι ἤδη
> Ἀργείους καὶ Τρῶας, ἐπεὶ κακὰ πολλὰ πέπασθε

---

[16] 9.17ff., 14.65ff.

εἵνεκ' ἐμῆς ἔριδος καὶ Ἀλεξάνδρου ἕνεκ' ἀρχῆς·
(3.98-100.)

With the response to Menelaus' call for an oath, the narrator continues this
commentary on the people: "So he spoke, and the Achaians and the
Trojans rejoiced/ hopeful to cease from the sorrowful war" (ὣς ἔφαθ', οἱ δ'
ἐχάρησαν Ἀχαιοί τε Τρῶές τε,/ ἐλπόμενοι παύσασθαι ὀιζυροῦ πολέμοιο. 3.111f.)
This is hardly the only time that the two peoples are grouped together in
the Book; the possibility for peace binds them together just as they are
bound together through conflict, as in Helen's tapestry:

> …she was weaving the many struggles
> of the horse-breaking Trojans and the bronze-clad Achaians,
> who, for her sake, had suffered much at the hands of Ares.

> πολέας δ' ἐνέπασσεν ἀέθλους
> Τρώων θ' ἱπποδάμων καὶ Ἀχαιῶν χαλκοχιτώνων,
> οὓς ἕθεν εἵνεκ' ἔπασχον ὑπ' Ἄρηος παλαμάων.
> (3.126-8)

Priam, too, comments on the two armies together:

> Come, dear girl, so that you might see the wondrous acts
> of the horse-breaking Trojans and the bronze-clad Achaians,
> who before bore lamentable Ares against one another
> on the plain, eager for destructive war,
> but now they sit in silence, and the fighting has stopped.

> δεῦρ' ἴθι νύμφα φίλη, ἵνα θέσκελα ἔργα ἴδηαι
> Τρώων θ' ἱπποδάμων καὶ Ἀχαιῶν χαλκοχιτώνων,
> οἳ πρὶν ἐπ' ἀλλήλοισι φέρον πολύδακρυν Ἄρηα
> ἐν πεδίῳ ὀλοοῖο λιλαιόμενοι πολέμοιο·
> οἳ δὴ νῦν ἕαται σιγῇ, πόλεμος δὲ πέπαυται.
> (3.130-4)

The Trojan elders' feelings about Helen as she passes with Priam echo
Hector's earlier chiding of Paris as a πῆμα: "Even (as beautiful) as she is,
let her go as cargo in the ships / lest she is left behind as a pain to our
children" (ἀλλὰ καὶ ὣς τοίη περ ἐοῦσ' ἐν νηυσὶ νεέσθω,/ μηδ' ἡμῖν τεκέεσσί τ'
ὀπίσσω πῆμα λίποιτο. 3.159f.) With more weight placed on the twin pains
of the Trojans, Paris and Helen, we would expect that the Trojans would
be the side more eager for an end to the war. But the narrative continues to
show each side's joy at the thought of peace. In Idaius' speech to Priam,

the Trojan herald says, "Rise up, son of Laomedon, the best call you forth, both of the horse-breaking Trojans and of the bronze-clad Achaians,/ to come down into the plain, to cut the trusted oaths" (ὄρσεο, Λαομεδοντιάδη, καλέουσιν ἄριστοι/ Τρώων ϑ' ἱπποδάμων καὶ Ἀχαιῶν χαλκοχιτώνων/ ἐς πεδίον καταβῆναι, ἵν' ὅρκια πιστὰ τάμητε. 3.250-2). But then Idaius goes on to expand the descriptions of both peoples, with a striking inclusion of more peacetime formulae: "let us dwell, in fertile Troy, and the others return home / to horse-pasturing Argos, and Achaea with its lovely women" (ναίοιμεν Τροίην ἐριβώλακα, τοὶ δὲ νέονται / Ἄργος ἐς ἱππόβοτον καὶ Ἀχαιΐδα καλλιγύναικα. 3.257f.) Here each side is given the possibility of a future peace. This confluence of the two peoples through peace is completed in their prayers for the success of the oaths where we see the phrase "and thus someone, either of the Achaians or of the Trojans, would speak..." used twice, clearly illustrating their common interest (ὧδε δέ τις εἴπεσκεν Ἀχαιῶν τε Τρώων τε· 3.297, 3.319).[17]

The individuals in the scene are not lost in the peoples' desire for peace, and certain characters emerge as especially aware of what the possibility of peace means. Antenor's short narrative at 3.204ff., where he refers to the embassy of Odysseus and Menelaus to Troy in order to confirm Helen's identification of Odysseus, is not only a moment of nostalgia in a flashback to before the war began, but is also particularly poignant in its stressing of the diplomatic attempt to avoid the war. This recollection of mutual respect, coupled with Priam and Helen's flattering appraisals of the Achaian leaders, creates an air of civility that is well-suited to the imminent truce. This complements Menelaus' request that Priam be present at the oath-taking at 3.105-110. Not only does Menelaus obviously respect Priam, but he also believes that Priam will bring respectability to the proceedings.[18]

So, in Book 3 plot and character are intricately intertwined in the consideration of peace. Hector, Priam, Antenor, Menelaus, Odysseus, and even Helen and Paris emerge as somehow connected to the desire for peace that encompasses the whole of both armies, each character understanding their individual roles in the conflict while also seeing the broader implications that the present war has, and a future peace would have, for all their people.

While the single combat in Book 3 is coupled with an oath that suggests a lasting peace between two warring armies, the single combat in

---

[17] Cf. de Jong 1987, 69-84, "The Greek and Trojan soldiers are here presented as a collective..."

[18] Contrasted with his opinion of the sons of Priam, who are "ἄπιστοι" (3.106).

Book 7 between Aias and Hector has no such grand ambitions. Yet it ends more positively than the botched combat between Menelaus and Paris, and the broken truce between their respective armies, because it closes in a draw between the two warriors and the rejoicing of their peoples.

The proposal for single combat is inspired in Hector by the gods via Helenus, and he addresses both armies with the challenge. The odd thing about the proposal is that there is no mention of how the outcome will affect the course of the war; Hector merely propositions the Achaians that one of them fight with him, and then lays out the term that whoever wins the contest should return the corpse of the loser to his people for proper burial (7.67-91). Just as there is no obvious reason here for Hector to introduce the proposal, there is perhaps even less reason for the Achaians to agree to it, but here Pandarus' offence of breaking the truce of Book 3 is forgotten.[19] After "a long time" (ὀψέ, 7.94), Menelaus finally takes up the challenge (7.94-121), only to be replaced by Aias when lots are drawn (7.181-3). And then another odd thing happens; the Achaians pray for a tie.

> Thus someone would speak, looking into wide heaven,
> "Father Zeus, watching from Ida, most glorious and greatest,
> give glory to Aias, for the shining victory:
> but if you love Hector very much, and care for him,
> then give equal strength to both of them, and glory.

> ὧδε δέ τις εἴπεσκεν ἰδὼν εἰς οὐρανὸν εὐρύν·
> Ζεῦ πάτερ Ἴδηθεν μεδέων κύδιστε μέγιστε
> δὸς νίκην Αἴαντι καὶ ἀγλαὸν εὖχος ἀρέσθαι:
> εἰ δὲ καὶ Ἕκτορά περ φιλέεις καὶ κήδεαι αὐτοῦ,
> ἴσην ἀμφοτέροισι βίην καὶ κῦδος ὄπασσον.
> (7.201-5)

This stands out as a curious moment in a narrative where the scales of fate are rarely balanced.[20]

---

[19] See Traill 1990, 301 for a discussion of this scene's oddities. Traill goes on to suggest that the scene *can* be explained as part of a larger philhellenic agenda on Homer's part that sought to give key Greeks victories over Hector before their own humiliations. While I concede that the scene shows Hector as the lesser warrior, I do not believe that he is humiliated; Hector emerges from the scene in a favourable light.

[20] Cf. 3.71f., 3.92f., 3.281-7, 16.435-8, 18.305-9, 22.130,175f., 255-9. See esp. 22.209-213. Also Hector's own statement in this scene at 7.291.

This is especially true when we consider that even though the combat proposal failed to detail what was at stake, it does not mean that there is nothing at stake; Hector's death would most certainly signal the imminent destruction of Troy, just as it does later in the epic. This knowledge makes the Achaians' prayer for a tie extraordinary, and what happens next even more so. In the heat of the fighting, with Hector clearly struggling more than Aias, the two heralds, Idaius the Trojan and Talthybius the Achaian, stop the men, urging them to call off the fight because the light is fading (7.274-282). Aias responds by saying that the decision is Hector's and he will obey whatever Hector tells him to do (πείσομαι, 7.286). Hector decides that they should call the fight.[21]

Even this small truce between two lone warriors has implications for the Achaian and Trojan people that echo those found in the army-wide truce of Book 3, as Hector himself details to Aias:

> So you will bring joy to all the Achaians beside the ships,
> especially to those who are your kinsmen and your companions:
> and I in the great city of lord Priam
> will bring joy to the Trojans and the Trojan women, with their trailing robes,
> who will go to give thanks before the divine assembly for me.

> ὡς σύ τ' εὐφρήνῃς πάντας παρὰ νηυσὶν Ἀχαιούς,
> σούς τε μάλιστα ἔτας καὶ ἑταίρους, οἵ τοι ἔασιν:
> αὐτὰρ ἐγὼ κατὰ ἄστυ μέγα Πριάμοιο ἄνακτος
> Τρῶας εὐφρανέω καὶ Τρῳάδας ἑλκεσιπέπλους,
> αἵ τέ μοι εὐχόμεναι θεῖον δύσονται ἀγῶνα.
> (7.294-298)

Hector suggests here that for these two warriors staying alive is not an object in itself, but something that brings joy to those around them, and

---

[21] This episode is consistently compared to the Glaucus/Diomedes armour exchange in Book 6, but it is in fact a very different scenario, which depends not on ancient institutions and ancestral relations, but rather on the immediacy of the situation and the characters of the men involved. And while the truce called is independent of some longer standing tradition and also has fewer implications for the future, their gift exchange does not suggest a future reciprocity, nor does it imply an indefinite peace between the two, as in the case of Glaucus and Diomedes. In fact, quite the opposite, as Hector very pragmatically tells Aias, "We shall fight again later, until one of the gods chooses between us, and gives victory to one of us…" (ὕστερον αὖτε μαχησόμεθ' εἰς ὅ κε δαίμων/ ἄμμε διακρίνῃ, δώῃ δ' ἑτέροισί γε νίκην. 7.291-2).

hope.[22] This implies a peace that is not as wide, nor as comfortable as the homecomings and restored cities of armistice, but is still present in the reunion of loved ones and the broader hope for survival. If this does not suggest that life can go on as it did during peacetime, it at least suggests that life can go on.

Book 7 in general follows in the same vein. Beginning with the Trojans' debate where Antenor suggests that they should try to make restitution to the Achaians (7.7.348-353), it continues with the dialogue between Paris' refusal to return Helen (7.357-364) and Diomedes' defiant response (7.400-402). This "exchange" contrasts with Priam's request for a truce to retrieve the bodies (7.368-378)[23] and Agamemnon's dutiful sworn granting of that request (7.406-412). Even in the face of a peace denied, compromises are still found in temporary truce and a mutual interest in honouring the dead.

We will see in our last example, from Book 22, that this is not always the case. Achilles' refusals of Hector's request, and then supplication, that his body be treated with respect are probably the most violent, hopeless speeches in all the *Iliad* (22.261-272, 22.345-354).[24] These speeches stand out so strongly because the scene itself is laced with peaceful possibilities, romantic fantasy, and nostalgia for better times, bringing together many strands of what we have discussed so far.

As Hector stands outside the wall, waiting for the advancing Achilles to meet him in single combat, he has a panicked conversation with himself where he goes through every possible alternative to actually fighting Achilles. First, he thinks of returning to the city, but decides against it out of shame (22.99-108); then he thinks of trying to approach Achilles without his armour on, offering up Helen, and the treasures of the Trojans, for the Atreidai to take back with them (22.111-121). In the end, he stops himself from these thoughts, thinking that Achilles would probably kill him naked if he tried to approach him in surrender (22.123-5). And it is with this acceptance of the impossibility of peace that Hector has the most vivid fantasy of peace so far:

> There is no way now from behind a tree or a rock
> to whisper to him, like a girl and a young man,

---

[22] Cf. 7.306-312, esp. 7.310.

[23] It is worth noting here Priam's same use of Hector's line at 7.290f. and at 377f: while Paris' refusal denies the possibility of a lasting peace, Priam, like Hector, can still envision a temporary peace.

[24] Perhaps only comparable to Achilles' speeches to Lycaon, at 21.99-113, 21.122-135.

how a girl and a young man whisper to each other.

οὐ μέν πως νῦν ἔστιν ἀπὸ δρυὸς οὐδ' ἀπὸ πέτρης
τῷ ὀαριζέμεναι, ἅ τε παρθένος ἠίθεός τε
παρθένος ἠίθεός τ' ὀαρίζετον ἀλλήλοιιν.
(22.126-8)

What a poignant image, evoking spring-time, and young love, a moment filled with promise: the moment that is farthest away.[25]

The narrative then continues to thread this peacetime imagery around the impending death of Hector; as Hector runs desperately around the city, Achilles close after him, the narrator paints the geography as it was during peace:

> They raced along by the look-out point, and the fig tree, blown by the wind,
> always away from under the wall, along the wagon roads,
> and came to the two lovely-running springs...
> Beside these there are the well-flowing stone washing places,
> where the wives of the Trojans and their lovely
> daughters washed the clothes to shining,
> before, when there was peace, before the coming of the sons of the Achaians.

οἳ δὲ παρὰ σκοπιὴν καὶ ἐρινεὸν ἠνεμόεντα
τείχεος αἰὲν ὑπ' ἐκ κατ' ἀμαξιτὸν ἐσσεύοντο,
κρουνὼ δ' ἵκανον καλλιρρόω·
ἔνθα δ' ἐπ' αὐτάων πλυνοὶ εὐρέες ἐγγὺς ἔασι
καλοὶ λαΐνεοι, ὅθι εἵματα σιγαλόεντα
πλύνεσκον Τρώων ἄλοχοι καλαί τε θύγατρες
τὸ πρὶν ἐπ' εἰρήνης πρὶν ἐλθεῖν υἷας Ἀχαιῶν.
(22.145-7, 153-6.)

Just as we saw earlier with the similes, this digression serves not to distract from war, or its immediacy, but to throw it into relief, to make its immediacy all the more pressing when compared to the idyllic past. That Hector's death is framed in such a way should be no surprise to us; it is Hector, more than any other character, who carries the peacetime with him. On his shoulders is the weight of preserving the Trojan way of life. This includes everything from the salvation of his family to the wealth of

---

[25] See Taplin 1980, 8f. and 20 n. 25 for a discussion of Hector's language here. Also of note is Achilles' own appraisal of Hector at 21.280, where he creates himself and Hector as equals.

Troy, to the fig-tree beside the wall, and the lovely Trojan women. All of this is Hector's, all of this is his to lose, and the audience is always reminded of this.[26]

In this way, Hector becomes emblematic of the *Iliad* itself, since both represent a hope for peace while also embodying the impossibility of that peace. Yet, perhaps it is of particular significance that the *Iliad* ends not in the midst of battle, but with a truce agreed upon for the sake of Hector's funeral. Hector's individual death becomes a public focal point, a reminder to both sides of what can be, and too often is, lost in war. The compromise between Achilles and Priam, Achilles' sleeping with Briseis (24.675f.), the fear of Achaian ambush being pushed out of mind by the funeral feast (24.799-803); all are glimpses into peacetime at a point where we know that the war will continue, and that Troy's fate is already sealed.[27] In a way, this uneasy tension between peace and war that Book 24 neatly encapsulates correlates directly with what we have seen of Hector's own character: man-slaughtering Hector, with his gentle disposition, and his gentle words (σῇ τ' ἀγανοφροσύνῃ καὶ σοῖς ἀγανοῖς ἐπέεσσι, 24.772).

Just as the *Iliad* intersperses its narrative of war with images of peace, so it interrupts the battlefield exploits of its warriors with glimpses of their peacetime lives. Broader narrative references to peace, in similes and stories, and individual characters' own concern for peace, in truce proposals, nostalgic memories, and fantasies for a peaceful future, are united in the poem's use of the masses' own desire for peace. In illustrating the sameness of the hunger for peace in the face of destruction, no matter the side or the initial motivation for war, the poem suggests that peace is as much a facet of human desire as war. And in its construction of its heroes the poem reiterates this, creating warriors who prove that compromise is not cowardice, that valuing life is not weakness, and that hoping for a future peace does not always mean surrender.

---

[26] One might say that Hector fears death and yet fears shame more (6.441-3, 22.100, 105). I would say that Hector fears death because he knows that his death is not his alone (6.450-65, 22.104, 107). Futhermore, shame is of particular significance to Hector because he is acutely aware of how his fate is intertwined with that of those around him; because he is so firmly embedded in a social structure, he more keenly feels the shame that it evokes. Thanks to Hans van Wees for challenging my characterisation of Hector on this point.

[27] Many thanks to Alan Sommerstein for his fruitful ideas about how Book 24 represents many romantic, even "marital" themes, from the intimate reunion of Achilles and Briseis to the book's ending with a great feast.

Bibliography

Allen, T. W. *Homeri Ilias*. Oxford: Clarendon Press, 1931.

Bassett, S. E. "The Function of the Homeric Simile." *TAPA* 52 (1921): 132-147.

Caldwell, W. E. "Hellenic Conceptions of Peace." *Studies in History, Economics, and Public Law* 84.2, 195 (1919).

de Jong, I. "The Voice of Anonymity: *tis*-speeches in the *Iliad*." *Eranos* 85 (1987): 69-84.

Porter, D. H. "Violent Juxtaposition in the Similes of the *Iliad*." *CJ* 68 (1972): 11-21.

Traill, D. "Unfair to Hector?" *CP* 85 (1990): 299-303.

Taplin, O. "The Shield of Achilles within the *Iliad*." *G&R* 2nd ser. 27.1 (1980): 1-21.

van Wees, H. *Status Warriors: War, Violence, and Society in Homer and History*. Amsterdam: JC Gieben, 1992.

CHAPTER NINE

MOURNING GLORY?: THE DEPICTION OF FALLEN WARRIORS IN ATHENIAN BLACK-FIGURE VASE-PAINTING[1]

DAVID SAUNDERS

The idealisation of a warrior's death is a concept that justifies willing involvement in battle, and, for the Western world, can be traced back to the *Iliad*. In this context, the subject has been studied thoroughly, in particular by Jean-Pierre Vernant and Nicole Loraux.[2] Death on the Homeric battlefield secures the warrior's heroic reputation and fixes the deceased as forever ἥβη - not so much an age-category as a "state of superiority."[3] Though only certain, already pre-eminent characters, such as Patroclus and Hector, attain the ideal in the *Iliad*,[4] the same trope can be

[1] This article derives from my D.Phil. thesis, "Sleepers in the Valley: Athenian Vase-Painting 600-400 BC and 'Beautiful Death'" (Oxford, 2006), and I am indebted to Professor Donna Kurtz for her support and advice throughout. Ed Bragg kindly invited me to speak at the conference, and I am grateful to him, Elizabeth Macaulay-Lewis, and Lisa Hau for their help in bringing this article to press. Previous drafts have been read by Alexandra Alexandridou, Sir John Boardman, Andrew Clark, Mary Louise Hart, Kenneth Lapatin and Hans van Wees, and it is has been much improved by their comments. Any errors remain my own. For assistance with illustrations, I am grateful to Jackie Burns (Los Angeles, The J. Paul Getty Museum), Erin Schleigh (Boston, Museum of Fine Arts), Dr. Ann Brownlee and Kristine Paulus (Philadelphia, University of Pennsylvania Museum), Brigitte Tailliez (Paris, Musée du Louvre), Jan Jordan (Athens, Agora Museum), Dr. Ursula Kaestner (Berlin, Antikensammlung), and Charles Arnold and Sikelela Owen (London, British Museum).
[2] Vernant 1991; Loraux 1978.
[3] Vernant 1991, 61.
[4] On the "epitaphs" for the lesser figures, see Griffin 1980, 103-143.

found in Tyrtaeus' exhortatory poems (frr. 10-12), with a more explicit emphasis on dying for one's homeland.

The most obvious idealisation of a warrior's death is Priam's appeal to Hector:

νέῳ δέ τε πάντ' ἐπέοικεν
ἀρηϊκταμένῳ δεδαϊγμένῳ ὀξέϊ χαλκῷ,
κεῖσθαι· πάντα δὲ καλὰ θανόντι περ, ὅττι φανήῃ·[5]

The "beautiful death" is essentially an ethical valuation, and καλός can be taken as "fine" or "noble." But in Priam's speech, καλός has a visual aspect too.[6] Objectively, the corpse is no more than "mute clay."[7] To his comrades, however, the bloodied body validates the fallen warrior's willingness to fight to the death and so is a good thing to behold. It is worthwhile to consider, therefore, whether this theme manifests itself in the extensive corpus of battle-scenes on painted pottery. I focus here on Athenian black-figure pottery of the sixth century BC, given the quantity of extant examples. Both Knittlemayer and Ellinghaus have made clear that a heroic, if not Homeric, paradigm is essential for the understanding of these scenes.[8] But while images of violence have received particular attention of late, the only close analysis of the depiction of corpses is Halm-Tisserant's.[9] Her study offers much that is useful, particularly regarding the motifs used to denote death, yet her conclusion that the corpse is shown without valour is, in light of the literary background, problematic.

Halm-Tisserant has a number of criteria that lead her to suggest that the presentation of the dead on vases is a "vision dévalorisante,"[10] including the body's position in the picture-field, its obscuring, and its

---

[5] *Il.* 22.71-73 "For a young man it is wholly fitting, when he is slain in battle, to lie mangled by the sharp bronze; dead though he is, all is fair that can be seen" (trans. Murray, A. T., *Homer, Iliad*, revised Wyatt, W. F. [1999]).

[6] Adkins 1960, 163-164 notes that an opposition between aesthetic and ethical aspects only appears in the late fifth century. On its own, physical beauty is not a criterion for excellence, *Il.* 3.44-45. See also Robertson 2003.

[7] *Il.* 24.54.

[8] Knittlemayer 1997, 57-60 and 71-73, who sees the presentation of the corpse as positive, in so far as negative traits are lacking (73); Ellinghaus 1997, *passim*. See also Mennenga 1976, 15-20.

[9] Halm-Tisserant 1993, although Vermeule 1979 remains valuable, esp. 83-117. Recent studies of depictions of violence include Fischer and Moraw 2005, Borg 2006, and Muth 2006.

[10] Halm-Tisserant 1993, 223.

vulnerability to being trampled on. Her illustrations suggest, however, that this conclusion is based on the consideration of fallen bodies detached from their pictorial context. Following a close analysis of the details of their depiction, I hope to demonstrate that it is rather the setting in which the fallen warriors appear that provides the most reliable interpretive framework. And while most of the images do not explicitly assert the Homeric ideal of "beautiful death," by no means is it plausible to ascribe a negative status to fallen bodies in battle-scenes.

I pass over images of fallen warriors being carried off from the battlefield or being deposited for burial since their positive connotations can hardly be doubted—the care devoted to the deceased is another key aspect of the "beautiful death."[11] Instead, I will explore the depiction of bodies *before* they are taken from the battlefield. In particular, I wish to focus on a recurrent composition in Athenian black-figure, the *battle over a fallen warrior*, in which warriors (usually a pair) clash over a body at their feet.

A Protoattic stand in Munich provides the earliest extant example.[12] In many respects, this depiction is an inauspicious beginning and would seem to support Halm-Tisserant's thesis. The body is small, seemingly inserted as an afterthought and barely visible behind its shield and helmet. But these are not pictorial traits that persist. There are other battle-scenes on Protoattic pottery,[13] but despite these native precursors (the battle-scenes on Athenian Geometric vases constitute a self-contained group and do not appear to influence later scenes), Corinth will be found to be a more important influence on Athenian black-figure vase-painters. A Siana cup attributed to the C Painter is perhaps our earliest extant example,[14] and it displays similarities to two Middle Corinthian—and most likely earlier—scenes.[15] By the mid-sixth century the composition is fully established, first on hydriae, and then amphorae and neck-amphorae (fig. 9-1). The last continue to be produced into the early fifth century. Besides hydriae, other shapes are used infrequently, and though cups and lekythoi regularly bear

---

[11] Cf. Vernant 1991, 67-74.

[12] Munich, Antikensammlungen 8936 (Vierneisel 1967, figs. 1-3).

[13] Notably the stand fr., Athens, National Archaeological Museum, number unknown (Morris 1984, 70-72, pl. 17) that depicts a battle over a fallen body. Morris 1984 argues that many of the Protoattic vases were made on Aegina.

[14] London, Private, Leventis Collection (Brijder 1983, pl.14c, BAD 6230).

[15] Middle Corinthian skyphos, Braunschweig, Herzog Anton Ulrich Museum 235 (*CVA* Braunschweig, Herzog Anton Ulrich Museum, pl. 3.1, BAD 1001785) and Middle Corinthian krater fr., Basel, Market (Münzen und Medaillen A.G. 1956, pl.15, no. 74).

battle-scenes, the *battle over a fallen warrior* is scarce, most likely because of space. In spite of the examples in the Corinthian repertoire, it is curious that the scene is rarely preserved on Athenian kraters and lebetes, for these shapes often carried prestigious scenes such as marriage and athletics. Among the scenes that accompany the *battle over a fallen warrior* the Heraclean and Dionysiac are popular (and perhaps meaningful; e.g. Heracles' apotheosis might be a heroising foil for the battle-scene), as are other military-scenes, especially if departures are included.[16]

The *battle over a fallen warrior* seems at first glance to be virtually absent from red-figure vases, despite its production in contemporary black-figure.[17] I know of only a handful of examples, one of the latest being the battle of Achilles and Memnon over Melanippus on a calyx-krater in Boston (Fig. 9-2).[18] But three-figure battle-scenes, with the central warrior defeated and falling, are far from lacking.[19] As I will argue below, in this context there is little meaningful difference as to whether the defeated figure is clearly marked as a corpse or simply fallen or falling. Why they are rarely depicted in red-figure as corpses remains unclear. It could be, in part, a practical matter. Cups are the major bearers of early red-figure scenes, and in contrast to the relatively flat picture-field of an amphora or a hydria's shoulder, their curved exteriors are ill-suited for depicting a corpse lying on the ground-line (although the figure would be more easily visible when the cup is lifted or hung on a wall).

The *battle over a fallen warrior* is an elaboration of the *duel* composition,[20] and just one of many different types of battle-scene. In

---

[16] Cf. Spiess 1992, 143-150, who records that 17% of the vases bearing a departure-scene have Heracles-scenes on the other side, 16% repeat the departure motif, and 11% carry battle-scenes.

[17] Halm-Tisserant 1993, 216 notes that black-figure is the primary extant medium for corpses, but does not pursue this. Cf. Recke 2002, 18.

[18] Boston, Museum of Fine Arts 97.368 (*ARV*[2] 290.1, 1591, *Para* 355, *Add*[2] 210, BAD 202631). See also, the r-f cups, Berlin, Antikensammlung F2264 (*ARV*[2] 60.64, *Para* 326, *Add*[2] 164, BAD 200457) and Palermo, Museo Archeologico Regionale V654 (*ARV*[2] 74.41, *CVA*, Italy 14 Palermo 1, III Ic, pl. 7.1, BAD 200485).

[19] E.g. r-f cup, Tarquinia, Museo Archeologico Nazionale 689 (*ARV*[2] 480.3, Kunisch 1997, no.10, pl. 8, BAD 205027). Additional figures can be included, see e.g. r-f cup, Berlin, Antikensammlung F2288 (*ARV*[2] 438.130, 1701, *Add*[2] 239, Buitron-Oliver 1995, no. 175, pl. 98, BAD 205176).

[20] Examples occur side by side on the Protocorinthian aryballos, Syracuse, Museo Archeologico Regionale Paolo Orsi 20967/B323 (Amyx 1988, 38.4). On the *duel*, see Recke 2002, 13-20; Mennenga 1976, 12-20. Within the Greek repertoire, the

other words, we should not think of a fallen body as an essential element in representations of battle. But, in the case of a Protocorinthian aryballos in Paris, not only is the fallen warrior at the centre of the action, but warriors from either side tug at the body (fig. 9-3).[21] Far from being left for dead, like the piles of dead warriors on Athenian Geometric kraters,[22] this figure is clearly valued. A similar interpretation can be applied to the *battle over a fallen warrior* scenes in Attic black-figure, and Recke draws a helpful comparison with boxing-scenes,[23] where a prize-amphora can be added between the competitors. As the prize over which the boxers are fighting, its presence raises the stakes. Although the scene is comprehensible without it, the amphora is nonetheless more than a mere embellishment. It is the object of the boxers' attentions and is, by its very presence, shown to be valuable and valued. The same is true for the fallen warrior that is fought over. Obviously, he has perished in battle, and now comrade and foe meet over him, either to rescue (and so guarantee funerary rites) or to abuse him. Based on the pictorial context alone, it is difficult to accept Halm-Tisserant's suggestion that the fallen warriors in these scenes are shown in a negative fashion. What I will explore here is whether there are any distinctive features in their depiction that confirm or counter this supposition.

Posture types

Within the basic composition outlined above, details may vary widely, and a number of posture-types for the dead body are distinguishable. The early group of Athenian black-figure scenes (mostly) on hydriae are attributed to the Painter of Louvre F6 and his workshop and bear corpses

---

representation of the duelling pair doubtless has chronological precedence; for Attic Geometric scenes, see e.g. the krater, New York Metropolitan Museum 34.11.2 (Ahlberg 1971, 51, fig. 50).

[21] Paris, Musée du Louvre CA 931 (Amyx 1988, 38.6, BAD 1006365). In this case, the fallen warrior still holds his spear, so he may not be dead yet. But compare Athenian examples: b-f amphora, Leipzig, Antikenmuseum der Universität Leipzig T2176 (*CVA*, Germany, Democratic Republic 2 Leipzig 2, pll. 11.1-3, BAD 1908), b-f neck-amphora, Karlsruhe, Badisches Landesmuseum B2423 (*ABV* 100.65, 684, *Add²* 27, *CVA* Germany 7 Karlsruhe 1, pll. 5.5, 6.3-4, BAD 310064), and b-f Merrythought cup, Manisa Museum 2137 (Ramage 1983, pl. 64.1-4, BAD 8420).

[22] E.g., Paris, Musée du Louvre A519 (Ahlberg 1971, 15-17, figs. 6-8).

[23] Recke 2002, 18-19.

of a common type, each *covered by a shield* (fig. 9-4).[24] Precursors can be found in both Protoattic and Protocorinthian wares.[25] The type continues to be used by black-figure vase-painters: a number of examples occur on belly-amphorae attributed to (the circle of) the Swing Painter, the Princeton Painter, and the Painter of Berlin 1686.[26] Other instances occur outside this group,[27] but a third (and final) phase is made up of lekythoi of the late sixth century attributed to the Groups of the Arming Warrior and the Departing Warrior (the Phanyllis Class).[28]

It is this corpse-type that Halm-Tisserant notes as giving the dead warrior the look of a "pantin désarticulé."[29] No doubt the arrangement of three frontal shields rendered the execution of the scene straightforward, but to consider the representation in negative terms seems to overlook the value accorded to the hoplite shield — not only as a sign of wealth in itself, but as a marker that the body is yet to be stripped. More generally, Halm-Tisserant interprets the position of the body in the background as another negative factor.[30] But the incising of the duelling warriors' legs over the fallen body indicates that the latter was one of the first figures to be painted on the vase—in one respect an integral part of the composition, unlike the body on the Munich stand.[31]

---

[24] E.g. b-f hydriae, Paris, Musée du Louvre CA3001 and F6 (*ABV* 123.2 and 123.3, *Para* 51, *Add*² 34, BAD 300898 and 300899).

[25] See above, nn. 13 and 21 (fig. 9-3). I do not know of other Corinthian examples until the Late Corinthian hydria fr., Vatican City, Museo Etrusco Gregoriano Vaticano, Astarita 653 (*LIMC* VII, *s.v.* Sarpedon 2*; discussed by Wachter 2001, 308-310), but it would not be surprising if appearance of the *covered by a shield* type in Athenian black-figure owed more to Corinth than to the native tradition, since vases attributed to the Painter of Louvre F6 and associated hands bear close comparison with Corinthian vase-painting in other respects (see Kleinbauer 1964).

[26] E.g. the b-f amphorae, Chicago, Art Institute 1978.114 (Moon and Berge 1979, no.31, BAD 5170), Munich, Antikensammlungen J324 / 1390 (*Para* 133.17bis, *Add*² 80, BAD 340555) and Vatican City, Museo Gregoriano Etrusco Vaticano 34549/G36 (*ABV* 304.1, *Add*² 79, BAD 301481). The shared figure-type suggests a link between these hands (cf. Böhr 1982, 53-55), and that there may be grounds for suspecting a connection with the earlier hydria painters.

[27] E.g., the b-f column-krater excavated at Orphani (*BCH* 122 (1998) 857, fig. 214, BAD 24002).

[28] E.g. the b-f lekythoi, Palermo, Museo Archeologico Regionale 1860; and Vienna, Kunsthistorisches Museum 87/IV (Giudice 1983, pll. 40.7 and 20.7, BAD 11249 and 9856).

[29] Halm-Tisserant 1993, 221.

[30] Halm-Tisserant 1993, 220.

[31] See above, n. 12.

Turning to other posture-types, further suggestions of Corinthian influence can be found among *prostrate* bodies.[32] *Supine* bodies had also occurred in earlier Corinthian vase-painting, usually with both legs drawn up.[33] Most Athenian black-figure examples tend to show one or both legs outstretched.[34] These figures often lie with an arm flexed over the head.[35] The gesture connotes disarray, perhaps conveying a posture similar to the figure seen from an unusual perspective on a red-figure fragment in Bryn Mawr.[36] The *supine* type is the closest to the bodies depicted in *prothesis* scenes. Might its use in a battle context be an allusion that the deceased will receive his funerary rites? This positive reading is attractive for a named hero like Patroclus (fig. 9-5),[37] and does seem a plausible approach to black-figure Ransom of Hector scenes (alluding to the successful outcome), but it becomes problematic for an "enemy" like Cycnus on an oinochoe in Berlin.[38] And if there were any validity to such a positive reading, it would be reasonable to expect that the *supine* figure-type would be more widespread, or particular to a certain shape, neither of which is the case.

The most commonly occurring posture I term the *conventional fallen* type. The basic schema is a frontal or unspecific torso with a supine lower

---

[32] E.g. b-f neck-amphora, Malibu, The J. Paul Getty Museum 86.AE.73 (*CVA*, J. Paul Getty Museum 1, pl. 22.1, BAD 12684) (fig. 9-1), b-f Little-Master band-cup, Paris, Private, Stavros Niarchos AO31 (Vos 1963, pl. 2a, BAD 11106). Cf. Middle Corinthian cups, Athens, National Archaeological Museum 641/CC623, and 992/CC621 (Amyx 1988, 194, A2 and 200, A1, pl. 83.1b).

[33] E.g. late Corinthian column-krater, Paris, Musée du Louvre E636 (Amyx 1988, 262, A1, Payne 1931, no. 1456, pl. 41.4).

[34] E.g. the b-f calyx-krater, Athens, Agora Museum AP1044 (*ABV* 145.19, *Para* 60, *Add²* 40, BAD 310401).

[35] E.g. b-f amphora, Düsseldorf, Hetjens-Museum 804/1962.29 (*Para* 57.4bis, *Add²* 37, BAD 350442). There are numerous variations on the posture, and it can sometimes look as if the hand is being held to the head, e.g. b-f amphora, type A, Karlsruhe 61.89 (*Para* 135.1bis, *Add²* 84, BAD 351011). Brize notes that this gesture occurs first for Eurytion, as he reaches for the arrow fixed in his forehead (Brize 1985, 86). Since the examples met for warriors do not seem to refer to any wound, a further significance is plausible. For the hand to the head is a typical mourning gesture, and perhaps alludes to the lamentation with which the deceased's demise would be met.

[36] Bryn Mawr College, Ella Riegel Memorial Museum P 936 (*ARV²* 438.131, *Add²* 239, BAD 205177).

[37] As on the calyx-krater noted above, n. 34.

[38] B-f oinochoe, Berlin, Antikensammlung F1732 (*ABV* 110.37, 685, *Para* 44, 48, *Add²* 30, BAD 310183).

body.[39] Halm-Tisserant refers to "la disposition antinaturelle du cadaver".[40] The term "antinaturelle" is problematic, for it risks misunderstanding the schemata that underpin compositions in the black-figure technique. Conversely, Halm-Tisserant herself notes that rotated limbs are distinctive of a corpse and that there are instances where painters do add details that contribute to the plausibility of their scenes, e.g. the indication of curling fingers, a feature that occurs when the muscles relax in death.[41]

Examples of the *conventional fallen* type range from the likes of the figure on an amphora in London (fig. 9-6),[42] who is still living, armed, and looking at one of the duellers, to those clearly marked as corpses, e.g. on a cup in Berlin (fig. 9-7).[43] The latter are characterised by signs of lifelessness that are consistently found in combination. The head is turned away, indicating that the warrior no longer plays a part in the action. The arm falls across the chest, and without a weapon or shield the warrior is shown to be ineffectual and so (as good as) dead.[44]

As for the fallen warriors that are not clearly marked as corpses, there is no indication that they should be contrasted with those that are; compare e.g. the scenes on two amphorae in Tarquinia.[45] In terms of our limited evidence, the most plausible factor for these variations in pose and details seems to be the preference of the painter. Examples appear on the same shapes and the duellers are not presented differently. In the *Iliad*, most warriors cease to be of interest once they are defeated. There is little likelihood that they will get up or fight back—whether or not the poet mentions explicitly that they are dead. Since they can no longer play a role

---

[39] As on the Siana cup noted above, n. 14.

[40] Halm-Tisserant 1993, 219.

[41] As on the Düsseldorf amphora noted above, n. 35.

[42] B-f amphora, type A, London, British Museum B199 (*ABV* 367.89, BAD 302084).

[43] B-f cup, Berlin, Antikensammlung F1672 (Schefold 1992, fig. 323, BAD 258). See also e.g. b-f amphorae, Tarquinia, Museo Nazionale Tarquiniese RC1816 (Tronchetti 1983, pl. 36, BAD 8230), and Tarquinia, Museo Nazionale Tarquiniese RC5166 (*ABV* 258.3, *Add*² 67, Tronchetti 1983, pl. 33, BAD 302235), and the b-f hydria fr., Jena, University 188 (*Para* 116.31bis, BAD 340455).

[44] Professor Boardman has alerted me to the similarity between a number of figures of this type and depictions of the Egyptian Earth divinity, Geb, lying beneath Nut. If it is not coincidental or remotely indebted to Oriental influences on Corinthian vase-painting, it would not be the only instance of Athenian vase-painters making use of Egyptian motifs, cf. Littauer 1968.

[45] Museo Nazionale Tarquiniese 649 (Tronchetti 1983, pl.37, BAD 8231) and RC5166 (above n. 43).

in the narrative, they count as dead or as good as. The same is true of the bodies in *battles over a fallen warrior*. No longer upright, they cannot play an active part in the fight.[46]

Identity, nudity and beards

It is difficult to conclude that the posture of a fallen body could be a bearer of meaning. Perhaps other iconographical details will be more significant. The role of nudity inevitably attracts attention.[47] It may serve as an indication of bodily strength, even beauty—or evoke pathos (the two need not be mutually exclusive). But by no means is every fallen body that is fought over nude, and any interpretation must take into account the fact that a straightforward differentiation between "nude" and "not nude" becomes difficult given the range of arms and attire that can be found between these two extremes.[48] But whatever their state, the bodies are found in the same fought-over context, and should be viewed in light of manly and aristocratic values. If anything, a "sliding-scale" is more appropriate, with which there are different ways of representing the same thing:[49] armour is costly and a sign of economic status; the marking of the penis (even where the figure is armed) asserts masculinity; and full nudity has aristocratic associations with bodily training.[50] Like the range of postures for the fallen figure, these variations appear to have little obvious effect on the scene's significance; I have not found any correspondences with variables such as vase-shape, identity, or iconographic details.

But the attire of the fallen does differ frequently (if to a varying extent) from that of the warriors fighting over them. The possibility that they have been stripped seems to conflict with the idea of a positive presentation. But despoiling the body is not a prominent theme in these scenes; if it were, we might expect more emphasis on the deceased's arms. Himmelmann's suggestion that the nudity of the dead Giants on the north Siphnian Treasury frieze is proleptic is more helpful.[51] Taken to apply to all *battle over a fallen warrior* scenes, nudity—whether full or partial—-

---

[46] Cf. Hölscher 2003, 11.

[47] On which see most recently Hallett 2005, 5-14; Daehner 2005; and Hurwit 2007.

[48] Entirely nude figures seem more numerous later in the sixth century, but the *conventional fallen* and *corpse covered by a shield* types, neither of which is ever fully nude, exist alongside in large quantities.

[49] Compare Sourvinou-Inwood's approach to funerary monuments (Sourvinou-Inwood 1995, 269-270).

[50] Bonfante 1989, esp. 547-556.

[51] Himmelmann 1990, 38.

indicates that the body *could* be stripped. It need not be viewed negatively. As seen on numerous occasions in the *Iliad*, a threat to the corpse, even if unfulfilled, heightens its valuation.

Recke notes that armed bodies tend to be bearded, and nude bodies beardless.[52] Given the emphasis in the literary sources on youth, the absence of facial hair might be meaningful.[53] But beards are found on entirely nude bodies too,[54] and their presence or absence can not be related to any other factors, such as posture or vase-shape. It is notable that bodies that are named or identifiable as Patroclus are beardless,[55] but it would be implausible to argue that all beardless bodies are Patroclus, or that bearded bodies are in some way less heroic—compare, for example, the body of Antilochus on an amphora in Philadelphia, where, unusually, his comrades chase away their opponents (fig. 9-8).[56]

This brings us to a final variable, that of identity. On an East Greek plate from Cameirus,[57] the figures are named: Euphorbus, fought over by Menelaus and Hector. Other heroes can be named or identified as participants in the *battle over a fallen warrior*,[58] and it is likely that the

---

[52] Recke 2002, 16, although his corpus of scenes is restricted to those he identifies as mythical.

[53] E.g. the b-f hydriae, London, British Museum B302 (*ABV* 261.40, 691, *Para* 115, *Add²* 68, BAD 302272) and London, British Museum B339 (*ABV* 264.1, 670, 678, BAD 302301), and the calyx-krater noted above, n. 34.

[54] E.g. b-f amphorae, Copenhagen, Ny Carlsberg Glyptothek 2652 (*CVA*, Copenhagen 1, pl. 3.1, BAD 43953), b-f lebes, Cleveland, Museum of Art 1971.46 (*CVA*, Cleveland pl. 65.2, BAD 5166), Tarquinia, Museo Nazionale Tarquiniese RC1816, and the b-f hydria, Jena University 188 (both above, n. 43). For the more fully attired, the issue is even less clear, e.g. the very similar scenes on the b-f amphora, London, Market, Sotheby's (*Sotheby's sale catalogue 14/7/1986* no.152, BAD 15846) where one body is bearded, the other not.

[55] Named on the b-f calyx-krater and the r-f cup in Berlin (above, nn. 34 and 18); identifiable based on the identities of other figures on the b-f amphora, Munich, Antikensammlungen J53/1408 (*ABV* 368.106, *Para* 162, *Add²* 98, BAD 302101) and the b-f cup, formerly Depoletti Collection (*ABV* 675.4, BAD 306472).

[56] Philadelphia, University of Pennsylvania, Museum MS 3442 (*ABV* 145.14, *Para* 60.14, *Add²* 40, BAD 310396). In so far as this composition indicates that the fallen body will be safe, it is noteworthy that it remains much less widespread than the evenly balanced battle.

[57] London, British Museum 1860.4-4.1 (*LIMC* IV, *s.v.*Euphorbos I 1*).

[58] On Athenian vases, e.g: Patroclus: see above, n. 55; Melanippus: see above, n. 18; Phocus: b-f neck-amphora, Private Collection, *c.*560-540; *LIMC* VII, Phokos V 1; BAD 19721. Askalaphos: b-f neck-amphora, Berlin, Antikensammlung F1879 (*Para* 221, *Add²* 122, BAD 360895; see *CVA*, Germany 45 Berlin 5, 59, cf. *Il.* 13.526-539). Antilochus: see above, n. 56.

more numerous scenes without inscriptions evoke these mythical and heroic paradigms.[59] This brings Halm-Tisserant's negative conclusions further into question. On the other hand, there is no sense that the identifiable bodies are, in terms of their rendering, in any way a class apart from their unnamed counterparts. Any elements that seem consistent appear less significant when considered alongside the many unidentifiable bodies, and I have not been able to discern any trends regarding particular posture-types, hair or beard-style, and the range of attire.

Fallen bodies that are not duelled over

I have analysed certain details that could have been of importance in interpreting the representation of dead warriors; posture, attire, age, and identity. Such approaches do not allow us to identify positive or negative trends, and the pictorial variables are best interpreted as painters' preferences. To some extent, it might be mistaken to seek iconographical consistency; details of a carefully rendered scene on an unusual vessel, such as the calyx-krater from Athens depicting the battle over Patroclus, might not be pertinent among mass-produced neck-amphorae that are often found in Etruria. But having covered a range of examples, some wider aspects—associated with the composition as a whole, rather than the rendering of the fallen body—are evident. Scarcely any of the fallen warriors that are fought over are mistreated by the combatants, and though birds attacking dead bodies—a common threat in the *Iliad*—are depicted in the art of other Mediterranean peoples,[60] nothing similar is preserved in these Attic battle-scenes.[61] And despite their vulnerable position, the bodies are hardly ever shown to be trodden on.[62] The "piétinement des

---

[59] Cf. Lissarrague 1990, 72-82.

[60] E.g. *Il.* 11.454-455. See Steuernagel 2005, 221-222 on a Faliscan stamnos and for references to similar scenes in Near Eastern Art and on Tenian-Boeotian relief pithoi. In Etruscan vase-painting, see e.g. Etruscan black-figure olpe, Rome, Museo Nazionale Etrusco di Villa Giulia 56029 (Szilágyi, 1992, 244, no.5, pl. 107a-b). See also Pipili 1987, 39-40.

[61] The motif is found in the parodic context of the Geranomachy, e.g. b-f cup, Taranto, Museo Archeologico Nazionale G4435 (*ABV* 159.1, *Para* 67, BAD 310529).

[62] Although defeated warriors may be trodden on in other Athenian battle compositions (notably Heracles against the Amazons), in the *battle over a fallen warrior* examples are exceptional, e.g. b-f neck-amphora, London, British Museum B240 (Kunze-Gotte 1992, pl. 61, BAD 5), and I know of no instance in which the head of the defeated is trodden on as it is in the Gigantomachy, b-f amphora frr., Athens, National Archaeological Museum, Akro*polis* Collection 1.2211 (Graef and

guerriers" that Halm-Tisserant notes is most obviously a feature of different composition that involves chariots (fig. 9-9). The composition of a body fallen beneath the horse-team appears to come from the Near East (I know of no Corinthian examples).[63] About to be trampled by their hooves, it is a position of complete subordination, a theme that is not present in the *battle over a fallen warrior*.

As might be expected from the preceding, it is difficult to identify iconographical features that are specific to bodies fallen beneath chariots, although there are some hints; full nudity is rare, for example. The composition finds a particular use in Gigantomachies, and this might suggest a genuine distinction between warriors fallen in battle and the opponents of the gods.[64] But Athenian vase iconography is rarely so tidy, and the chariot-composition is used without gods and giants too, i.e. with figures that can only be identified as "male warriors." I would be wary of claiming that those fallen in this setting are somehow less "heroic" than those that are fought over. But the *battle over a fallen warrior* does at least privilege the defeated figure in a way that the chariot scene does not, and if we are to make any conclusions as to the way the fallen are rendered, a more nuanced view that appreciates the pictorial context in which they appear is necessary.

One feature worthy of further investigation goes some way to support this, namely the presence of "clearly marked" corpses. In reference to the *battle over a fallen warrior* I played down the distinction between bodies that are clearly marked as corpses, and those that are simply "fallen". In the chariot-scenes, however, a much smaller proportion of the bodies are

---

Langlotz 1925-1933, pl. 94, no. 2211, BAD 3363). On two Chalcidian vases, the amphora, Melbourne, National Gallery of Victoria 1643/4 (Trendall 1958, pl. IIIb) and the oinochoe, Private, Hirschmann Collection (Isler 1983, pl. 8), the fallen body is not fought over, but trodden on and stabbed. The closest Athenian comparanda are two b-f hydriae, Rimini, Museo Civico (*ABV* 261.36, 257, 665, *Para* 115, BAD 302268) and Oxford, Ashmolean Museum V222 (*ABV* 281.7, *Add²* 73, BAD 320227). Unlike the Chalcidian examples, however, the fallen are not deserted by their comrades.

[63] E.g. London, British Museum WA 124546; relief from the North West Palace of Ashurnasirpal II (883-859 B.C.) (Barnett, 1960 pl. 15).

[64] See the scenes paired on the b-f amphora, Vatican City, Museo Gregoriano Etrusco Vaticano 16445 (A365) (*ABV* 311.1, *Para* 135, BAD 301601). Note, however, the clash of warriors and charioteers over a corpse on the b-f dinos, Athens, National Archaeological Museum, Akro*polis* Collection 1.606/ 15116 (*ABV* 81.1, 682, *Para* 30, *Add²* 22, BAD 300754). Datable to the second quarter of the sixth century, the composition—not least on account of space—does not appear to have been popular.

explicitly shown to be dead; most must simply be termed "fallen".[65] The same appears to be the case in other Gigantomachies (without chariots), Amazonomachies, Cycnus-scenes[66] and scenes in which a body is fallen beneath two rearing horse riders. Again, the fluid ways in which iconographical motifs are distributed prevent any dogmatic assertions, but the stronger tendency to show bodies as clearly dead when they are fought over does suggest that their presence in evenly matched battles had some significance.

Conclusion

Before concluding, it is necessary to mention a final aspect; the depiction of injuries. I will deal with this subject fully in a forthcoming study,[67] but to foreshadow my observations, the representation of wounds is essentially a painterly choice, and their presence, though by no means negative, does not appear to have been intrinsic to the presentation of the dead warrior. There are cases where injuries seem to have been toned down, suggesting a positive gloss on the realities of battle. For example, the depiction of spilling entrails, a feature of Homeric battle, is restricted to bodies fallen under the Calydonian boar. But I have not been able to identify any sign that wounds were used as a means of characterisation, which might be expected in light of the differentiation between wounds to the front and back in literary sources.[68]

As regards the presentation of dead warriors, therefore, the depiction of wounds seems to accord with the study of other details. It has not been possible to identify any iconographical trends that support an argument, for example, that nudity was important, or that youthfulness was a key

---

[65] As far as painters' preferences may be a factor, there does seem to be a differentiation among vases attributed to (or near to) Group E between *fought-over* bodies and those *under a chariot*. Compare e.g. the b-f amphorae Kassel, Staatliche Museen, Antikensammlung T674 (*Para* 56.31*bis*, *Add²* 36, BAD 350427) and Düsseldorf 804/1962.29 (see above, n. 35) with Copenhagen, National Museum 322 (*ABV* 135.33, *Add²* 36, BAD 310293) and Manchester, City Art Gallery and Museum 1885.21.AA45 (*ABV* 142.4, *Add²* 38, BAD 310372). But in the few other cases that a quantity of relevant vases is attributed to (or near) one hand, there is no such consistency.

[66] The oinochoe attributed to Lydus (see above, n. 38) uses the *battle over a fallen warrior* composition at an early stage in the scene's establishment in the black-figure repertoire. But presenting Cycnus as a corpse does not appear to have caught on.

[67] Saunders 2008.

[68] E.g. *Il.* 13.288-291.

feature, in the presentation of warrior death. If we are to assess the significance of this theme on the vases, the answers are better sought in a broader understanding of the *battle over a fallen warrior* and how the scene operates in the society in which it is used. Naturally, the best evidence would be vases that carry images of dead warriors buried in, or associated with, graves of warriors. The case presented by Marconi in relation to a grave in Acragas indicates that this is no idle speculation.[69] Where known, the majority of findspots for vases with the *battle over a fallen warrior* scene is Etruscan (Vulci in particular). Evidently, the military theme translated easily and was appreciated,[70] but further research is required to ascertain whether we could make more precise assertions as to how this particular scene was interpreted in Etruria.

Turning to Athens, where these vases were produced and some, at least, remained,[71] involvement in military activity in the sixth century BC seems to have been primarily a role associated with the leisured classes,[72] and even after Cleisthenes' reorganisation of the military infrastructure[73] arms and material means remain connected. Furthermore, up until the closing decades of the sixth century, Athenian experiences of large-scale hoplite battle seem to have been limited,[74] and without suggesting that the sixth century was a period of peace, or underestimating the effect that a warrior's death would have had on his family and community, this should inform the interpretation of the abundant battle-scenes. Far from illustrating reality, these images express élite (or élite-aspiring) ideals, and support the suggestion that the *battle over a fallen warrior* presents death on the battlefield in a positive fashion.[75]

---

[69] Marconi 2004. Recent excavations on Paros have unearthed what seems to be an eighth century burial of a group of warriors, and amongst the finds are two neck-amphorae that depict battle-scenes (see Zaphiropoulou 2002, 283-284). Comparable are also the fifth century Athenian "battle-loutrophoroi", particularly those recently found in the region of the Demosion Sema (see *Archaeological Reports for 1997-1998*, 8-10 and Oakley 2004, 216-217 with n. 5).

[70] See e.g. Jannot 1985, 127-141.

[71] As well as the b-f calyx-krater (see above, n. 34), see e.g. two b-f lekythoi from the Cerameicus (where each is the only grave-gift): Athens, Cerameicus Museum inv. 8668 and 8717 (*AM* 81 (1966) pl. 20.1-2, BAD 294 and BAD 257).

[72] On compulsory military service see van Wees 2004, 55-57.

[73] See Ostwald 1988, 332-334.

[74] Frost 1984.

[75] On the paradigmatic role of images on vases, cf., Scheibler 1987.

Figures

Figure 9-1. Neck-amphora, J. Paul Getty Museum 86.AE.73.

Figure 9-2. Calyx-krater, Boston, Museum of Fine Arts 97.368.

Figure 9-3. Aryballos, Paris, Musée du Louvre CA 931.

Figure 9-4. Hydria, Paris, Musée du Louvre F6.

Figure 9-5. Calyx-krater, Athens, Agora Museum AP1044.

Figure 9-6. Amphora, London, British Museum B199.

Figure 9-7. Cup, Berlin Antikensammlung F1672.

Figure 9-8. Amphora, Philadelphia, University of Pennsylvania, MS 3442.

Figure 9-9. Neck-amphora, London, British Museum B251.

Bibliography

Adkins, A. W. H. *Merit and Responsibility.* Oxford: Clarendon Press, 1960.

Ahlberg, G. *Fighting on Land and Sea in Greek Geometric Art.* Stockholm: Svenska institutet i Athen, 1971.

Amyx, D. A. *Corinthian Vase-Painting of the Archaic Period.* Berkeley: University of California Press, 1988.

Barnett, R. D. *Assyrian Palace Reliefs and their Influence on the Sculptures of Babylonian and Persia.* London: Batchworth Press, 1960.

Böhr, E., *Der Schaukelmaler.* Mainz am Rhein: Philipp von Zabern, 1982.

Bonfante, L. "Nudity as Costume in Classical Art." *AJA* 93 (1989): 543-70.

Borg, B. "Gefährliche Bilder? Gewalt und Leidenschaft in der archaischen und klassischen Kunst." In *Gewalt und Ästhetik. Zur Gewalt und ihrer Darstellung in der griechischen Klassik,* edited by B. Seidensticker and M. Vöhler, 223-257. Berlin and New York: Walter de Gruyter, 2006.

Brijder, H. A. G. *Siana Cups I and Komast Cups*. Amsterdam: Allard Pierson Series, 1983.

Brize, P. "Samos und Stesichoros zu einem früharchaischen Bronzeblech." *AM* 100 (1985): 53-90.

Buitron-Oliver, D. *Douris*. Mainz am Rhein: Philipp von Zabern, 1995.

Daehner, J. "Grenzen der Nacktheit. Studien zum nackten männlichen Körper in der griechischen Plastik des 5. und 4. Jahrhunderts v. Chr." *JdI* 120 (2005): 155-300.

Ellinghaus, C. *Aristokratische Leitbilder, Demokratische Leitbilder*. Münster: Scriptorium, 1997.

Fischer, G. and Moraw, S. (eds.) *Die andere Seite der Klassik. Gewalt im 5. und 4. Jahrhundert v. Chr.* Stüttgart: Steiner, 2005.

Frost, F. J. "The Athenian Military before Cleisthenes." *Historia* 33 (1984): 283-294.

Giudice, F. *I Pittore della classe di Phanyllis: organizzazione, produzione, distribuzione dei vasi di un' officina di eta pisistratideo-clistenica*. Catania: Università di Catania, Istituto di Archeologia, 1983.

Graef, B. and Langlotz, E. *Die antiken Vasen von der Akropolis zu Athen* I-II. Berlin: Walter de Gruyter, 1925-1933.

Griffin, J. *Homer on Life and Death*. Oxford: Clarendon Press, 1980.

Hallett, C. *The Roman Nude: heroic portrait statuary 200 B.C.-A.D. 300*. Oxford, Oxford University Press, 2005.

Halm-Tisserant, M. "Iconographie et Status du Cadavre." *Ktema* 18 (1993): 215-226.

Himmelmann, N. *Ideale Nacktheit in der Griechischen Kunst*. Berlin: Walter de Gruyter, 1990.

Hölscher, T. "Images of War in Greece and Rome: Between Military Practice, Public Memory and Cultural Symbolism." *JRS* 93 (2003): 1-17.

Hurwit, J. "The Problem with Dexileos; Heroic and other Nudities in Greek Art." *AJA* 111 (2007): 35-60.

Isler, H.-P. "Zwei chalkidische Vasen in schweizer Privatbesitz." *Antike Kunst* 26 (1983): 17-21.

Jannot, J.-R. "Les Cités Étrusques et la Guerre. Remarques sur la Fonction Militaire dans la Cité Étrusque." *Ktema* 10 (1985): 127-141.

Kleinbauer, W.E. "The Dionysios Painter and the "Corinthio-Attic" Problem." *AJA* 68 (1964): 355-370.

Knittlemayer, B. *Die Attische Aristokratie und ihre Helden: Untersuchungen zu*

Darstellungen des trojanischen Sagenkreises im 6. und frühen 5. Jarhundert v. Chr. Heidelberg: Verlag Archäologie und Geschichte, 1997.

Kunisch, N. *Makron.* Mainz am Rhein: Phillip von Zabern, 1997.

Kunze-Gotte, E. *Der Kleophrades-Maler unter Malern schwarzfigurer Amphoren. Eine Werkstattestudie.* Mainz am Rhein: Phillip von Zabern, 1992.

Lissarrague, F. *L'Autre Guerrier — archers, peltastes, cavaliers dans l'imagerie attique.* Paris and Rome: École Française de Rome, 1990.

Littauer, M.A. "A 19th and 20th Dynasty Heroic Motif on Attic Black-Figured Vases." *AJA* 72 (1968): 150-152.

Loraux, N. "Mourir devant Troie, tomber pour Athènes; de la gloire du héros à l'ideé de la cite." *Information sur les Sciences Socials* 17.6 (1978): 801-818.

Marconi, C. "Images for a Warrior. On a Group of Athenian Vases and their Public." In *Greek Vases: Images, Contexts and Controversies,* edited by C. Marconi, 27-40. Leiden: Brill, 2004.

Mennenga, I. P. *Untersuchung zur Komposition und Deutung homerischer Zweikampfszenen in der griechischen Vasenmalerei.* Berlin: 1976.

Moon, W. G. and Berge, L. (eds.) *Greek Vase-Painting in Mid Western Collections.* Chicago: Art Institute of Chicago, 1979.

Morris, S. P. *The Black and White Style: Athens and Aigina in the Orientalizing Period.* New Haven: Yale University Press, 1984.

Münzen und Medaillen A.G. *Kunst der Antike 16.* Basel: Münzen und Medaillen, 1956.

Muth, S. "Als Gewaltbilder zu ihrem Wirkungspotential fanden." In *Gewalt und Ästhetik. Zur Gewalt und ihrer Darstellung in der griechischen Klassik,* edited by B. Seidensticker and M. Vöhler, 259-293. Berlin and New York: Walter de Gruyter, 2006.

Oakley, J. H. *Picturing Death in Classical Athens.* Cambridge: Cambridge University Press, 2004.

Ostwald, M. "The Reform of the Athenian State by Cleisthenes." In *CAH*² vol. IV, *Persia, Greece and the Western Mediterranean c.525-479 BC,* edited by J. Boardman, N. G. L. Hammond, D. Lewis and M. Ostwald, 301-346. Cambridge: Cambridge University Press, 1988.

Payne, H. *Necrocorinthia: a study of Corinthian art in the Archaic Period.* Oxford: Clarendon Press, 1931.

Pipili, M. *Laconian Iconography of the Sixth Century BC.* Oxford: Oxford University Committee for Archaeology, 1987.

Ramage, N. H. "A Merrythought Cup from Sardis." *AJA* 87 (1983): 453-460.

Recke, M. *Gewalt und Leid*. Istanbul: Ege Yayinlari, 2002.

Robertson, G. I. C. "The Andreia of Xenocles: *Kouros, Kallos* and *Kleos*." In *Andreia: Studies in Manliness and Courage in Classical Antiquity*, edited by R. M. Rosen and I. Sluiter, 59-75. Leiden: Brill, 2003.

Saunders, D. A. "Dead Warriors and their Wounds in Athenian Black-Figure Vase-Painting." In *Festschrift for Eleni Hatzivassiliou*, edited by D. C. Kurtz, Oxford: Archaeopress, 2008.

Schefold, K., *Gods and Heroes in Late Archaic Greek Art*, translated A. Griffiths. Cambridge: Cambridge University Press, 1992.

Scheibler, I., "Bild und Gefäss: zur Ikonographisches und Funktionalen Bedeutung der Attischen Bildfeldamphoren." *JdI* 102 (1987): 57-118.

Seidensticker, B. and Vöhler, M. (eds.) *Gewalt und Ästhetik. Zur Gewalt und ihrer Darstellung in der griechischen Klassik*. Berlin and New York: Walter de Gruyter, 2006.

Sourvinou-Inwood, C. *"Reading" Greek Death; to the end of the classical period*. Oxford: Clarendon Press, 1995.

Spiess, A. B. *Der Kriegerabschied auf attischen Vasen der archaischer Zeit*. Frankfurt am Main: Lang, 1992.

Steuernagel, D. "Sieger und Besiegte in der etruskischen und mittelitalischen Bildkunst." In *Die andere Seite der Klassik. Gewalt im 5. und 4. Jahrhundert v. Chr.*, edited by G. Fischer and S. Moraw, 211-223. Stuttgart: Steiner, 2005.

Szilágyi, J. G. *Ceramica Etrusco-Corinzia Figurata* I. Florence: Olschki, 1992.

Trendall, A. D. *The Felton Greek Vases*. Canberra: Australian Humanities Research Council, 1958.

Tronchetti, C. *Ceramica attica a figure nere: grandi vasi, anfore, pelikai, crateri. Materiale del Museo Archeologico Nazionale di Tarquinia* V. Rome: G. Bretschneider, 1983.

van Wees, H. *Greek Warfare: Myths and Realities*. London: Duckworth, 2004.

Vermeule, E. *Aspects of Death in Early Greek Art and Poetry*. Berkeley: University of California Press, 1979.

Vernant, J.-P. "A Beautiful Death and the Disfigured Corpse in Homeric Epic." In *Mortals and Immortals: collected essays,* edited by F. I. Zeitlin, 50-74. Princeton: Princeton University Press, 1991.

Vierneisel, K. "Neuewerbungen Staatliche Antikensammlungen und Glyptothek." *Münchner Jahrbuch der bildenden Kunst* 18 (1967): 241-245.

Vos, M. F. *Scythian Archers in Archaic Attic Vase Painting*. Gröningen: J. B. Wolters, 1963.

Wachter, R. *Non-Attic Greek Vase Inscriptions.* Oxford: Oxford
    University Press, 2001.
Zaphiropoulou, P. "Recent Finds from Paros." In *Excavating Classical
    Culture*: *recent archaeological discoveries in Greece,* edited by M.
    Stamatopoulou and M. Yeroulanou, 281-284. Oxford: Beazley Archive
    and Archaeopress, 2002.

CHAPTER TEN

CIVIL WAR IN THE *RES GESTAE DIVI AUGUSTI*: CONQUERING THE WORLD AND FIGHTING A WAR AT HOME[1]

CARSTEN HJORT LANGE

Nowadays there seems to be a tendency to approach the *Res Gestae* as a means of revealing Augustus and his deceptive ways, what might be called the right-or-wrong approach to history.[2] The German epigraphist Alföldy rightly observes that the *Res Gestae* is different from biographies, and in continuation of this point stresses that inscriptions did not normally focus on the negative qualities of the honorand.[3] That Augustus does stress civil war more than once seems not to have distracted him from that

---

[1] I am very grateful to Dr Andrew Bayliss, Dr Alison Cooley, and Prof. John Rich for comments. An article of this length cannot possibly engage with all theories and approaches to the *Res Gestae*. For the immense bibliography, see Ramage 1987; Kienast 1999, 208-212; and Ridley 2003. All translations in the article of the *Res Gestae* are by Brunt and Moore 1967.
[2] There is a tendency among historians to try to make known, to expose, something that has been concealed. See Hedrick 2000, 133. Syme 1939 (1952), 522 stresses the *Res Gestae* as "the hall-mark of official truth". Similarly Yavetz 1984, 23; Jones 1977[2], 168f; Ramage 1987, 32-37. On page 36, he mentions that only Augustus is given credit for building in Rome and Italy, but the inscription is about the *Res Gestae* of Augustus. Eder 1990, 71 and Osgood 2006, 182 stress civil war issues omitted from the *Res Gestae*. Of course the *Res Gestae* constitutes Augustus' truth, his ideology, but what is missing from the modern debate is an explanation for why he wrote as he did. Already in the eighteenth century the moderate policy of Augustus was thought by some to be intended to conceal the realities of despotism. See Erskine-Hill 1983, 249-266, who describes this appropriately as 'the spread of a Tacitean view'.
[3] Alföldy 2005, 32. To be fair, Alföldy 1991 is a brilliant example of the difference between approaching inscriptions and historical writing.

conclusion.[4] One might say that the ending of the civil wars is accentuated, but the good ending only makes sense as a counterbalance to the not so good, i.e. the civil war itself. The question is what is expected from the *Res Gestae*.

This article will look at approaches to the *Res Gestae* and will suggest that negative things are not left out, but used to stress the coming of a new and better age of universal peace. Had Augustus tried to deceive, he would have jeopardised his *res gestae*. Not to mention the negative sides of Octavian would be absurd; it is by addressing the negative aspects that justification becomes possible.[5]

A reconsideration of Heuss' article on the ideology of the *Res Gestae* will be used to exemplify this approach. According to Heuss, the inscription should be used in its entirety, not just for cherry-picking. Surprisingly, he does not think a connection between the chapters was important for Augustus. Chapter 28 is thus misplaced because the mentioning of colonies should not be part of the section on foreign politics.[6] This might seem rather unimportant, but that is far from the case. Heuss dismisses information instead of trying to find out why the information is in the chapter in question. This article will try to focus on the colonies of chapter 28 and the problem of why colonies are mentioned in this chapter; this will be the key to understanding that, apart from expansion and war, a subject of the *RG,* is the return to normality after civil war. In *RG* 3.3 foreign and civil wars are mentioned, as are indeed colonies; there is right from the outset a clear connection between civil war and colonies.

How to approach an inscription

As Bosworth argues in his article on apotheosis in the *Res Gestae*, it is a good start to accept that the conquest of the world is a primary theme.[7] The genre of the *Res Gestae* is a very different question, as are its purposes and multiple levels, not to mention the audiences of the

---

[4] Most clearly *RG* 3.1, 34.1

[5] Morgan 1999, 128: propaganda cannot or should not ignore the prevailing mood of the public. Similarly Johnson 1976, 7f.

[6] See also *RG* 3.3, 16.1 and Heuss 1975, 56-62.

[7] Bosworth 1999, 1. Similarly Nicolet 1991, 9, 74, who stresses it as a geographical survey and makes a connection to the map of Agrippa in the *Porticus Vipsania* (Plin. *HN* 3.17, Cass. Dio. 55.8.3-4). But why is the map not at or close to the Mausoleum of Augustus?

inscription or even inscriptions.[8] One model might be the traditional Roman *elogium*, but the scope and length of the *Res Gestae* make it so very different.[9] Because of its length and its use of first person, the inscription is best looked at as something unique.[10] Perhaps this is the reason that no other *princeps* in Rome "dared" to put up something similar.

Stating the obvious will perhaps clarify the discussion: it was a document written by Augustus, presented to the world as such,[11] and read in the Senate after his death. The documents kept by the Vestal Virgins, including the *Res Gestae*, were sealed, and the instructions were simple; the intention was to have the document, the *Res Gestae*, inscribed on bronze tablets in front of Augustus's mausoleum on the *Campus Martius*.[12] Suetonius mentions them as *tabulae*; they were set up *ante Mausoleum*, not on the building. There was also a document with instructions for his funeral; nothing was left to chance. This is the context Augustus chose for himself; the *Res Gestae* is an inscription, a fact too often overlooked by modern scholars who write as if the *Res Gestae* was a literary text. Unlike a literary text, an inscription is always part of a

---

[8] Yavetz 1984, 14-20, stressing the *iuventus* of Italy and Rome. This is supported by Millar 1988, 18, using the *Tabula Siarensis*. But why does the inscription not spell it out if the audience is a specific one? For multiple purposes see Bosworth 1999, 1.

[9] Regarding *elogia*, see Gagé 1950[2], 29. Nicolet 1991, 31-33 mentions the *elogium* of Pompeius Magnus as a possible model (Diod. Sic. 40.4, Plin. *HN* 7.97-8). The conquest of the world is a definitive connection, but the length is a difference and Pompeius' inscription is not written in the first person. According to Kraus 2005, 192, the *commentarii* of Caesar "serve the *Res Gestae* as ground text" She also refers the inscription back to the Hellenistic biographical tradition (191 n. 25), which misses the point that it is an inscription.

[10] Mommsen 1887a, 393; Syme 1939 (1952), 524. One theory tries to connect the *Forum Augustum* and the *Res Gestae*, see Frisch 1980, 93-98 and Luce 1990, esp. 127-128. Augustus in both instances wanted to stress that he has surpassed the *res gestae* of all great men in Roman history, but an ideological connection should also take into account the physical distance beween the monuments. For the *summi viri*, see Suet. *Aug.* 31.5. These *elogia* are also much shorter than the *Res Gestae*.

[11] Suet. *Aug.* 101.1-4; Cass. Dio 56.33.1.

[12] Suet. *Aug.* 101.4. Amm. Marc. 17.4.16 mentions two obelisks, perhaps Augustan or perhaps later, as they are not mentioned by Strabo and Pliny. Buchner, in a recent excavation, has found two bases, the level most likely being Augustan; thus there are four bases, and so the *Res Gestae* can have been placed *ante Mausoleum* with the obelisks placed close by as well. See Buchner 1996, 163-167; Rehak 2006, 62-95.

monument.[13] Millar points out that we ought to look up from our book and doing so, we would see the Mausoleum with the statue of Augustus. Millar concludes that nobody, in antiquity that is, would be clever enough to read it as a republican "document".[14] This is the ideology of Augustus; this is how he wanted to be perceived by posterity.[15] Elsner, in a more provocative manner, but rightly so, observes that Mussolini "grasped the essentially monumental quality of the *Res Gestae* as a text designed to be inscribed on or in front of buildings".[16] Mussolini inscribed the *Res Gestae* on the building containing the *Ara Pacis*, a building situated today by the mausoleum of Augustus. Thus one conclusion to be made already is the difference in audience between the document and the inscription, the document being Augustan and the inscription Tiberian, the inscription being set up in a garden open to the public, the document being read out only to the Senate.[17]

There is no reason to believe that the chapter divisions do not go back to the original inscription and Augustus' draft. Thus a reading of structure is possible.[18] Therefore, a theory about the *Res Gestae* should in principle be in agreement with all chapters of the inscription, but also with the historical and ideological context, and the surroundings on the northern parts of the *Campus Martius*.

The Augustan Peace altar is mentioned in *RG* 12. The next chapter mentions the closing of the temple of Janus, the honour after the victories of Antonius and Cleopatra that pleased Augustus the most.[19] The *Ara*

---

[13] Ramage 1987 and Ridley 2003 both ignore the context of the inscription. Rehak 2006 accepts that the context of the *Res Gestae* is the Mausoleum (54-58), but oddly sees a difference between the monarchical buildings of the *Campus Martius* and the "Republican" *Res Gestae* (8). Alföldy 1991, 292 stresses that an inscription always belongs to a monument. Similarly Woolf 1996, 28. The heading of the *Res Gestae* was, according to Gagé 1950[2], 9: *res gestae divi Augusti, quibus orbem terrarum imperio populi Romani subiecit, et impensae quas in rem publicam populumque Romanum fecit*. Volkmann 1969, 10; Ramage 1987, 13 both suggest there might be no "title." One problem is of course the deification in prescript, but that could easily have been changed after the deification itself. From Suet. *Aug.* 101 (on the will) and *Aug.* 50 Augustus emerges a pedant. He would hardly have forgotten a heading and at the same time not mention his name in the first line.
[14] Millar 1984, 58.
[15] *RG,* 8.4 does mention posterity. Similarly the *Senatus Consultum de Cn. Pisone Patre* 165-170 (*posterorum memoriae*).
[16] Elsner 1996, 34-35.
[17] Suet. *Aug.* 100.4, 101.
[18] See Brunt and Moore 1967, 2.
[19] Cass. Dio 51.20.4.

Pacis is put up later, but the inscription's chronology is relative. According to *RG* 13, the temple of Janus was closed *cum per totum imperium populi Romani terra marique esset parta victoriis pax* ("When victories had secured peace by land and sea throughout the whole empire of the Roman people"). Similar statements appear in Livy 1.19.3 on Actium and the inscription from the victory monument at Actium itself: Actium meant peace.[20]

The *Horologium* commemorates the capture of Egypt, as mentioned in the inscription on the base. The obelisk is of course Apollo's, Augustus' patron god and helper at Actium.[21] The mausoleum is best looked at in the context of 32 BC and the will of Antonius, with his wish to be buried in Alexandria next to Cleopatra. The Mausoleum in Rome is the perfect counterpart to Alexandria.[22] The field of Mars is turned into the field of peace, Augustus' peace after his victories. Importantly, the entrances of both the Mausoleum and the Augustan Peace Altar point inwards to the *Campus*, not to the *via Flaminia* or the Tiber.

According to Buchner the birthday of Augustus was central to the area and on the 23rd September a shadow from the obelisk would point to the centre of the Peace Altar. Sadly, this theory did not stand the test of time and a physicist from Tübingen.[23] However, Gabba observes how odd it is

---

[20] See Murray and Petsas 1989, 76. According to Rosenstein 2007, 232 the Romans did not use the term *pax* for reconciliation after civil war, but *concordia*. But in fact the term *concordia* is not used in the *Res Gestae*, civil war and peace are. To make no connection between the two in the inscription makes little sense.

[21] The dedication of the inscription reads "*Soli donum dedit*" (*CIL* VI 702; Taf.109.1), and also mentions *Aegypto in potestatem populi Romani redacta*, closely resembled in *RG* 27.1. Sol points to Apollo, see Champlin 2003, 114. For Apollo as divine helper at Actium see Verg. *Aen.* 8.704. On Apollo as the patron god of Octavian see Hekster and Rich 2006.

[22] Suet. *Aug.* 100.4 mentions that the structure was built in his sixth consulship: *sexto suo consulatu extruxerat.* Clearly it could not have been built in 28 BC, and Cass. Dio 53.30.5 even suggests it was not finished in 23 BC. 32 BC is by far the most likely candidate looking at context, even though no source mentions that year. The struggle with Antonius and his will mentioning his own future burial at Alexandria instead of Rome is mentioned by Cass. Dio 50.3.5 and Plut. *Vit. Ant.* 58.4. Octavian did choose to finish the tomb of Antonius and Cleopatra in Alexandria and allow them to be buried there (Suet. *Aug.* 17.4). For 32 BC see Kraft 1967 and Rehak 2006, 35-53.

[23] Buchner 1982 and 1988, 240-245. For the criticism see Schütz 1990, 432-457, comprehensively refuting the measurements of Buchner. Schütz 1990, 451 stresses that even if Buchner was correct, the shadow to pierce the *Ara Pacis* on the birthday of Augustus would have been invisible six meters from the monument. Buchner 1996, 161-168 has tried to hit back, but his theory seems tenuous. See

that Augustus mentions his own birth in *RG* 13; Roman history is divided into two parts and Augustus' birth is the turning point. This makes Augustus a godlike person, perhaps sent by the gods.[24] Earlier the birthday of Caesar had been celebrated in public and the fourth *Eclogue* of Virgil, the calendar of the province Asia, and the *fasti* of the Arvals tell the story of a period obsessed with birth.[25] According to Gradel the *Res Gestae* might be Augustus' argument, his *apologia*, for state divinity.[26] Perhaps the "proposition" did not come as a surprise for anybody: the victory in the war against Cleopatra and Antonius meant peace for Rome, all visible on the *Campus Martius* when the *Res Gestae* was inscribed as Augustus' last alteration to the area, a peace that was only possible with Augustus.

The Triumviral assignment

The inscription seems to have an introduction and a conclusion: chapters one and two, perhaps including chapter three and chapters 34 and 35. Ramage is right in stressing a chronological coherence, with the nineteen year old *privatus* who becomes *pater patriae*.[27]

Appian, trying to define the triumvirate, stresses that three men were in possession of all power in the *Res Publica*,[28] although he also observes they were given the powers of consuls.[29] This appears contradictory, but

---

also Rehak 2006, 62-95 and Barton 1995, especially 44-46 for criticism of Buchner.

[24] In the interpretation of Gabba 1995, 11-14. This bears resemblance to the idea of the Messiah. See Suet. *Aug.* 100.3, 94.3.

[25] Weinstock 1971, 211 on Caesar; Coleman 1977 on the fourth *Eclogue*; Degrassi 1963, 13.2, 512 on the *fasti* of the Arvals; and *EJ* 98 on the new calendar of Asia Minor based on Augustus' birthday (9 BC).

[26] Gradel 2002, 281. See also Weber 1936, 102-104.

[27] *RG* 1.1, 35.1; Ramage 1987, 19. According to Mommsen 1887b, V, the *Res Gestae* must be divided into three sections: *honores* (1-14), *impensae* (15-24) and *Res Gestae* proper (25 to the end). Hardy 1923: 14-18 stresses *RG* 1-3 as the introduction. Weber 1936: 150 makes chapters 1-2 stand out, together with 34-35 (217-224). Gagé 1950,[2] 13-16 on the triple division of the *Res Gestae* (*RG* 34-35 as conclusion). Yavetz 1984, 14-15 observes that we ought not to rigorously accept the three parts. According to Kornemann the *Res Gestae* is written in stages: *RG* 1-4 constitutes the "Urmonument" (1921, 28-40). The *Res Gestae* was begun 28 BC according to Kornemann (1921, III), perhaps because this is the year the Mausoleum was built according to Suetonius. This is difficult to determine, and the document seems to have been edited to a final version (See Gagé 1950, 16).

[28] App. *B Civ.* 5.1.

[29] App. *B Civ.* 4.7.

the reason for this difference is with all probability that the triumvirs were trying to avoid the title of dictator.[30] There is a difference between the formal vote, the *Lex Titia*, and "Realpolitik". Importantly, the purpose of the new magistracy was to constitute the *Res Publica* and end the civil wars, thus also avending Caesar.[31]

According to Mommsen, the renewed triumvirate was extended to the end of 33 BC, but it did not expire until given up by its holders, and in the end this was done by Octavian on 13 January 27 BC.[32] This view was challenged by Kromayer as early as 1888: the triumvirate did lapse in 33 BC and that was the end of it. Thus 32 BC constitutes a *coup d'état*.[33] Similarly to Mommsen, Fadinger suggests that Octavian was not a triumvir in 32 BC, but was still in possession of the triumviral *potestas*. What is given back in 27 BC is the triumviral *potestas* as observed by Mommsen.[34]

That the triumvirs at various points did speak of laying down the triumviral powers suggests that the triumvirate did not lapse automatically.[35] But again, the main problem is the *Res Gestae* itself: Why would Augustus say that he was triumvir for 10 years if this was not so? Fadinger is thus most likely right.

---

[30] App. *B Civ*. 4.2; Cass. Dio 46.55.3.

[31] Avenging Caesar, see App. *B Civ*. 4.8f. and Cass. Dio 46.56.1ff. On the termination of the civil wars, see App. *B Civ*. 4.2. Both factors are to be found in Cass. Dio 53.4.4. Reynolds 1982, n. 9 line 12 and n. 8 line 80, may point to the triumvirs being conceived as promagistrates, not magistrates, and thus contradictory to App. *B Civ*. 4.2.7. But, as pointed out by Rich 1992, 113, we cannot be certain that their powers in respect to the provinces were proconsular.

[32] Mommsen 1887b, 702-742, especially 718-719. This idea has found support; see Girardet 1990, 324 n. 4 on the German scholarship. See also Brunt and Moore 1967, 48-49 and Rich 1992, 114. The triumvirate, instituted 27 November 43 BC, did initially terminate at the end of 38 BC (*EJ* 32). It was renewed for 5 years at the meeting at Tarentum in the autumn 37 BC (App. *B Civ*. 5.95, Cass. Dio 48.54.6). The terminal date is thus the end of 33 BC. This is favoured by Augustus in *RG* 7.1. See also Suet. *Aug*. 27.1. Livy *Per*. 132 may stress the same, but is problematic. App. *Ill*. 28.80 states that the triumvirate ended 32 BC. Even if a conclusion is uncertain because of the sources, Augustus in the *Res Gestae* did state that he was a triumvir for ten years.

[33] Kromayer 1888, 2-21, stating that the triumvirate did lapse in 32 BC (9), and thus the actions of Octavian in 32 BC equal a "Staatsstreich" (15). It was not the triumviral powers given back in 27 BC (11f). Similarly Syme 1939 (1952), 225, 270-1.

[34] Fadinger 1969, especially 143-145.

[35] App. *B Civ*. 5.73, 132; Cass. Dio 49.41.6, 50.7.1, Livy *Per*. 132.

In *RG* 1, the tyranny of a faction turns a coup into something legitimate. Ridley comments on this in a chapter called "Lies", but in fact Augustus does explain that he was a *privatus* who raised an army, and then goes on to give his view of why this was acceptable. The obverse legend *Libertatis P R Vindex* on a cistophorus from 28 BC, whose reverse commemorates *pax*, and the *corona obsidionalis*, a military distinction given to Octavian for saving the community, point to the defence of the liberty of the Roman people. This is close to *RG* 1.1, and the justification is the same as later with the triumvirate: Augustus did what he did to save the *Res Publica*. All this material must be seen in relation to the war against Antonius and Cleopatra.[36]

RG 2 reads:

Qui parentem meum trucidaverunt, eos in exilium expuli iudiciis legitimis ultus eorum facinus, et postea bellum inferentis rei publicae vici bis acie.

I drove into exile the murderers of my father, avenging their crime through tribunals established by law; and afterwards, when they made war on the republic, I twice defeated them in battle.

RG 3.1 constitutes in many ways a small conclusion to the inscription right at the outset. It reads:

Bella terra et mari civilia externaque toto in orbe terrarum saepe gessi...

I undertook many civil and foreign wars by land and sea throughout the world...

This is very close to *RG* 13 and the slogan of peace through victory. And in *RG* 34, the conclusion of the *Res Gestae*, the ending of the civil wars appears prominently.

RG 34.1 reads:

In consulatu sexto et septimo, postquam bella civilia extinxeram, per consensum universorum potens rerum omnium...

In my sixth and seventh consulship, after I had extinguished civil wars, and at a time when with universal consent I was in complete control of affairs...

---

[36] Rich and Williams 1999, 184-185. *Libertatis P R Vindex,* Cistophori, see *RIC* 1² 476. *Corona obsidionalis*, Plin. *HN* 22.13 and Cass. Dio 51.19.5.

The *Res Gestae* does seem to reveal itself as Augustus' "commentaries" on the civil wars. The triumvirate is only very loosely defined in *RG* 1.4, but taken together with chapter two and 34 a picture emerges: Caesar is avenged in chapter two, and the civil war ended in chapter 34. *RG* 2 constitutes a partial success in the constituting of the *Res Publica*. This is very close to the information given by especially Appian (*B Civ.* 4.2).

The civil wars

The question that remains unanswered is whether Actium, the turning point in history, was a civil or a foreign war? But again, let us begin by stating the obvious: *RG* 27.1 stresses *Aegyptum imperio populi Romani adieci* ("I added Egypt to the empire of the Roman people"). The victory over Egypt and Cleopatra cannot constitute the ending of the civil wars as mentioned in *RG* 34, at least not on its own.

RG 25.2 reads:

> *Iuravit in mea verba tota Italia sponte sua, et me belli quo vici ad Actium ducem depoposcit.*

> The whole of Italy of its own free will swore allegiance to me and demanded me as leader in the war in which I was victorious at Actium.

Next is chapter 24, which reads:

> *In templis omnium civitatium provinciae Asiae victor ornamenta reposui quae spoliatis templis is cum quo bellum gesseram privatim possederat.*

> After my victory, I replaced in the temples of all the cities of the province of Asia the ornaments which my late adversary, after despoiling the temples, had taken into his private possession.

Ridley in his recent book on the *Res Gestae*, discussing *RG* 24.1 and *is cum quo bellum gesseram*, writes: "He has revealed the gender of his real opponent in a civil war and thus undone years of official propaganda." The opponent is a man.[37] To believe this was unintentional is very odd indeed and very negative in its approach. One might ask a different question: why

---

[37] Ridley 2003, 125 for the quotation. Ridley looks at "omissions", "defensible statements", and "lies". The assumption seems to be that we can judge the *Res Gestae*, not a piece of historical writing, by modern historical standards alone.

did Augustus mention the civil war in the *Res Gestae*, even when implicit as here. This might indeed be what makes the inscription truly unique.

The chapter is datable since it begins with "after my victory", the context showing it most likely to be Actium. It might relate to his return from Asia in 30/29 BC, but the victory must surely refer to Actium. The wrongs of Antonius, the unmentioned adversary, are made right by Octavian, returning temple ornaments to their rightful owners. And Augustus mentions that he had statues of himself in Rome melted down and put the money gained to use, by giving golden offerings to Apollo, the patron god of Octavian and helper at Actium. This is a counterbalance to Antonius' wrongdoing, not about Asia Minor.[38]

This is the last chapter of the *impensae* section of the inscription; the first chapter of the *Res Gestae* proper on wars is *RG* 25, mentioning Actium.[39] The civil war is not mentioned in this chapter because of the triumph of 29 BC, a triumph is in principle not possible after civil war.[40] The adversary in *RG* 24 is the same as in *RG* 25 and again not mentioned; the adversary is Antonius.

The subject here is "*damnatio memoriae*", or perhaps more correctly, the omission of the name of Antonius; of course none of the enemies of Augustus are mentioned in the *Res Gestae*, but the fact remains that the recipients must have suspected Antonius and this was the point. The ideas put forward by Hedrick regarding the Late Roman Empire can be used for the Augustan age as well: Antonius was not mentioned by name, not to forget him, but to dishonour him.[41] Why would Augustus stress Antonius so often in the *Res Gestae* if he was trying to make everybody forget him?[42] The result of the "*damnatio memoriae*" is clearly visible in other sources where Antonius is not mentioned by name. This seems later to have changed partly, for Antonius is mentioned in book eight of the *Aeneid* (685).

---

[38] According to Elsner 1996, 35 the text was exported, but nothing suggests involvement from Augustus. Alföldy 2003, 7 observes that all three copies are from one and the same province, which suggests the involvement of the provincial governor. The appendix would have been odd as a postscript after the conclusion. The appendix stresses the provinces more than the main text, and importantly, the total of expenses in section 1 is not given in sesterces as in the *Res Gestae*, but in *denarii*. See Brunt and Moore 1967, 80-81.

[39] *RG* 25.2.

[40] Val. Max. 2.8.7, Cic. *Phil*. 14.22f.

[41] Hedrick 2000, chapter 4, especially 114. For the more traditional view of '*damnatio memoriae*', a very flexible concept, see Vittinghoff 1936 and Flower 2006.

[42] *RG* 1.1.

Returning to the powers of the triumvirate, the inscription may reveal even more. Augustus in *RG* 34.1 describes his own powers in 28-27 BC as *potens rerum omnium* ("I was in possession of all things").[43] As mentioned above, the likely scenario is the continuation and retention of the triumviral *potestas*, but detached from the magistrate itself.[44] All the powers in the *Res Publica* cannot be explained within the powers of the consul. The termination of the triumvirate is the end of 33 BC; *RG* 7.1 states *triumvir per continuos annos decem*. Octavian was not triumvir in the year 32 BC.

One way of saving the legitimacy of Octavian in 32 BC has been put forward by some scholars, as part of a trend to normalise the triumvirate: the triumvirs only retained powers in the provinces, i.e. as proconsuls.[45] During a senate meeting in early 32 BC Octavian did in fact sit between the consuls,[46] but it is believed the meeting was outside the *pomerium*. But the proconsuls were not allowed to sit between the consuls, and the triumvirate would hardly have degraded into a proconsulate.[47] One might add that the powers of a proconsul cannot be spoken of as *potens rerum omnium* either.[48]

Potens rerum omnium clearly focuses on Octavian's position prior to the surrender of these powers in 28-27 BC and not 32 BC, but since no decision is known giving Octavian all powers in the state, this most likely

---

[43] Botteri 2003, 264 has found a new fragment of the *Res Gestae*. This fragment from Antiochia shows that *potens* is the correct reading of *RG* 34.1, not *potitus*. See also Drew-Bear and Scheid 2005, esp. 233-236. Lebek 2004, 60 points out that the idea of *potens* goes back to Kassel. See Krömer 1978, 135 for this. See Lebek for scholarship on the issue. The reading *per consensum universorum* [*potitus rerum omn*]*ium* goes back to Mommsen 1883. See also Ramsey and von Premerstein 1927, 95 and Tab.XIV, with a fragment containing the letters M and OM. On the vast amount of scholarship on *RG* 34, see Ramage 1987, 154-157.

[44] Regarding the period between 32 BC and 27 BC see Fadinger 1969, 144, 302f. Fadinger also observes that it is impossible to see any difference in relation to Octavian's powers between the year 33 BC and 32 BC (137).

[45] Girardet 1990, esp. 338-342; 1995, 151; Lewis 1991, esp. 61; and Bleicken 1990, 38-39 and 57-62. On normality, see Gruen 1974; Millar 1973 and 1998. Ungern-Sternberg, 2004, in a German approach to the question, stresses the normality, but defines this as a question of a "crises without an alternative" quoting Meier's *Res publica amissa* (1997). According to Ungern-Sternberg, the main participants did not propose a different constitution (106).

[46] Cass. Dio 50.2.

[47] Rich 1992, 114; Millar 1973, 59.

[48] *RG* 34.1.

happened after the victory over Antonius. There is no new command in
RG 25 or in our external sources.

The oath of allegiance to Octavian in the year 32 BC is best seen as
some kind of political justification. In the *Res Gestae* Augustus does not
set out to describe his powers and positions in constitutional terms. This is
also the reason for relating that more than seven hundred senators served
under him during the battle of Actium.[49] This oath leads to *per consensum
universorum potens rerum omnium*.[50] The consensus justified the fact that
Octavian was still in possession of the triumviral powers; it justified him
fighting for the *Res Publica* against the enemies Cleopatra and Antonius.[51]
This is similar to the way in which the two triumvirs divided the *potestas*
of Lepidus in 36 BC; Octavian now was in complete possession of all
powers in the *Res Publica* because he had defeated Antonius in battle.[52]
The powers that had been shared between the triumvirs devolved to
Octavian, which made him in effect *potens rerum omnium*.

That Octavian was fighting for the *Res Publica* is visible in the
external sources as well. Part of the inscription of Octavian's victory
monument at Actium reads:

> *vacat Imp · Caesa]r · Div[i · Iuli ·]f · vict[oriam · consecutus · bell]o ·
> quod · pro [·r]e[·]p[u]blic[a] · ges[si]t · in · hac · region[e]*

> Imperator Caesar, son of the Divine Julius, following the victory in the war
> which he waged on behalf of the *res publica* in this region...[53]

"*Pro republica*" does seem to point in the same direction as *RG* 2. This
is also close to "*re publica conservata*" on an inscription firmly dated to
29 BC, found in the Forum Romanum, and most likely to have come from
the Actian arch. Similarly, the 1st Augustus 30 BC, the day of the capture
of Alexandria, was *feriae* because Octavian "freed the res publica from
very grave danger" (*rem publicam tristissimo periculo liberavit*).[54]

---

[49] *RG* 25.

[50] *RG* 34.1.

[51] Von Premerstein 1937, 60ff; Fadinger 1969, 315-332; Kienast 1999, 67-69.

[52] App. *B Civ.* 5.1. Mommsen 1996 (German ed. 1992), 91; Fadinger 1969, 296ff.

[53] See Murray and Petsas 1989, 76, 86 for translation. For the inscription in general
see Zachos 2003, 76, who has found a new block with the letters TI · NEP and thus
likely restored as [*MAR*]*TI · NEPTUNO* [*QUE*]. Mars thus needs to be placed
before Neptune. The traditional reading goes back to Suet. *Aug.* 18.2: "*Neptuno ac
Marti*".

[54] Rich 1998, 100-114 and Rich and Williams 1999, 184-185 on the inscription (*EJ*
17) and the arch. For the first August see *EJ*, 49.

The triumvirate had indeed constituted the *Res Publica*. *RG* 34 constitutes the giving back of the powers of the triumvirate to the *Res Publica*. The assignment had been accomplished successfully, the civil war was terminated.

Conquering the world and fighting a war at home

According to Gruen "The *Res Gestae* places emphasis not on peace but on pacification."[55] He stresses foreign, not civil wars. The heading of the inscription states beautifully:

> *Rerum gestarum divi Augusti, quibus orbem terrarum imperio populi Romani subiecit.*

> The achievements of the Divine Augustus, by which he brought the world under the empire of the Roman people.

However, Weinstock demonstrated many years ago that the peace of the Augustan era was not only a question of expansion, but also a question of civil war: *pax* is both internal and external.[56] Dio comes closest of the sources to understanding the context of Actium and the war against Antonius and Cleopatra, stating that the war was declared on Cleopatra, in reality of course, against Antonius.[57] There was going to be a civil war, the question was who was going to start it. In the end Antonius and Cleopatra did, moving their troops close to Italy (Actium and Patras); when Antonius in the end did help Cleopatra at Actium, he became automatically an enemy of Rome. He started the civil war.

As shown in this paper, the triumviral assignment, including the civil war, is the setting in the preface and conclusion of the *Res Gestae*. Moreover, these parameters are found in the three opening chapters of the main sections of the *Res Gestae* (*RG* 3, 15, and 25), *honores* (*RG* 3-14), *impensae* (*RG* 15-24), and *Res Gestae* proper (*RG* 25-33): *RG* 3 on the civil wars, *RG* 15 on the giving of money to the poor in Rome in accordance with the will of Caesar, and *RG* 25 on Naulochus and Actium. Similarly for the closing chapters: *RG* 24 as already mentioned, *RG* 33

---

[55] Gruen 1985, 54; see also Syme 1989, 116.
[56] Weinstock 1960, 45. On *pax* and victory, see Rich 2003. The blurring of civil and foreign war is obvious in Verg. *Aen.* 8.685ff,, which mentions both Antonius and Cleopatra as the enemies. According to DeBrohun 2007, 256, the Romans made a clear distinction between foreign and civil war. This is clearly wrong.
[57] Cass. Dio 50.4.5.

focuses on the fruits of peace, with *RG* 14.1 mentioning Gaius and Lucius as the possible exception. Even if the traditionally perceived tripartite structure of the inscription should be dismissed as too rigid, it is still necessary to explain why specific things are mentioned and in what context.[58]

It is time to return to Heuss and the misplaced chapter 28, time to put it into context. Reading the section *Res Gestae* proper (*RG* 25-33), an alternative possibility appears, one of universal peace and the return to normality after civil war. *RG* 25 concerns the justification of the war against Sextus Pompeius and Actium. Chapter 26 is about the expansion of the Roman Empire without waging an unjust war. The information is specifically about the war in the Alps, but the implications are general for all Augustus' wars. The result, or one of them, is the victory over Egypt (*RG* 27) and the death of Cleopatra and Antonius. Therefore, the context of the inscription only allows one conclusion, namely that Octavian's participation in the civil wars (*RG* 34) was justified: the civil war began with Antonius helping Cleopatra. Chapter 29 is concerned with the regaining of the lost standards and the claiming of victory over the Parthians. *RG* 30 mentions what happened when Augustus was *princeps*. The implicit message is clear: these victories would not have been possible without his person. The chapters 31 to 33 are about the *Imperium Romanum* as the centre of the *oikoumene*. This is truly a list of the positive consequences of the termination of the civil wars with the Roman Empire assuming its rightful place in the world. Once his ending of the civil wars had been celebrated as the establishment of universal peace, Augustus then moved on to an explicit programme of pacification, inaugurated in 27 BC. Again we have a blurring of civil and foreign war.[59]

In *RG* 28 the context of the colonies must briefly be explained. The major programmes of colony foundation took place not only immediately after Actium, but also in 14 BC (*RG* 16.1). Some of them were founded to settle the veterans recruited for the Actium war, but this was later followed up with new military service regulations on his return in 13 BC.[60] By these means he sought finally to banish the spectre of the army in politics by recruiting soldiers on the basis that on discharge they would be given not land, but cash to set themselves up on land they would purchase themselves. It was most likely no accident that these regulations were

---

[58] Dr Alison Cooley kindly brought my attention to the possibility that the traditional tripartite structure might be too rigid. But even so, it remains a useful starting point for understanding context.

[59] See Rich 2003 on the pacification after 27 BC.

[60] Cass. Dio 54.25; Brunt 1971, 332ff.

promulgated at the same time as the decision was taken to found the Altar of *Pax Augusta*. So the second wave of colonies and the ensuing military regulations completed outstanding civil war business.

Chapter 28 thus becomes part of the ending of the civil wars: when wars are won and peace secured, the legionaries are sent to colonies. This is a symbol of peace and the return to normality. Heuss is clearly wrong; the chapter is not misplaced. Of course the *Res Gestae* is about conquering the world, but there is more to it. That both the introduction and the conclusion are so blatantly referring to the civil war is a surprise. Instead of criticising Augustus for omitting the negative sides of his reign, scholars ought to be positively surprised that he did not do so, at least not entirely. The *Res Gestae* is after all not history writing, and ought not to be approached as such. It is a monumental inscription and its main focus is Augustus and what he did for the *Res Publica*, as told by himself.

Bibliography

Alföldy, G. "Augustus und die Inschriften: Tradition und Innovation. Die Geburt der imperialen Epigraphik." *Gymnasium* 98 (1991): 289-324.

—. "Die Rapräsentation der kaiserlichen Macht in den Inschriften Roms und des Imperium Romanum." In *The Representation and Perception of Roman Imperial Power. Proceedings of the Third Workshop of the International Network Impact of Empire (Roman Empire, c. 200 B.C.-A.D. 476,* edited by L. De Blois *et al.*, 3-19, Amsterdam: Brill, 2003.

—. "Inschriften und Biographie in der römischen Welt." In *Biographie und Prosopographie. Internationales Kolloquium zum 65. Geburtstags von Anthony R. Birley,* edited by K. Vössing, 29-52. Stuttgart: Franz Steiner Verlag, 2005.

Barton, T. "Augustus and Capricorn: Astrological Polyvalency and Imperial Rhetoric." *JRS* 85 (1995): 33-51.

Bleicken, J. *Zwischen Republik und Prinzipat. Zum Charakter des Zweiten Triumvirats.* Göttingen: Vandenhoech & Ruprecht, 1990.

Bosworth, B. "Augustus, the *Res Gestae* and Hellenistic Theories of Apotheosis." *JRS* 89 (1999): 1-18.

Botteri, P. "L'Integrazione Mommseniana a *Res Gestae* Divi Augusti 34,1 "Potitus Rerum Omnium" e il Testo Greco." *ZPE* 144 (2003): 261-267.

Brunt, P. A. *Italian Manpower 225 B.C. - A.D. 14,* Oxford: Oxford University Press, 1971.

Brunt, P. A. and Moore, J. M. *Res Gestae Divi Augusti. The Achievements of the Divine Augustus.* Oxford: Oxford University Press, 1967.

Buchner, E. *Die Sonnenuhr des Augustus. Nachdruck aus RM 1976 und 1980 und Nachwort über die Ausgrabung 1980/81*, Mainz am Rhein: Verlag Philipp von Zabern, 1982.

—. "Horologium solarium Augusti." In *Kaiser Augustus und die Verlorene Republik*, edited by E. La Rocca *et al.*, 240-245. Mainz am Rhein: Verlag Philipp von Zabern, 1988

—. "Ein Kanal für Obelisken. Neues vom Maosoleum des Augustus in Rom," *Antike Welt* 27.3 (1996): 161-168.

Champlin, E.. *Nero*. Cambridge (MA) and London: The Belknap Press of Harvard University Press, 2003.

Coleman, R. *Vergil Eclogues*, Cambridge: Cambridge University Press, 1977.

DeBrohun, J. B. "The Gates of War (and Peace): Roman Literary perspectives." In *War and Peace in the Ancient World*, edited by K. A. Raaflaub, 256-278. Oxford: Blackwell, 2007.

Degrassi, A. *Fasti anni Numani et Iuliani, Inscriptiones Italiae 13.2.* Rome: Istituto Poligrafico dello Stato, 1963.

Drew-Bear, T. and Scheid, J. "La Copie Des *Res Gestae* D'Antioche De Pisidie," *ZPE* 154 (2005): 217-260.

Eder, W. "Augustus and the Power of Tradition: The Augustan Principate as Binding Link between Republic and Empire." In *Between Republic and Empire. Interpretations of Augustus and His Principate*, edited by K. A. Raaflaub and M. Toher, 71-122. Berkeley, Los Angeles and London: University of California Press, 1990.

Ehrenberg, V. and Jones, A. H. M. *Documents illustrating the Reigns of Augustus and Tiberius.*[2] Oxford: Oxford University Press, 1955.

Elsner, J. "Inventing Imperium: Texts and the propaganda of monuments in Augustan Rome." In *Art and Text in Roman Culture*, edited by J. Elsner, 32-53. Cambridge: Cambridge University Press, 1996.

Erskine-Hill, H. *The Augustan Idea in English Literature*. London: Edward Arnold, 1983.

Fadinger, V. *Die Begründung des Prinzipats. Quellenkritische und staatsrechtliche Untersuchungen zu Cassius Dio und der Parallelüberlieferung.* Berlin: Rudolf Habelt Verlag, 1969.

Flower, H. *The Art of Fogetting. Disgrace and Oblivion in Roman Political Culture*. Chapel Hill: The University of North Carolina Press, 2006.

Frisch, P. "Zu den Elogien des Augustusforums." *ZPE* 39 (1980): 91-98.

Gabba, E. "Riflessione sul Cap. 13 della *Res Gestae* Divi Augusti." *In Leaders and Masses in the Roman World. Studies in honour of Zvi*

Yavetz, edited by I. Malkin and Z. W. Rubinsohn, 11-14. Leiden: Brill, 1995

Gagé, J. *Res Gestae Divi Augusti.*[2] Paris: Belles Lettres, 1950.

Girardet, K. "Der Rechtsstatus Oktavians im Jahre 32 V.Chr." *RhM* 133.1 (1990): 322-350.

—. "Per continuos annos decem (res gestae divi Augusti 7,1). Zu Frage nach dem Endtermin des Triumvirats." *Chiron* 25 (1995): 147-161.

Gradel, I. *Emperor Worship and Roman Religion*. Oxford: Oxford University Press, 2002.

Gruen, E. S. *The Last Generation of the Roman Republic*. Berkeley, Los Angeles and London: University of California Press, 1974.

—. "Augustus and the Ideology of War and Peace." In *The Age of Augustus*, edited by R. Winkes, 51-72. Louvain-la-Neuve: Art and Archaeology Publications, Collège Erasme 1985:

Hardy, E. G. *The Monumentum Ancyranum*. Oxford: Oxford University Press,1923.

Hedrick Jr., C. W. *History and Silence. Purge and Rehabilitation of Memory in Late Antiquity*. Austin; University of Texas Press, 2000.

Hekster, O. and Rich, J. "Octavian and the Thunderbolt: The temple of Apollo Palatinus and Roman Traditions of Temple Building," *CQ* 56.1 (2006): 149-168.

Heuss, A. "Zeitgeschichte als Ideologie. Bemerkungen zu Komposition und Gedankenführung der *Res Gestae* Divi Augusti." *Monumentum Chiloniense. Studien zur augusteischen Zeit. Kieler Festschrift für E. Burck zum 70. Geburtstag*, edited by E. Lefévre, 55-95. Amsterdam: Adolf M. Hakkert, 1975.

Johnson, J. R. *Augustan Propaganda: The Battle of Actium, Mark Antony's Will, the Fasti Capitolini Consulares, and Early Imperial Historiography*, Ph.D. diss., University of California, Los Angeles, 1976.

Jones, A. H. M. *Augustus.*[2] London: Chatto and Windus, 1977.

Kienast, D. *Augustus. Princeps und Monarch.*[2] Darmstadt: Wissenschaftliche Buchgesellschaft, 1999.

Kornemann, E. *Mausoleum und Tatanbericht des Augustus*. Leipzig: Teubner, 1921.

Kraft, K. "Der Sinn des Mausoleums des Augustus." *Historia* 16 (1967): 189-206.

Kraus, C. S. "From Exempla to Exemplar? Writing History around the Emperor in Imperial Rome." In *Flavius Josephus and Flavian Rome*, edited by J. Edmondson, 181-200, Oxford: Oxford University Press, 2005.

Kromayer, J. *Die Rechtliche Begründung des Principats*. Marburg: R. Friedrich, 1888.

Krömer, D. "Textkritisches zu Augustus und Tiberius (*Res Gestae* c. 34-Tac. ann. 6,30,3)," *ZPE* 28 (1978): 127-144.

Lebek, W. D. "*Res Gestae* Divi Augusti 34,1: Rudolf Kassels Potens Rerum Omnium und ein Neues Fragment des Monumentum Antiochenum." *ZPE* 146 (2004): 60.

Lewis, R. G. "Rechtsfrage II: Octavian's powers in 32 BC." *LCM* 16.4 (1991): 57-62.

Luce, T. J. "Livy, Augustus and the Forum Augustum." In *Between Republic and Empire. Interpretations of Augustus and his Principate*, edited by K. A. Raaflaub and M. Toher, 123-138. Berkeley, Los Angeles and London: University of California Press, 1990.

Meier, C. *Res publica amissa. Eine Studie zu Verfassung und geschichte der späten römischen Republik.*[3] Frankfurt am Main: Suhrkamp Verlag, 1997.

Millar, F. "Triumvirate and Principate." *JRS* 63 (1973): 50-67.

—. "State and Subject: The Impact of Monarchy." In *Caesar Augustus. Seven Aspects*, edited by F. Millar and E. Segal, 37-60.Oxford: Oxford University Press, 1984.

—. "Imperial Ideology in the Tabula Siarensis." In *Estudios sobre la Tabula Siarensis*, edited by J. Gonzales and J. Arce, 11-19. Madrid: Consejo Superior de Investigaciones Cientificas, Centro de Estudios Historicos, 1988.

—. *The Crowd in Rome in the Late Republic*, Ann Arbor: The University of Michigan Press, 1998.

Mommsen, T. *Res gestae divi Augusti. ex monumentis ancyrano et apolloniensi.*[2] Berlin: Weidmann, 1883.

—.1887a: "Der Rechenschaftsbericht der Augustus." *HZ* 57 (1887): 385-397.

—. 1887b: *Römisches Staatsrecht.*[3] Leipzig; Hirzel, 1887.

—. *A History of Rome under the Emperors*. London: Routledge, 1996.

Morgan, L. (1999) *Patterns of Redemption in Virgil's 'Georgics.'* Cambridge: Cambridge University Press, 1999.

Murray, W. M. and P. M. Petsas. *Octavian's Campsite Memorial for the Actian War'* Philadelphia: The American Philosophical Society, 1989.

Nicolet, C. *Space, Geography, and Politics in the Early Roman Empire*. Ann Arbor: University of Michigan Press, 1991.

Osgood, J. *Caesar's Legacy. Civil War and the Emergence of the Roman Empire*. Cambridge: Cambridge University Press, 2006.

von Premerstein, A. *Vom Werden und Wesen des Prinzipats.* Munich: Verlag der Bayerischen Akademie der Wissenschaften, 1937.

Ramage, E. S. *The Nature and Purpose of Augustus' "Res Gestae."* Stuttgart: Franz Steiner Verlag, 1987.

Ramsey, W. M. and von Premerstein, A. *Monumentum Antiochenum. Die Neugefundene Aufzeichnung der Res Gestae Divi Augusti im Pisidischen Antiochia.* Weisbaden: Klio. Beiträge zur alten Geschichte, 1927.

Rehak, P. (Edited by Younger, J.G.) *Imperium and Cosmos. Augustus and the Northern Campus Martius,* Madison: University of Wisconsin Press, 2006.

Reynolds, J. *Aphrodisias and Rome.* London: Journal of Roman Studies Monographs, 1982.

Rich, J. W. "The Second triumvirate. Review of Jochen Bleicken." *CR* 42 (1992): 112-114.

—."Augustus's Parthian Honours, the Temple of Mars Ultor and the Arch in the Forum Romanum." *PBSR* 66 (1998): 71-128.

—. "Augustus, War and Peace." In *The Representation and Perception of Roman Imperial Power. Proceedings of the Third International Network Impact of Empire (Roman Empire, c. 200 B.C.-A.D. 476),* edited by L. De Blois *et al.*, 329-357. Amsterdam: Brill, 2003.

Rich, J. W. and J. H. C. Williams. "Leges et Iura P.R. Restituit: A New Aureus of Octavian and the Settlement of 28-27 BC." *NC* 159 (1999): 169-213.

Ridley, R. *The Emperor's Retrospect. Augustus' Res Gestae in Epigraphy, Historiography and Commentary.* Leuven; Peeters Publishers, 2003.

Rosenstein, N. "War and Peace, Fear and Reconciliation at Rome." In *War and Peace in the Ancient World,* edited by K. A. Raaflaub, 226-244. Oxford: Blackwell, 2007.

Schütz, M. "Zur Sonnenuhr des Augustus auf dem Marsfeld." *Gymnasium* 97 (1990): 432-457.

Syme, R. *The Roman Revolution,* Oxford: Oxford University Press. 1939; 1952.

—. "Janus and Parthia in Horace." In *Studies in Latin Literature and its Tradition in Honour of C. O. Brink,* edited by J. Diggle *et al.*, 113-124. Cambridge: Cambridge University Press, 1989.

Ungern-Sternberg, J. "The Crisis of the Republic." In *The Cambridge Companion to The Late Republic,* edited by H. Flower, 89-109. Cambridge: Cambridge University Press, 2004.

Vittinghoff, F. *Der Staatsfeind in der römischen Kaiserzeit: Untersuchungen zur "damnatio memoriae."* Berlin: Junker und Dünnhaupt, 1936.

Volkmann, H. *Res Gestae Divi Augusti. Das Monumentum Ancyranum.* Berlin; Verlag Walter de Gruyter und Co, 1969.

Weber, W. *Princeps. Studien zur Geschichte des Augustus, Band 1.* Stuttgart and Berlin: Verlag W. Kohlhammer, 1936.

Weinstock, S. "Pax and the '*Ara Pacis.*' " *JRS* 50 (1960): 44-58.

—. *Divus Julius*, Oxford; Oxford University Press, 1971.

Woolf, G. "Monumental Writing and the Expansion of Roman Society in the Early Empire." *JRS* 86 (1996): 22-39.

Yavetz, Z. "The *Res Gestae* and Augustus' Public Image." In *Caesar Augustus. Seven Aspects*, edited by F. Millar and E. Segal, 1-36. Oxford; Oxford University Press, 1984.

Zachos, K. "The tropaeum of the sea-battle of Actium at Niko*polis*: interim report." *JRA* 16 (2003): 65-92.

CHAPTER ELEVEN

THE FRUITS OF VICTORY: GENERALS, PLANTS, AND POWER IN THE ROMAN WORLD

ELIZABETH MACAULAY-LEWIS

We tend to think of symbols of victory as being permanent, man-made structures or spaces. Trajan's column, the Arch of Septimius Severus, and the *Forum Augustum* all celebrate the achievements of successful generals and emperors. In late Republican Rome, victorious generals began to construct public complexes—often parks or gardens enclosed by porticos—*ex manubiis*, as a means for celebrating their deeds and promoting their political ambitions.[1] While scholars have acknowledged the creation of politically and ideologically charged gardens in Rome,[2] little work has been done on the political importance of *flora*. If gardens were politicized, could their plants also be political? This paper explores the use of plants by Pompey in his triumph and the use of the balsam and palm by Vespasian and Titus as political symbols of military victories and as economic booty in order to understand whether plants were important political tools in the late Republic and early Empire.

Origins in ancient Egypt, the ancient Near East, Alexandria and the Hellenistic world

The connections between plants, displays of power, and kings are as old as civilization itself. Many Egyptian and Near Eastern rulers imported and displayed exotic *flora* as a means of displaying wealth or control of

---

[1] On the *Porticus Pompei/Pompeiana*, see Gleason 1994; Kuttner 1999; Gros 1999,148-149. On the Mausoleum of Augustus, See Rehak 2006; Zanker 1998, 135-156; Davies 2004. On the Porticus Metelli, see Viscogliosi 1999a, 130-132; on the *Porticus Octavia*, see Viscogliosi 1999b, 139-141.

[2] Gleason 1994; Kuttner 1999.

distant lands.[3] Hatshepsut sent an expedition to the mythical land of Punt; the expedition returned with incense trees.[4] After her, Egyptian rulers imported exotic plants from Punt. The Queen of Sheba famously visited King David and brought with her myrrh and frankincense.[5] While these examples are not overtly militaristic, they highlight the political and economic power of plants. The ability to possess expensive plants was a testament to the power of a ruler. In ancient Persia and the Hellenistic world, these connections between plants, gardens, generals and kings continued.[6] In ancient Persia, plants often served as a form of tribute, and attacks on gardens became a way to rebel against a hated ruler or to demonstrate a military victory.[7] Alexander the Great also took an active interest in botany, allowing botanists and naturalists to accompany his army. They recorded a staggering number of plants new to the West.[8] It seems highly likely that the army returned with specimen plants, which may have been intended for Alexander's royal palace complex in Alexandria and for Aristotle's garden in Athens. Thus, long before the Romans, specific plants served as symbols of victory and had economic value.

Politics and plants in Rome

Rome had a long garden tradition;[9] however, the return of Roman generals from the East with incredible wealth in the late second century BC resulted in the establishment of the first monumental public and private gardens in Rome. These generals, such as Scipio Africanus, established luxurious villa estates with elaborate gardens on the Bay of Naples.[10] Under Pompey the Great and the other generals of the late Republic, plants and gardens were transformed into political tools and expressions of power. As the competition for power intensified in Rome, all available avenues for political advertisement and advancement were used. Plants and gardens became new tools in the Roman political arsenal.

---

[3] Foster 1998, 320.

[4] Wilkinson 1998, 48; Singer 2007, 4.

[5] 1 Kings 10:1-13; cf. 2 Chronicles 9:1-12.

[6] Stronach 1994. For a survey of much of the recent work done on Hellenistic and Near Eastern gardens, see Bedal 2004, 121-170.

[7] Diod. Sic. 26.41.2-5, Xen. An., I.iv.10-11; Plin. HN, 12.80; Hdt. 3.97. For a discussion of chopping down trees in war in Greece, see Hanson 1998.

[8] Theophr., Caus. pl. 4.4.13.

[9] Jashemski 1979; Jashemski 1992.

[10] D'Arms 1970; Nielsen 1999, 164-180.

Horti, monumental peri-urban estates of which gardens were a large component, were constructed around Rome at this time.[11] These estates and their gardens often served as pleasurable retreats, but also as political staging grounds; both Caesar and Pompey used the gardens of their *horti* for political ends.[12] Upon his return to Rome, Pompey reportedly bribed the plebs to vote for Afranius in the consular election within the bounds of his *horti* on the *Campus Martius*.[13] Caesar also made good political use of his *horti trans Tiberim*. First, he received Cleopatra here when she arrived in Rome.[14] Second, when the first civil wars ended in 45 BC, Caesar celebrated his Spanish triumph and his victory over Pompey at Munda. He commemorated these victories by offering Chian and Falernian wines to the plebs and by inviting them into his *horti trans Tiberim* to feast with him.[15] Upon his death, Caesar left his *horti* to the Roman people.[16] Clearly, private gardens could serve as venues for political intrigues and events.

Pompey in particular revolutionized the use of plants and gardens in Rome. His *horti* served as a political staging ground, Pompey erected Rome's first public park, the *Porticus Pompei*, his victory monument and a highly politicized space.[17] Most relevant to this paper is his display of plants and a representation of a foriegn landscape in his triumph.

Pompey's Triumphal Plants

Exposed to the use of gardens and plants by eastern rulers, Pompey utilitized plants to celebrate his victories in his triumph over Mithridates, Asia, Pontus, other eastern kingdoms, and the pirates in 61 BC.[18] Before Pompey's chariot, the standard ranks of *manubii*,[19] including 1,000 captives, 85 million drachmas in coined money and gold, and placards

---

[11] For a general discussion of Rome's *horti* see Cima and La Rocca 1986 and 1998; Purcell 1987, 1996, and 2001; D'Arms 1998; Hartswick 2004.

[12] D'Arms 1998, 33-43.

[13] Plut. *Vit. Pomp.* 44.3; Papi 1996, 55-56.

[14] Purcell 1996, 132.

[15] Val. Max. 9.15.1. An inscription fragment of the consular *fasti* of Cupra Maritima also recorded this; see D'Arms 1998, 41.

[16] There is some dispute over whether the second *horti* on one of the Hills of Rome actually belonged to him. We have no evidence that anything political or otherwise notable went on at Caesar's other *horti*.

[17] Gleason 1994, 13-27.

[18] Plin. *HN* 7.98, 37.12-16, 37.18; App. *Mith.* 17.117.

[19] Versnel 1970, 95.

detailing the nations he had defeated were displayed.[20] For the first time, plants and representations of foreign landscapes were marched.

In his triumphal procession, Pompey paraded a golden pyramid that depicted a foreign landscape.[21] While Pliny the Elder did not assign a particular name or genre to this landscaped artifact, his description (*montem aureum quadratum cum cervis et leonibus et pomis omnis generis circumdata vite aurea*) implies that the "geo-depiction" on Pompey's golden pyramid was a παράδεισος.[22] One must imagine a portable pyramid with stags, lions, plants, and vines carved in an elaborate scene on its three sides, shimmering in the sun, as a cart or slaves carried it. It was, in the words of A. Kuttner, an "Asian landscape... a great gold pyramid (*quadratus*) model of a paradisal mountain, rising from an encircling vine, on which stags and lions ran through fruited trees."[23] This pyramid was unlike any object seen in Rome before and must have been a great spectacle.

This παράδεισος landscape was a particularly Asian landscape.[24] In ancient Persia, a παράδεισος was either an elaborate garden associated with a royal palace that had an official purpose, or it was a royal or aristocratic hunting park. The inclusion of the stags and lions in vegetal depictions recalled hunts of Asian kings and aristocrats in their παράδεισοι.[25] Such a scene sharply contrasted with Rome's urban landscape. While *horti* had begun to dominate many of Rome's hills, hunting was a rural, aristocratic pursuit, which most Romans had never experienced. Pompey had not only conquered Asia, but he had conquered a specific landscape—that of kings.

A parade of living specimens complimented the landscape on Pompey's pyramid. According to Pliny, Pompey inaugurated the tradition of leading trees in a triumph.[26] Pliny reported that a rare type of tree, possibly ebony, which was pure, free of knots, of dark hue, and from India, (*rarum id quod melius, arboreum, purae et enodis materiae nigri splendoris ac vel sine arte protinus iucundi, alterum fruticosum cytisi modo et tota India dispersum*) and other trees (*arbores*) were present in

---

[20] Plut. *Vit. Pomp.* 45.1-5.

[21] Plin. *HN* 37.6.14.

[22] Plin. *HN* 37.6.14.

[23] Kuttner 1999, 345.

[24] Carroll 2003; Bedal 2004, 121-170.

[25] For example, consider the large stone reliefs, taken from a range of Assyrian palaces, which are now in the British Museum. Many of these reliefs show elaborate hunting scenes. See Barnett 1970.

[26] Plin. *HN* 12.54.111-112.

Pompey's triumph.[27] While Pliny is not more specific, *arbores* suggests that many trees, possibly of different species, were paraded.[28] Ebony reportedly had symbolic importance. It was not native to Asia Minor, but came from India. Pompey, like Alexander, had even conquered India, a parallel noted by Pliny.[29] The exhibition of captured trees served as another means to represent a distant, conquered land, now obedient to Rome. While there is no evidence that Pompey specifically gained from the possession of ebony, ebony also certainly had an economic value; it was extremely expensive. The economic power of plants will be returned to later in this paper.

Parading trees in a triumph may have been a variation on the tradition of displaying trophies. Armour trophies, in particular cuirasses, were often displayed on trunks of oak trees as victorious votive offerings to the Roman gods.[30] By the late Republican and early Imperial period, the tradition is well attested. There are numerous references to trophies affixed to trunks in the landscape in the *Aeneid*; Plutarch reports that Marcellus even paraded his trophy (on a trunk) to Jupiter.[31] Such trophies also existed in the sculptural record; a trophy sculpted in marble was reportedly displayed in the *horti Sallustiani* and is now on show in Rome's Centrale Montemartini Museum (Inv. No. MC00042); an example of such trophies can also be seen on the front of this volume. Furthermore, the decision to place a cuirass on an oak trunk may have been significant, because the oak was associated with Jupiter and victory. The ancient sources often portray cutting down trees as a symbolic act of violence against an enemy.[32] For example, Lucan associated Pompey with the oak;[33] therefore, Caesar's action of felling a grove of oaks has been interpreted as a symbolic foretelling Caesar's defeat of Pompey.[34]

While these trophies or the symbolic action of felling trees may have served as a precedent for Pompey's use of trees, his inclusion of living trees and a representation of an Asian landscape in his triumph were highly original. Rome not only controlled Mithridates' kingdom, but Rome even dominated her landscape. By parading the botanical bounty of a distant land that was now Roman, Pompey celebrated his victory over

---

[27] Plin. *HN* 12.9.20, 12.54.111-112.
[28] Plin. *HN* 12.9.20.
[29] Plin. *HN* 12.9.20.
[30] Picard 1957.
[31] Verg. *Aen.* 10.420-4, 11.1-30; Plut. *Vit. Marc.* 8.1-5.
[32] Augoustakis 2006, 634-638; Luc. 1.135-43, 3.399-452.
[33] Luc. 1.135-43.
[34] Augoustakis 2006, 634 n. 2.

Mithridates and firmly established his role as conqueror of Asia. The use of plants in Pompey's triumph also demonstrates that plants could serve as potent political symbols of a conquered land, just like a defeated queen, king, or other human captive could. The sight of marching trees and a παράδεισος landscape was not only a remarkable spectacle, heralding Pompey's success, but it also established the political and militaristic symbolism of plants outside a garden context. Pompey's successful deployment of plants for political ends transformed plants into political symbols in Rome.

Laurels wreaths, groves, and tall trees:
Augustus and symbolic plants

The use of plants as political tools and symbols continued under Rome's first emperor. Because scholars have explored the symbolic role of the laurel at length,[35] this section briefly examines Augustus' use of the laurel and other plants as political and militaristic symbols. Since the early Republic, laurel wreaths and branches were bestowed upon victors.[36] By associating himself with the laurel, Augustus evoked this Republican tradition.[37] Equally important for Augustus was the association of the laurel with Apollo, Augustus' patron god. After lightening struck Augustus' Palatine residence, he constructed a temple to Apollo and planted laurel trees that flanked the entrance to his home.[38] He also used the laurel in his coinage. The longevity of Augustus and his successors was also intrinsically linked with the fate of a particular laurel grove. The ancient sources record the famous story that one day an eagle dropped a white chicken holding a laurel sprig in Livia's lap just north of Rome.[39] Here she built her villa *ad Gallinas*, which is generally accepted as the villa at Prima Porta.[40] Just before the death of Nero, the grove withered away, and the offspring of the original hen died, symbolizing the end of the Julio-Claudians.[41] This short summary demonstrates that plants played an important role in Augustan ideology and propaganda.

---

[35] Klynne 2005; Reader 1997a; 1997b; 2001; Kellum 1994; Zanker 1998, 92ff.
[36] Zanker 1998, 92-93.
[37] Zanker 1998, 92-93.
[38] Zanker 1998, 93.
[39] Dio. Cass. 48.54.3-4; Plin. *HN* 15.136-7.
[40] Klynne 2005; Messineo 2001; Klynne and Liljenstolpe 2000; Liljenstolpe and Klynne, 1997-1998; Reeder 1997, 89-118; Calci and Messineo 1984.
[41] Suet. *Galb.* 1.

Plants also played an important role in one of his largest and most important constructions: his mausoleum in the northern *Campus Martius*.[42] The mausoleum was set into a monumental, public park.[43] The complex was a space where Augustus could articulate his political ideas to Rome's urban populace. It was a celebration of Augustus' successes, achievements and life. Not only was there an Egyptian obelisk that functioned as a gnomon for a monumental sundial, but the plants of the complex also reflected Augustan policies. The mausoleum's dome was planted with tall evergreens, probably cypresses.[44] Cypresses were appropriate trees for the mausoleum, as they are funerary trees.[45] They, with the highly visible sculpture of Augustus atop the mausoleum, also dominated the landscape of the upper *Campus Martius*.[46] A grove of black poplars, also funerary trees, surrounded the *ustrinum*.[47] The lower frieze of the *Ara Pacis* featured an array of plants in bloom, even though the plants depicted flowered at different times of year. This *pankarpia* testified to the blossoming and blooming of the Roman world under the auspices of Augustan peace[48] and was a symbol of the *concordia* of the gods, which was also brought about by Augustan peace.[49] While this is only the briefest of summaries of Augustan uses of plants as political symbols, the wide-ranging use of the laurel on coinage and at his Palatine residence as well as his use of plants on the *Ara Pacis* and in his mausoleum suggest that plants had political currency.

---

[42] On the Mausoleum of Augustus complex see Rehak 2006; Davies 2004; Zanker 1998, 135-156, esp. 144; von Hesberg 1996, 234-237; Macciocca 1996, 237-239. See Lange's paper in this volume for a discussion of the *Res Gestae*, a copy of which was displayed in front of the mausoleum.

[43] The park associated with the Mausoleum of Augustus can also be thought about as a monumental tomb garden.

[44] Richardson 1992, 247 does not think that the trees were cypresses, because the root systems of these trees would have been too big and heavy to be supported.

[45] Strabo 5.3.8, Plin. *HN* 16.40.139-140

[46] Tac. *Ann.* 3.9.

[47] Von Hesberg 1996, 234-237; Macciocca 1996, 237-239.

[48] Castriota 1995, 31; La Rocca 1983. It is possible that these plants may have been merely decorative; however, considering the use of plants as symbols in Augustan coinage and propaganda, coupled with the use of the natural world and its fertile bounty as a metaphor for Augustan peace and stability in the literature of the time, it seems unlikely that these plants were just visual garnish without meaning.

[49] Castriota 1995, 21-22; La Rocca 1983.

Balsam and the Date Palm: Judaea and Flavian success

Considering the potency of plants as symbols of victory, it is unsurprising that the use of plants in this capacity continued under the Flavians. The Flavian dynasty staked its claim to imperial power because of its suppression of the Jewish Revolt of AD 66-70.[50] In Rome, the Arch of Titus, erected by Domitian, and the *Templum Pacis*, Vespasian's monumental porticoed garden/museum complex, celebrated these victories.[51] The Arch showed Titus's triumphant return into Rome and his booty, which included the menorah from the Second Temple, while the *Templum Pacis* actually displayed these items.[52] These monuments have been an obvious focus for scholars interested in Flavian displays of victory. In addition to erecting permanent monuments to their dynasty's success and military prowess, Vespasian and Titus, like Pompey and Augustus, used plants as a way to display their victory over the Jews. Specifically, Vespasian and Titus displayed balsam in their triumphs, and the date palm played an important role in the iconography of their coinage. This section explores the presentation of balsam and palms in the literary record and depiction of palms on Flavian coinage.

In their joint triumph in AD 71, Vespasian and Titus exhibited balsam[53] (*ostendere arborum hanc urbi imperators Vespasiani, clarumque dictu, a Pompeio Magno in triumpho arbores quoque duximus*).[54] The inclusion of balsam in the triumph was significant. The display of a plant linked Vespasian and Titus with Pompey and Augustus; they were continuing in the tradition of using plants as symbols. More importantly balsam was a plant specifically associated with Judaea; Pliny claims it only grew in two gardens in Judaea, one of which belonged to the king of Judaea.[55] While Pliny's assertion about the presence of balsam in a mere two gardens cannot be confirmed and is probably unlikely, the close

---

[50] Levick 1999, 31ff; Goodman 1987, 235-6; Goodman 1998, 7; Goodman 2007, esp. 11-29 for a summary of the revolt; Joseph. *BJ* 7.158-62.

[51] Coarelli 1999, 67-70. The Flavian Amphitheatre, better known as the Colosseum, was also in some sense a victory monument, owing to its situation atop the previous site of the *stagnum* in Nero's *Domus Aurea*.

[52] Coarelli 1999, 67-70. Two detailed studies on the Arch of Titus are Yarden 1991 and Pfanner 1983. On the recent excavations of the *Templum Pacis*, see La Rocca 2001, 171-213; Rizzo 2001, 215-244.

[53] Balsam is a plant that grows in both a tree and shrub form. Ancient balsam is now extinct; however, balsam related to this ancient variety still grows in the Levant today.

[54] Plin. *HN* 12.111.

[55] Plin. *HN* 12.111.

connection between balsam and the kings of Judaea is well attested. In 30 BC, balsam plantations were among the property returned to Herod by Octavian.[56] Furthermore, the archaeological remains of a plant that was probably balsam from the Ionic colonnade garden at Herod's winter palace at Jericho seems to confirm the close connection between the kings of Judaea and balsam.[57] By displaying balsam, it was made apparent to all that Vespasian and Titus had conquered the distant, exotic land of Judaea. Unlike the palm, which I will discuss below, few people in Rome would ever have seen a balsam tree. Pliny's language speaks to the power of plants as symbols of victory; he also saw the balsam as a symbol of the Jewish people. In *HN* 12.111-112, the balsam plants were led in triumph (*duximus*), like human captives. Like the Jewish people, the balsam became subject to Rome and had to pay tribute to her (*servit nunc haec ac tributa pendit cum sua gente*). Here, the balsam ceases to be a plant, it has assumed the position of a defeated nation.

The rarity and economic value of balsam not only made it a potent symbol of Vespasian and Titus' victory, but the possession of balsam contributed to the wealth of Rome. Balsam was highly valuable; the Romans prized balsam for its scent above all other plants (*sed omnibus odoribus praefertur balsamum*);[58] as such, it was used in the production of perfumes and incense. Pliny praises the Roman care for and cultivation of balsam. He claims that during the revolt the Jews ravaged their balsam, just as they had treated themselves (*saeviere in eam Iudaei sicut in vitam quoque suam*).[59] While this claim might sound odd, in the context of a fierce rebellion it makes sense. By destroying balsam, one of the most valuable, if not the most valuable, plant grown in Judaea, the Jews prevented the Romans from harvesting the flourishing stocks of balsam for their own economic benefit. Destroying balsam was an act of economic warfare against the Romans; by killing their balsam plants the Jews denied Romans their fruits of victory—at least temporarily. In the end, the Romans protected the balsam groves; Pliny reports that there were even battles to defend balsam (*contra defendere Romani et dimicatum pro frutice est*).[60] The Romans were not ardent environmentalists, rather they had an economic interest in the survival of balsam; it was a valuable source of revenue. From this point onwards, agents of the emperor were

---

[56] Joseph. *BJ* 1.396, *AJ* 15.217.
[57] Gleason 1993, 156-167.
[58] Plin. *HN* 12.111.
[59] Plin. *HN* 12.111.
[60] Plin. *HN* 12.113.

responsible for the cultivation of balsam.[61] Although balsam never grew very tall under the Romans, Pliny claims that balsam was never as plentiful as it was after the defeat of the Jews.[62] Thus in the end, the Romans, or at least the imperial estate, reaped the fruits of victory.

The date palm also had a special association with the Jews.[63] Much of the iconography of the coinage issued by Vespasian and, to a lesser extent, Titus focuses on their victory over Judaea.[64] Before I discuss the role of the date palm in the iconography of certain Vespasianic coins, a few words about the choice of a palm tree are essential. Why the date palm? Palm branches had long been a symbol of victory in the Roman world, but the inclusion of a whole palm with fruit was new.[65] Cody argues that the palm "at first may be a reference to victory as well as, or instead of, a geographical allusion."[66] Certainly, it is both, but the root question of "why the date palm?" remains unaddressed. The Romans valued the palm for its ability to add scent to unguents and perfumes.[67] It and its fruit provided many of the eastern provinces with wine, bread, and even cattle fodder if we are to believe Pliny the Elder.[68] Reportedly only in very warm climates did the palm bear fruit. Not all palms were equal; the palms of

---

[61] The Latin reads *seritque nunc eum fiscus, nec umquam fuit numersior; proceritas intra bina cubita subsistit* (Plin. *HN* 12.113). Here I follow Millar's definition of the *fiscus* as the Imperial Estate. See Millar 1963, 29.

[62] Plin. *HN* 12.113.

[63] For example, both the palm tree and branch were used on coinage as symbols of Tiberias, which Herod Antipas founded in AD 19. The coinage issued during the Bar-Kokhba revolt, AD 132-135, also uses palm trees. See Mershorer 2001 for a detailed study of Jewish coinage.

[64] Cody 2003, 103-123. Some of the coinage issued by Agrippa II after the defeat of Judaea also features palm branches on the reverse of coinage with obverses of Titus and Domitian. See Meshorer 2001, nos. 150, 160, 169, and 173 (all bronze coinage) all show either Titus and Domitian on the obverse with a reverse of Nike walking, holding a palm branch, presumably symbolizing the Flavian victory over Judaea. For example, no.156 features a Bust of Domitian with a palm tree on the reverse (Meshorer 2001). Agrippa II may have been showing his loyalty to Rome since it was his province that had rebelled. These examples are by no means exhaustive; for more examples, see Meshorer 2001. Nerva also used the palm tree as a symbol of Judaea in his coinage that celebrates the abolition of the Jewish tax. See Meshorer, 1982, 145; Samuels, Rynearson and Meshorer 2000, 77, no. 152.

[65] Stylized stumps or minaturized palm tree served as marble supports in late Republic sculpture.

[66] Cody 2003, 107.

[67] Plin. *HN* 13.26.

[68] Plin. *HN* 13.26.

Judaea were the most famous (*Iudaea vero incluta est vel magis palmis*).[69] Unlike the palms of Europe, the palms of Judaea were fertile.[70] These palms, in particular those found in Jericho and in the valleys of Archelais, Phaselis and Livias, were exceptional. They were prized above all others for their juice, which had a sweet, wine-like flavour (*dos iis praecipua suco pingui lactentibus quodamque vini sapore ut melle praedulci*).[71]

Thus the date palm was one of the agricultural jewels of Judaea, comparable to balsam. Therefore it is not surprising that Vespasian (and Titus) selected this specific tree for their coinage. The palm was a highly recognisable image, making it a suitable image for coinage.[72] The date palm was not merely a symbol of and geographic reference to the victory over Judaea. It symbolized the agricultural fruits and wealth of Judaea, which could not be cultivated at Rome, but once again were brought under the helm of the Roman Empire to enhance the glory and wealth of the Flavians. Lastly, the choice to place a palm tree rather than balsam or another plant on Flavian coinage is significant. As noted above, palms were well known outside of Judaea. The trunk, frons and hanging fruits of palms are distinct and easily recognized. Therefore, the high level of visual recognition of palms made Vespasian's message of victory clear to all. Furthermore, during the Jewish revolt, a palm branch and a citron, which were used in celebration of the Tabernacles, were depicted on coinage issued in Jerusalem.[73] Thus, the choice of a palm may not only speak to Vespasian and Rome's reclamation of Judaea but also to victory of Roman religion over Judaism.

Cody identified two coin designs, the *prouincia capta* type and the *supplicatio/adoratio* types, in whose iconography palm trees are very

---

[69] Plin. *HN* 13.26.

[70] Plin. *HN* 13.26.

[71] Plin. *HN* 13.44.

[72] It is interesting to note, however, how rarely plants are used on Roman coinage as symbols for provinces or people. The laurel, as noted above, was used on Augustan coinage, but it was among the most important plants and symbols in the Roman world. Therefore, it seems unsurprising that it should appear. However, most plants, even the most famous, from the provinces would have only been recognisable to very few, thereby lessening their ability to convey political messages. A crocodile, known from the Egyptianising Roman art from the mid and late Republic, was a far better, more easily read symbol of Egypt on Augustan coinage than a papyrus plant would have been. Thus, the choice of the Flavians to use the palm is a considered one. Balsam would not have been recognised by as wide an audience as the palm, so perhaps for this reason, it was not selected for the use on Flavian coinage.

[73] Goodman 2007, 18, n. 9.

important.[74] As Cody observed, the *capta* coinage type conveyed a strong political message. In the Roman *capta* types of coins, the defeated is portrayed as totally subjugated, while the victor is almost omnipotent.[75] This image suited Vespasian and Titus' political needs. While their imperial power certainly derived from their victory over Judaea, it should be remembered that Vespasian had fought a civil war. Thus, the emphasis on the defeat of a foreign enemy as a source of power and legitimacy rather than an internal Roman enemy was critical; it was similar to Augustus' use of Egypt after his victory in the civil war against Antony.[76] That said, it should be noted that not all coins that depicted the palm tree and a seated female captive fall into either one of these types.[77] Because Cody treats the *prouincia capta* type in detail, I will focus on other types of Vespasianic coinage. An exploration of the depiction of the palm tree and its role on specific examples from the coinage of Vespasian suggests that the natural world and her plants were potent ways to express political, military, and economic success. However, before I discuss other depictions of the palm on Vespasianic coinage, a few additional comments on the *capta* type are needed.

Cody observed that on the *Judaea Capta* coins, the palm tree replaced the trophy,[78] which is typically included in the *capta* scenes of previous and later emperors, but she did not explore this idea further (fig. 11-1). As noted above, the use of trees in triumphs, as objects of victory, may derive from armour trophies. Therefore, Vespasian's choice to use the palm tree as well as trophies on his coins, may suggest that the palm and trophy were a part of the same vocabulary. The trees themselves may have been the trophies, the spoils of victory.

On a Vespasianic *quadrans*, a lone palm tree appears on the obverse (with the inscription *IMP VES PASIAN AVG*) and a *vexillum* on the reverse (with the inscription *P M TR P P P COS III* and *SC* (fig. 11-2).[79] The presence of a palm tree rather than Vespasian's head on the obverse is striking. A palm tree not only alludes to Judaea and its defeat, but it also seems as if it could represent Vespasian, not just his victory over Judaea. On a number of these coins, the palms bear fruit, which hangs heavily down from their branches. The presence of fruit might seem a nice artistic

---

[74] Cody 2003, 105, 107-112, 116.

[75] Cody 2003, 105.

[76] Goodman 1987, 235.

[77] For example, *BMC* 2.44, 2.78, 2.83; *BMC* plates 2.1 no. 13; *BMC* 2.2 nos. 10 and 14.

[78] Cody 2003, 107.

[79] *BMC* 2.618, 2.619; *BMC* 2, plate 24, nos. 1-3; 6.

touch; however, in a small space such as the face of a coin, the choice to include fruit is deliberate. As discussed above, the date palm was valued for its fruit and for its use in perfumes and unguents. This small detail— the inclusion of fruit—was a reminder of the economic contribution that Vespasian had made to the Roman Empire by bringing Judaea back into the fold. On the reverse, the *vexillum* reminds the viewer of Vespasian's military prowess and victories.

Another prominent reverse on a *sestertius* of Vespasian is a Victory, inscribing a shield, which is fixed to a palm tree (fig. 11-3); the inscription on the reverse reads *VICTORIA AUGUSTI*.[80] In many depictions of Victories inscribing shields, the shields are not fixed to trees; rather they float in space or rest upon a non-descript base, as on the Column of Trajan.[81] The inclusion of the date palm tree, therefore, is significant. The palm tree immediately alerts the audience to the fact that this image refers to Vespasian's victory in Judaea. The use of a scene with Victory inscribing a shield, a common scene in Roman imperial art, has been adapted to suit the needs of Vespasian. Here, the *Victoria Augusti* is specified through the inclusion of the palm tree. Interestingly and ironically, perhaps, the coinage of Judaea issued under Agrippa II, during the reigns of Titus and Domitian, minted coins that included palm branches and wreaths, often borne by Nike, in their iconography.[82] Although it is beyond the scope of this paper to discuss these coins in detail, it is clear that the inclusion of the palm tree proclaimed Vespasian's victory.[83]

Conclusions

In first century BC Rome, plants became a part of the visual and symbolic language of victory. They were a way for the victorious to display and symbolize their achievements. This tradition of using plants to

---

[80] For example *BMC* 2.637; 2.638. Compare also *BMC* 2, Plate 32.5. No number is given for this coin; it is worth noting that on the reverse of this coin, a captive seated below the palm is also present.

[81] See Settis *et al.*1998, 395, Plate 137 for an image of a Victory inscribing a shield on the Column of Trajan. For an introduction to the Column of Trajan see Hannestad 1988, 154-167.

[82] See above, nn. 64-5.

[83] Palm branches continue to appear with Victories on the reverses of coins after the Flavians. There is a Severan coin, from Britain, that shows a Victory inscribing a shield attached to a palm tree. Perhaps, by this time, the palm tree had become a generic symbol of victory. Per. Comm. R. Abdy.

express power and ideologies seems to have a long history in ancient Egypt and in the ancient Near East. Although Rome had a long garden tradition, its use of gardens and plants for political purposes originated in the first century BC. Conquest may have served as a means to exchange ideas about gardens in the ancient world. The *agrimensores*, or Roman land surveyors, had often served in the army and may have gained employment as "landscape architects" after their military careers, bringing with them a knowledge of exotic *flora*. Plants, however, were not only symbols of victory. The possession of ebony financially benefited Pompey, while the control of palms and, more importantly, balsam enriched Vespasian and the imperial coffers. These plants, while symbolic of military victories and defeated lands, were the economic fruits of victory.

Acknowledgements

I would like to thank Ed Bragg for asking me to give this paper at the Beyond the Battlefields Conference, for organizing the conference, and for asking me to help with this volume. Also special thanks to Lisa Irene Hau for her suggestions and comments. The comments of audiences in Oxford, Newcastle and London that heard versions of this paper greatly improved it. Andreas Kropp's amazingly detailed coin sheets on the coinage of the Near Eastern client kings were particularly helpful in identifying earlier and later uses of the palm in Jewish coinage. Janie Anderson's suggestions on trophies were very useful. Thanks to Helen Whitehouse, John Baines, and Stephanie Dalley, who provided guidance on the Egyptian and Ancient Near Eastern material, although it appears in a much reduced form. Richard Abdy of the Coin and Medal Department of the British Museum was very kind to speak with me about palms and palm branches on Roman coinage. Thank you lastly to Saskia Stevens, and Profs. Bettina Bergmann, Kathryn Gleason, and Brian Campbell, whose comments greatly improved this paper. All errors remain my own.

Figures

Figure 11-1. A *sestertius* with Head of Vespasian on the obverse and on the reverse, Victory standing inscribing a shield attached to a palm tree (*BMC* 2.638 (p. 141), Plate 25, No. 4.) Photograph © the Trustees of the British Museum.

Figure 11-2. A Vespasianic *quadrans*, a lone palm tree appears on the obverse (with the inscription *IMP VES PASIAN AVG*) and a *vexillum* on the reverse (with the inscription *P M TR P P P COS III* and *SC*. Photograph © the Trustees of the British Museum.

Figure 11-3. A Vespasianic *sestertius* with a victory on the reverse, inscribing a shield which is fixed to a palm tree. The inscription on the reverse reads *VICTORIA AUGUSTI*. Photograph © the Trustees of the British Museum.

Bibliography

Augoustakis, A. "Cutting Down the grove in Lucan, Valerius Maximus and Cassius Dio." *CQ* 56 (2) (2006): 634-638.

Bedal, L.A. *The Petra Pool-Complex: a Hellenistic Paradeisos in the Nabataean Capital*. Piscataway, N.J., Gorgias Press, 2004.

Barnett, R. D. *Assyrian palace reliefs in the British Museum. London* : British Museum, 1970.

Buchner, E. *Die Sonnenuhr des Augustus: Nachdruck aus RM 1976 und 1980 und Nachtrag über die Ausgrabung 1980/1981*. Mainz am Rhein: Von Zabern, 1982.

Calci, C. and Messineo, G.. *La Villa di Livia a Prima Porta*. Rome: De Luca, 1984.

Carroll, M. *Earthly Paradises: Ancient gardens in history and archaeology*. London: The British Museum Press, 2003.

Castriota, D. *The Ara Pacis Augustae and the imagery of abundance in later Greek and early Roman imperial art*. Princeton: Princeton University Press, 1995.

Claridge, A. *Rome: an Oxford archaeological guide*. Oxford: Oxford University Press, 1998.

Cima, M. and La Rocca, E. (eds). *Le tranquille dimore degli dei: la residenza imperiale degli horti Lamiani.* Venice: C. Marsilio, 1986.

—. (eds.) *Horti Romani.* Rome: L'Erma di Bretschneider, 1998.

Coarelli, F. "Pax, Templum." In *LTUR* IV, 67-70. 1999.

Cody, J. M. "Conquerors and Conquered on Flavian Coins." In *Flavian Rome: Culture, Image, Text,* edited by A. J. Boyle and W. J. Dominik, 103-123. Leiden; Boston: Brill, 2003.

Davies, P. J. *Death and the emperor: Roman imperial funerary monuments from Augustus to Marcus Aurelius.* Austin: University of Texas Press, 2004.

D'Arms, J. H. *Romans on the Bay of Naples: a social and cultural study of the villas and their owners from 150 B.C. to A.D. 400.* Cambridge: Harvard University Press, 1970.

—. "Between Public and Private: The *Epulum Publicum* and Caesar's *Horti Trans Tiberim.*" In *Horti Romani,* edited by M. Cima and E. La Rocca, 33-43. Rome: L'Erma di Bretschneider, 1998.

Goodman, M. *The ruling class of Judaea: the origins of the Jewish revolt against Rome, A.D. 66-70.* Cambridge: Cambridge University Press, 1987.

—. "Jews, Greeks and Romans." In *Jews in a Graeco-Roman world,* edited by M. Goodman, 3-14. Oxford: Clarendon Press, 1998.

—. "Coinage and Identity: The Jewish Evidence." In *Coinage and Identity in the Roman Provinces,* edited by C. J. Howgego, V. Heuchert, and A. M. Burnett, 163-6. Oxford: Oxford University Press, 2005.

—. *Rome and Jerusalem: the clash of ancient civilizations.* London: Allen Lane, 2007.

Foster, K. "Gardens of Eden: Exotic Flora and Fauna in the Ancient Near East." In *Transformations of Middle Eastern Natural Environments: Legacies and Lessons,* edited by J. Albert, M. Bernhardsson, and R. Kenna, 320-329. New Haven: Yale University Press, 1998.

Hanson, V. D. *Warfare and Agriculture in Classical Greece.* Berkeley; London: University of California Press, 1998.

Hartswick, K. J. *The Gardens of Sallust: a changing landscape.* Austin: University of Texas Press, 2004.

Gleason, K. L. "A Garden Excavation in the Oasis Palace of Herod the Great at Jericho." *Landscape Journal* 12(2) (1993): 156-167.

—. "*Porticus Pompeiana*: a New Perspective on the First Public Park of Ancient Rome." *JGH* 14 (1) (1994): 13-27.

Gros, P. "Porticus Pompei." In *LTUR IV,* 148-149. 1999.

Jashemski, W. F. *The gardens of Pompeii: Herculaneum and the villas destroyed by Vesuvius I.* New Rochelle, N.Y.: Caratzas Brothers, 1979.

—. *The gardens of Pompeii: Herculaneum and the villas destroyed by Vesuvius II*. New Rochelle, N.Y.: Caratzas Brothers, 1992.

Goodman, M. *The ruling class of Judaea: the origins of the Jewish revolt against Rome, A.D. 66-70*. Cambridge: Cambridge University Press, 1987.

—. "Jews, Greeks and Romans." in *Jews in a Graeco-Roman world*, edited by M. Goodman, 3-14. Oxford: Clarendon Press, 1998.

—. "Coinage and Identity: The Jewish Evidence." In *Coinage and Identity in the Roman Provinces*, edited by C. J. Howgego, V. Heuchert, and A. M. Burnett, 163-6. Oxford: Oxford University Press, 2005.

—. *Rome and Jerusalem: the clash of ancient civilizations*. London: Allen Lane, 2007.

Kellum, B. "The Construction of Landscape in Augustan Rome: The Garden Room at the Villa ad Gallinas." *ArtB* 76(2) (1994): 211-224.

Klynne, A. and Liljenstolpe, P. "Investigating the Gardens of the Villa of Livia." *JRA* 13 (2000): 220—233.

Klynne, A. "The laurel grove of the Caesars: looking in and looking out." In *Roman villas around the* Urbs. *Interaction with landscape and environment. Proceedings of a conference held at the Swedish Institute in Rome, September 17—18, 2004. The Swedish Institute in Rome. Projects and Seminars, 2,* edited by B. Santillo Frizell and A. Klynne, 1-9. Rome: The Swedish Institute in Rome. Projects and Seminars, 2, 2005. (www.svenska-institutet-rom.org/villa/ (accessed June 8th 2006.)

Kuttner, A. L. "Culture and History at Pompey's Museum." *TAPA* 129 (1999): 343-373.

La Rocca, E. *Ara Pacis Augustae: in occasione del restauro della fronte orientale*. Rome: L'ERMA di Bretschneider, 1983.

—. "La Nuova Immagine dei Fori Imperiale." *RM* 108 (2001): 171-213.

Liljenstolpe P. and Klynne, A. "The Imperial Gardens of the Villa of Livia at Prima Porta: a Preliminary Report on the 1997 Campaign." *OpRom,* 22—23, (1997-1998): 130—134.

Macciocca, M. "Mausoleum Augusti: Le Sepolture." In *LTUR* III, 237-239. 1996.

Mattingly, H. *BMC Vol.2, Vespasian to Domitian*: London: British Museum Publications for the Trustees of the British Museum, 1930.

Meshorer, Y. *Ancient Jewish coinage, Vols. I- II*. Dix Hills, N.Y: Amphora Books, 1982.

—. *A Treasury of Jewish Coins from the Persian Period to Bar Kokhba*. Jerusalem and Nyack, NY: Amphora, 2001.

Messineo, G. (ed.) *Ad Gallinas Albas: Villa di Livia*. Rome: "L'Erma" di Bretschneider, 2001.

Millar, F. "The Fiscus in the First Two Centuries." *JRS* 53 (1-2) (1963), 29-42.

Nielsen, I. *Hellenistic palaces: tradition and renewal.* Aarhus: Aarhus University Press, 1999.

—. "The gardens of Hellenistic palaces." In *The Royal Palace Institution in the first Millennium BC*, edited by I. Nielsen. 165-87. Athens: The Danish Institute at Athens, 2001.

Papi, E. "Horti Caesaris (trans Tiberim)." In *LTUR* III, 55-56, 1996.

Picard, G. C. *Les trophées romains; contribution à l'histoire de la religion et de l'art triomphal de Rome.* Paris: Boccard, 1957.

Purcell, N. "Town in Country and Country in Town." In *Ancient Roman Villa Gardens. Dumbarton Oaks Colloquium on the History of Landscape Architecture* X, edited by E. B. MacDougall. 185-205. Washington D.C.: Dumbarton Oaks, 1987.

—. "The Roman Garden as a Domestic Building." In *Roman Domestic Buildings,* edited by I. Barton. 121-152. Exeter: Exeter University Press, 1996.

—. "Dialectical Gardening." *JRA* 14 (2001): 546-56.

Pfanner, M. *Der Titusbogen.* Mainz: Ph. von Zabern, 1983.

Reeder 1997a: Reeder, J.C. "The Statue of Augustus from Prima Porta and the Underground Complex," Studies in Latin Literature and Roman History, VIII. *Latomus* 239 (1997): 287-308.

—. (1997b): Reeder, J. C. "The Statue of Augustus from Prima Porta, the Underground Complex, and the Omen of Gallina Alba" *AJP* 118 (1997): 89-118.

—. *The Villa of Livia Ad Gallinas Albas: A study in the Augustan Villa and Garden.* Providence: Center for Old World Archaeology and Art, Brown University, 2001.

Rehak, P. *Imperium and Cosmos: Augustus and the northern Campus Martius*, edited by John G. Younger. Madison: University of Wisconsin Press, 2006.

Richardson Jr., L. *A New Topographical Dictionary of Rome.* Baltimore: John Hopkins University Press, 1992.

Rizzo, S. "Indagini nei Fori Imperiali." *RM* 108 (2001): 215-244.

Samuels, C. W., Rynearson, P., and Meshorer, Y. *The numismatic legacy of the Jews: as depicted by a distinguished American collection*, edited by Paul Rynearson. New York: Stack's Publications Numismatic Review, 2000.

Settis, S. *et al. La Colonna Traiana,* edited by S. Settis. Turin: G. Einaudi, 1998.

Singer, C. "The Incense Kingdoms of Yemen: An Outline History of the South Arabian Incense Trade." In *Food for the Gods: New Light on the Ancient Incense Trade*, edited by D. Peacock and D. Williams, 4-27. Oxbow: Oxford, 2007.

Stronach, D. "Parterres and Stones Watercourses at Pasargadae: notes on the Achaemenid contribution to garden design" *JGH* 14 (1) (1994): 3-12.

Versnel, H. S. *Triumphus: An Inquiry into the Origin, Development, and Meaning of the Roman Triumph.* Leiden: E. J. Brill, 1970.

Viscogliosi 1999a: Viscogliosi, A. "Porticus Metelli." In *LTUR* IV, 130-132, 1999.

—. 1999b: Viscogliosi, A. "Porticus Octavia." In *LTUR* IV, 139-141, 1999.

von Hesberg, H. "Mausoleum Augusti: das Monument." In *LTUR* III, 234-237, 1996.

Yarden, L. *The spoils of Jerusalem on the Arch of Titus: a re-investigation.* Stockholm: Svenska Institutet i Rom, 1991.

Zachos, K. L. "The *tropaeum* of the sea-battle of Actium at Niko*polis*: interim report." *JRA 16* (2003): 64-92.

CHAPTER TWELVE

PROMOTING CIVIL WAR: REWARDS AND LOYALTY IN THE DANUBIAN-BALKAN PROVINCES, AD 285-354[1]

CRAIG H. CALDWELL III

Despite the considerable amount of recent scholarship devoted to the late Roman army, analyses of recruitment remain insufficiently engaged with the issue of loyalty.[2] The longstanding debate over the "barbarization" of the army has construed loyalty as a result of recruitment patterns, not a fluid factor to be manipulated. In intra-imperial conflicts, however, loyalty was a vital, contested resource like manpower and money. The civil wars of the fourth century AD provide an occasion to inject loyalty into an investigation of the late Roman army. To move beyond the battlefields between 285 and 354, this paper considers the financial incentives of the late Roman soldier and weighs the effects of regional solidarity and imperial clemency upon loyalty. The Danubian-Balkan provinces form a focal point for these inquiries since they were an important source of soldiers as well as the decisive theater in most fourth century civil wars.

Battlefield success proved less important than the flexible loyalties of a rival's soldiers in the civil war of 285. At the battle of the Margus (Morava), the emperor Carinus, backed by troops from the Rhine army and Italy, attempted to suppress the usurpation of Diocletian, whose

[1] I would like to thank Prof. Brian Campbell, Dr. Alan Stahl, and Edward Bragg for reading and commenting on earlier versions of this paper. I am also grateful to the American Numismatic Society for access to its collection as well as permission to photograph several coins.

[2] For example Elton 1996; Southern and Dixon 1996; Nicasie 1998, 83-96; Richardot 2001[2]; Carrié 2004, 371-88.

support came from the eastern army.[3] But since Carinus was murdered by his own troops before the battle was decided, Diocletian, whose army was perhaps inferior to that of Carinus, emerged triumphant. Cycles of intra-imperial strife in the third century had demonstrated the escape clause of civil war: it ended if one rival emperor or the other had a nasty fall onto an extended sword. Following the aborted battle, the victorious army of Diocletian must have absorbed the rank and file of Carinus's forces, and the conquering emperor showed special favor to those who had facilitated his success, including Aristobulus, Carinus's praetorian prefect.[4]

At the battle of the Margus, the possibility of mercy and reward was a vital part of Diocletian's strategy, and the Petrijanec Treasure is an example of the largesse with which an emperor might propel troops to the battlefield, win over an army, or try to prevent his own soldiers from abandoning him. This cache of gold coins mounted as *phalerae* (military ornaments) and other jewelry was unearthed in 1805 in the Dravus (Drava) valley east of Poetovio (Ptuj). Scholars have supposed it to be the savings of one of Carinus's officers on his way to the Margus in 285 since the newest coins are of Carinus, his father, and his brother.[5] The quantity and quality of the items suggest a soldier of higher rank who buried some of his wealth rather than risk its loss. This wearable fortune had marked the owner of the Petrijanec Treasure as a loyal follower of the dynasty of Carus, and it obliged him to fight for Carus's son Carinus in 285. Moreover, such a decorated soldier was an inspiration to his comrades to emulate his devotion to the cause. But golden distinctions also promoted the envy of the enemy, and perhaps that rationale encouraged its deposit. This soldier's fate at the Margus is unknown, but certain of his comrades—perhaps those who had not received such favor from Carinus— sought greater rewards from Diocletian. Carinus's incentives for loyalty and victory were insufficiently convincing at the moment of decision.

But what constituted effective metallic motivation for a late Roman soldier? He received three types of support from the state: *stipendia* (regular pay), *donativa* (donatives) paid upon imperial accessions and five year anniversaries, and *annonae* (rations). Of these, the soldier's wage was the most meager, and it was paid in billon or bronze coins with limited

---

[3] Aur. Vict. *Caes.* 39.11 provides a version of events especially hostile to Carinus, while Eutr. *Brev.* 9.20.2 includes a more neutral account of the battle; see Bird 1976, 123-32.

[4] Aur. Vict. *Caes.* 39.15; *PLRE* 106 v. "T. Cl. Aurelius Aristobulus". Aristobulus later served as proconsul of Africa and urban prefect.

[5] Noll 1974, 62-63, pl. 40.

purchasing power.[6] His rations were a more substantial sum if the state commuted it to cash rather than issuing it in kind, but few lower-ranking troops would have managed to save much of it after purchasing their subsistence.[7] The soldier's joy was the donative, which was paid in precious metals in quantities that dwarfed his other income. In the middle of the fourth century, new emperors gave five golden *solidi* and a pound of silver to each man when they assumed the purple, and five *solidi* every five years thereafter.[8] Rewards in gold not only held their value in the marketplace, but they also indicated imperial connections and privileges.[9] Moreover, since five *solidi* constituted the pinnacle of a soldier's regular expectations, a *fibula* that contained the gold of more than thirty *solidi* (such as one unearthed at Taraneš, discussed below) exerted a magnetic pull on the rank and file. When rival emperors tried to sway their opponents' armies and bolster the loyalty of their own troops, civil wars provided the opportunity for soldiers to gain immense rewards relative to their everyday finances.

Incentives did not guarantee a swift decision, however. At the Battle of Campus Ergenus in 313, neither side won a victory like Diocletian had at the Margus.[10] Maximinus Daia and Licinius fought on the plain of the Ergenus in eastern Thrace in 313 for mastery of the territorial legacy of their tetrarchic "father" Galerius. Like Diocletian in 285, Maximinus drew his support from the eastern army, while Licinius gathered a smaller force at Adrianople from the Danubian troops.[11] Maximinus had military mass and momentum on his side, but his army's commitment to fighting Licinius was uncertain, so the wealth of the eastern Empire was Maximinus's weapon of choice.[12] Furthermore, purchasing someone else's

---

[6] Jones 1964, 623-24.

[7] Jones 1964, 629-30.

[8] Amm. Marc. 15.6.3 (Constantius II in 355), 28.6.12 (Valentinian I in 370).

[9] Banaji 2001, 79.

[10] For the site of the battle, see Gregoire 1938, 584-86 and Barnes 1982, 63 n. 6.

[11] Any history of this civil war must depend upon the account of Lactantius in *De mort. pers.* 45-47, and caution is certainly warranted with regard to the author's Christian partisanship and characterizations of the rival emperors. Furthermore, Lactantius had been a teacher of rhetoric under Diocletian, so he was a master at deploying selective evidence to serve his agenda. Even so, Lactantius was a contemporary of the events he narrates, and his desire to cast the victors as servants of the Christian God does not negate the factual value of his polemic.

[12] Eutr. *Brev.* 10.4. Licinius was one of the late emperor Galerius's comrades, and he had served ably during that emperor's campaigns against Persia in the 290s. Whether the eastern army would fight well against the loyal general of its old commander would have been in doubt.

soldiers was quicker and cheaper than enlisting new ones.[13] At Byzantium and Heraclea, important harbors along the coastal road of southern Thrace, Maximinus offered rewards if the Licinian garrisons surrendered to him, but no speedy capitulations followed. Maximinus lost several weeks by investing each city in turn and compelling the troops to yield by shows of force. Because Licinius merited the loyalty of these small forces in Thrace, he had a few weeks of precious time to gather his army.

Maximinus's strategy of cooption by coin failed again when he confronted Licinius's entire army in late April 313. Hoping to avoid battle, Maximinus had trusted in fear and gold to deliver the Licinian army to him, much as Diocletian had overthrown Carinus. Yet, even when Licinius's troops faced the twin threats of Maximinus's greater numbers and the glittering reward for defection, they did not yield. While Lactantius attributes the soldiers' steadfastness to a Christian prayer given to Licinius by Constantine, more mundane factors are also worthy of consideration.[14] The speed with which Licinius assembled his army must have produced an army of veteran Moesian and Thracian troops, and many of them would have already served together on the frontier.[15] But even if regional and unit solidarity kept Maximinus from easily dividing the Licinian troops, he only needed to buy a single sword in Licinius's camp to end the civil war. Along with his Diocletianic bodyguard, Licinius's origin may have saved him. A native of the province of Dacia, Licinius trusted his fate at Campus Ergenus to men who served in his home region.[16] If the imperative of haste had not dictated Licinius's choice of troops, Maximinus's economic incentives might have prevailed. Instead, he was compelled to hazard his fortune in actual battle where his generalship proved inferior to Licinius's. The expectation of a nearly bloodless victory gave way to prolonged carnage in which perhaps half of Maximinus's army was slain or wounded.[17] Regional affinities and a commander's reputation among the soldiers complicated the path to victory through economic incentives.

The battlefield success of Licinius's hastily assembled army is a reminder of the importance of the Danubian-Balkan region as a source of military manpower. Since the standing army in these provinces was well-equipped and experienced following decades of campaigning in the

---

[13] For the considerable expense and time involved in raising new units, see Elton 1996, 123-24.

[14] Lactant. *De mort. pers.* 47.

[15] Lactant. *De mort. pers.* 45.7.

[16] For Licinius's origin in (New) Dacia see Eutr. *Brev.* 10.4.

[17] Lactant. *De mort. pers.* 47.4.

presence of a reigning emperor, it was a resource that could tip the scales of civil war in favor of its master. Lactantius claims that Licinius had gathered 30,000 men from the Danubian-Balkan army to oppose Maximinus in 313, and that figure seems essentially sound.[18] Moreover, beyond the existing soldiers there, the territory was well known for the quality of its recruits.[19] Maximinus had sought to seize the region not only for its strategic position and wealthy southern cities, but also to deny its reserves of warlike men to Licinius. Even though he was outnumbered, Licinius had advanced on Maximinus in order to hinder his movement further into Thrace, thus protecting his centers of recruitment and supply. In 316, Thracian recruits came to Licinius's rescue again, reinforcing his battered army and preventing his total defeat by Constantine at the Battle of Campus Ardiensis.[20]

In many cases, the fourth century civil wars became contests between the principal regional commands to secure "their" emperor's claim to the purple. To oppose Licinius's Danubian-Balkan forces in 316, Constantine mobilized the Gallic army that defended the Rhine frontier. One issue of coinage from the Constantinian mint at Trier refers specifically to the role of regional solidarity in encouraging the troops, the *solidi* with the reverse legend VIRTVS EXERCITVS GALL(ICANI) (fig. 12-1).[21] Soldiers' appreciation of coin reverses is difficult to prove, but when they mounted gold coins like these *solidi* as *phalerae* to be worn, the settings did not obscure the reverses.[22] The resonance of the designation of "Gallic army" is more definite. The army of the Rhine frontier had won Constantine's victory at the Milvian Bridge in 312, and panegyrics and Constantine's triumphal arch had immortalized them as the saviours of the state.[23] After the Gallic soldiers won another great battle and seized much of Danubian-Balkan territories from Licinius in 316-17, Constantine issued *solidi* from the captured mint of Siscia with reverses relevant to the Gallic army. Rather than mere borrowing of outdated types from Trier, these GAUDIVM ROMANORVM FRANCIA and VIRTVS EXERCITVS GALL(ICANI) *solidi* minted at Siscia may have been intended to reward

---

[18] Lactant. *De mort. pers.* 45.7.

[19] *Exp. tot. mund.* 50 (Thrace); *Pan. Lat.* 10.2.4, 11.3.9 (Pannonia).

[20] Zos. *HN* 2.19.

[21] *RIC* VII, 192.

[22] For example Bruhn 1993, nos. 4-5, 40-41.

[23] *Pan. Lat.* 4.7.4, 4.19.4, on the devotion of Constantine to his army and vice versa.

the victorious soldiers who had marched from the Rhine.[24] Constantine also minted *solidi* without the divisiveness of regional promotion, the VICTORIA CONSTANTINI AVG(VSTI) reverse type (fig. 12-2).[25] Although Constantine and Licinius reconciled early in 317, Siscia produced this coinage only in Constantine's name, probably as a reward to those on the right side in the civil war and a reminder of the region's new master.

Retaining capable soldiers such as those of the Gallic army was essential in an age of civil wars. The grave of one of Licinius's soldiers excavated in the Republic of Macedonia provides evidence for a particularly ostentatious way of promoting loyalty. Among the various ornate weapons and other possessions of the deceased is a *fibula* that extols the Licinian dynasty.[26] Used to fasten the military cloaks favoured by late Roman soldiers, *fibulae* had been fashionable markers of rank and wealth in the late third century as well as the fourth. But while earlier *fibulae* were silent, the one from Taraneš proclaims, "Jovius Augustus, may you conquer; Jovius Caesar, may you live."[27] At a half-pound of Roman gold, such a *fibula* was both a sign of imperial favour and an advertisement of this soldier's commitment to the cause of Licinius. As a wearable statement of loyalty and store of wealth, it served the same purpose as a *fidem Constantino* ring.[28] Other means of bestowing imperial generosity included *largitio* silver plate, which bear the marks of mass production and seem to have been given to more humble soldiers as donatives.[29] Two hoards of silver plate produced for Licinius's *decennalia* in 317 were unearthed in the Danubian-Balkan provinces at Naissus (Niš in Serbia) and Červenbreg in Bulgaria. Silver gifts of this type evolved out of the issuing of donatives in the form of commemorative coinage, and they served a similar purpose in confirming the recipient's connection with the emperor.[30] Although coins were still mounted for wearing in the fourth century as they had been in the third century Petrijanec Treasure, larger and more prominent objects joined them as incentives during the period of rivalry between Constantine and Licinius.

---

[24] *RIC* VII, 29, 30. Bruun (*RIC* VII, 413) decided that these reverse types were "borrowed from another mint and struck at a time when their original purpose was outdated."

[25] *RIC* VII, 28.

[26] Ivanovski 1987, 81-90.

[27] Ivanovski 1987, 83: IOVI AVG(VSTE) VINCAS; IOVI CAES(AR) VIVAS.

[28] Schwinden 1995, 39-45.

[29] Leader-Newby 2003, 16-19.

[30] Leader-Newby 2003, 19.

The soldiers' identification of their own side and that of their opponents was an important part of their motivation, especially if intra-imperial conflict resulted in significant casualties rather than assassination. As a late Roman soldier prepared to fight other Romans, he reserved the identity of Romanness for himself. The funerary inscription of Valerius Victorinus from Ulmetum (Pantelimon de Sus) in Scythia (fig. 12-3), who was perhaps a guardsman of Licinius, makes this point clearly: "[he] died in the battle of the Romans against [their] enemies at Chalcedon."[31] Here a civil war is a struggle of Romans versus ostensibly non-Roman opponents.[32] The consequences of considering opponents in civil war to be non-Romans are evident in the later campaign of Magnentius, discussed below.

After the defeat of Licinius, Constantine reorganized the entire army in the Danubian-Balkan provinces, apparently sending some of the best units east to Asia Minor and the Persian frontier.[33] Not only was this shift part of a master plan for the transformation of imperial armed forces, it also diminished the military influence of the provinces whose troops had opposed him under Licinius. While Constantine had singled out the Gallic army for special praise and rewards, the Danubian-Balkan soldiers may have received a different sort of attention after 324. In a fourth-century civil war, defeat could lead to the decline of an entire region's stature in the Empire.

Since the post-Constantinian Danubian-Balkan provinces retained their strategic central position and some of their wealth but had a reduced standing army for defense, they became a tempting target for usurpers. When Magnentius set out to invade the region from northern Italy in 351, he used every available incentive to retain his soldiers' loyalty and attract more supporters. Magnentius's rival was Constantine's son Constantius II, who had dynastic legitimacy and the formidable eastern army on his side. In Italy, Magnentius cast himself as the liberator of the Roman state, and he advertised this role to the troops on huge gold coins minted at Aquileia (fig. 12-4).[34] Judging from the find spots of this issue near Emona (Ljubljana), Magnentius's soldiers probably received their rewards prior to the invasion, and some soldiers deposited them before their first battle

---

[31] *AE* 1976, 631; Speidel 1995, 84-87; Woods 1997, 85-93.

[32] See Macaulay-Lewis in this volume.

[33] Lydus *Mag.* 2.10, 3.31; Nicasie, 39-40; perhaps following the precedent of Licinius's reassignment of Maximinus's troops implied by Lactant. *De mort. pers.* 48.

[34] *RIC* VIII, 122.

with Constantius's forces.[35] Magnentius also paid out accession donatives in silver ingots, some of which found their way into the Kaiseraugst Treasure in Switzerland.[36] When Magnentius's forces seized the mint of Siscia from Constantius, his soldiers must have received another bonus from the plunder. But according to Julian, Magnentius made further promises to the troops:

> "[Magnentius] did not ... trust to the energy of his soul or his physical strength, but to the numbers of his barbarian followers, and he boasted that he would lay everything at their feet to plunder, that every general and captain and common soldier of his should despoil an enemy of corresponding rank of his baggage and belongings, and that he would enslave the owners as well."[37]

Writing a panegyric of his cousin Constantius, Julian claimed that Magnentius's troops were barbarians, a common aspersion in civil wars.[38] As the ethnic composition of Magnentius's army from Gaul in 351 probably differed little from Constantine's own in 312, this allegation is incidental to the more important accusation that Magnentius authorized the enslavement of his enemies. This action was possible because some soldiers conceived of their service in civil wars as actually a matter of Romans versus non-Romans; fighting other Romans could be glossed as a battle on Rome's behalf, as in earlier Roman history.[39] If Magnentius carried such an attitude to its logical conclusion, he could indeed have endorsed the behavior decried by Julian. Roman soldiers did own slaves, and the emperors even provided for their support through the soldiers' rations.[40] In the midst of a high-stakes contest for the purple, Magnentius's promise of slaves to his troops seems reasonable, though he would then eschew the addition of the defeated foes to his forces as additional manpower. Severity toward opponents in intra-imperial conflict was Magnentius's strategy to shore up the motivation of his troops, and thus to protect himself against their defection and defeat.

---

[35] Mirnik 1981, 80, no. 291.

[36] Cahn and Kaufmann-Heinimann 1984.

[37] Julian *Or.* 2.57A, trans. W.C. Wright: οὔτι μὴν ... τῇ ῥώμῃ τῆς ψυχῆς πίσυνος οὐδὲ ἀλκῇ τοῦ σώματος, τῷ πλήθει δὲ τῶν ξυνεπομένων βαρβάρων, οἷς δὴ καὶ λείαν ἅπαντα προθήσειν ἠπείλει, ταξίαρχον ταξιάρχῳ καὶ λοχαγὸν λοχαγῷ καὶ στρατιώτην στρατιώτῃ τῶν ἐξ ἐναντίας αὐταῖς ἀποσκευαῖς καὶ κτήμασιν, οὐδὲ τὸ σῶμα ἀφιεὶς ἐλεύθερον.

[38] Heather 1999, 239-40.

[39] For numerous examples in earlier Roman literature see Henderson 1998.

[40] Speidel 1989, 239-48; *CTh* 7.4.17.

While Constantius II notoriously dispensed cruel punishments for any hint of disloyalty during peacetime, he countered Magnentius with calculated acts of clemency. As in the earlier fourth century civil wars, manpower was a pressing concern, but the emperor's choice of strategies for expanding his ranks was a delicate one. Constantius had decreed stricter limits on leave and early discharges, but once news of a civil war had spread through the ranks, an inflexible emperor might meet his demise if his troops deserted to support a more charitable rival.[41] Constantius thus employed subterfuge and subversion to deny the Danubian-Balkan provinces to Magnentius, permitting the rise of a usurper sponsored by Constantius's sister Constantia.[42] The general Vetranio was a safe candidate for usurpation, a useful tool to assist Constantius in the important tasks of rewarding and recruiting. Vetranio aided Constantius by paying an accession donative to the Danubian-Balkan army, denying Magnentius the opportunity to buy his way into the region. The *solidi* of Vetranio from Siscia with the reverse legend SALVATOR REI PVBLICAE were part of this largesse, and Vetranio may have employed the unusual word *salvator* to distinguish himself from Magnentius the *liberator*.[43] Even though the forces of Illyricum were less impressive than they had been in Licinius's time, Constantius needed them to tip the scales against Magnentius. Vetranio's ten-month reign in 350 was sufficient to concentrate the units in the provinces and bring them up to strength through recruiting. The entirely new bronze coinage that Vetranio minted to pay his soldiers' annual wages indicated that they were fighting for the legacy of Constantine: HOC SIGNO VICTOR ERIS was the reverse legend. Moreover, Vetranio issued these coins (and all his bronze) in his name (fig. 12-5), as well as in Constantius's, acknowledging that his rule depended upon his claim to reign alongside the last son of Constantine.[44] When Vetranio abdicated after Constantius "persuaded" his soldiers to desert him at Naissus, he added more than 20,000 troops to the latter's army.[45] For his usefulness to Constantius in a time of civil war, Vetranio earned the clemency of a quiet retirement in Bithynia.[46]

Constantius found more allies through strategic generosity. Before he met Magnentius in battle at Mursa in 351, Constantius obtained the

---

[41] *CTh* 7.1.4.

[42] For a detailed study of Vetranio and his coinage see Dearn 2003, 169-91.

[43] *RIC* VIII, 260.

[44] *RIC* VIII, 275, 283, 287, 288, 292 (Vetranio); *RIC* VIII, 272, 278, 282, 286, 291 (Constantius).

[45] Julian *Or.* 2.77B.

[46] Zon. *EH* 13.7.

defection of Silvanus, one of Magnentius's tribunes.[47] This was no small accomplishment, since Silvanus brought with him some of Magnentius's elite troops, the *schola palatina armaturarum*. Silvanus was part of the Gallic army that had elevated Magnentius in 350, and he was of Frankish ancestry like Magnentius, so his loyalty must have seemed secure. But Constantius kindled opportunism and family loyalty in Silvanus, both of which were important motivations in civil war. The opportunism was straightforward; Constantius raised Silvanus from the rank of tribune to general, essentially promoting him in Magnentius's place. Constantius also made a subtler appeal to family loyalty. Silvanus was the son of the Frankish general Bonitus, who fought for Constantine I in the civil wars against Licinius.[48] Just as Silvanus's father had helped Constantius's father to victory in an epic war to reunite the empire, Silvanus would assist Constantius in achieving the same goal. Constantius's successful motivation of Silvanus helped to seal the fate of Magnentius at Mursa.

Even with Silvanus's defection, tens of thousands of Roman soldiers perished at the Battle of Mursa. As civil wars proved ever more costly, emperors frequently referred back to Constantine, who was never defeated in civil war, to reassure and inspire their soldiers. The sighting of a cross in the sky in Jerusalem prior to the Battle of Mursa recalled Constantine's vision before the battle of the Milvian Bridge.[49] Constantine the Great was the most potent and lasting symbol of victory in intra-imperial conflict. What late Roman soldier would not have been moved to fight if he thought that his army would receive divine reinforcements, as Constantine's troops had?[50] An oration of Julian comparing Constantius's triumph in civil war with his father's victory indicates the length of Constantine's shadow:

> "The trophy that you [Constantius] set up for that victory [over Magnentius] was far more brilliant than your father's. [Constantine] led an army that had always proved itself invincible, and with it conquered a miserable old man [Licinius]. But the tyranny that you suppressed was flourishing and had reached its height, partly through the crimes that had been committed, but still more because so many of the youth were on that side, and you took the field against it with legions that had been trained by yourself."[51]

---

[47] Amm. Marc. 15.5.33; *PLRE* 840-41 v. "Silvanus 2"; Nutt 1973, 80.

[48] Amm. Marc. 15.5.33.

[49] Bihain 1973, 264-96.

[50] *Pan. Lat.* 4.14.1.

[51] Julian *Or.* 1.37B, trans. W.C. Wright: Τρόπαιον δὲ ἀνέστησας ἐπὶ τῇ νίκῃ τοῦ πατρῴου λαμπρότερον· ὁ μὲν γὰρ τοὺς τέως ἀμάχους δοκοῦντας ἄγων ἐκράτει γέροντος δυστυχοῦς· σὺ δὲ ἡβῶσαν καὶ ἀκμάζουσαν οὐ τοῖς κακοῖς μόνον οἷς ἔδρα, τῇ νεότητι δὲ

Julian could not escape a reference to the unconquerable Constantine even as he praised Constantius for winning a more difficult civil war. But Julian also mentions a sobering reality of civil war in the fourth century: the erection of trophies after Romans conquered Romans.[52] As Julian put it in another oration, Constantius fought battles against as many of his own subjects as against foreign enemies, and Ammianus indicates that he commemorated them in similar fashion.[53] While the public glorification of partisan triumph might have served Constantius's interests by motivating his soldiers, it also reinforced the attitude expressed by Valerius Victorinus's funerary inscription. In private and public memory, enemies in civil wars were non-Romans, though this outlook placed the ideas of loyalty to Rome and Romanness at risk.

To survive his long reign, Constantius learned the lessons of late Roman rewards and recruitment well. His treatment of the Caesar Gallus while he traveled across the Danubian-Balkan region in 354 provides an opportunity to observe a skilled hand at work. Reports from the East had convinced Constantius that his cousin Gallus intended to rebel against him, so Constantius resolved to avoid a civil war by taking him prisoner. Constantius lured Gallus westward with promises that he would elevate him to the rank of Augustus, but Gallus's route would take him through the midst of the Danubian-Balkan army. Since Constantius could ill afford Gallus "taking measures for his own security" by recruiting a retinue of loyal soldiers, he ordered the garrisons out of all the towns on Gallus's route.[54] When Gallus reached Adrianople, however, some legions in nearby winter quarters sent messengers to him. By encouraging Gallus to remain in Thrace under their protection, these Theban troops wanted to place their bets on Gallus's bid for power. But Constantius had dispatched several trusted officers to escort Gallus, and they succeeded in keeping him unaware of the soldiers' support for him.[55] Constantius knew the dangers of fertile recruiting grounds and self-interested soldiers, and his foresight headed off a rebellion. Although Constantius had already deprived Gallus of his guardsmen, handling someone who wore the purple was still a delicate task if he did not abdicate or die on the battlefield. To strip Gallus of his rank at Poetovio, Constantius sent motivated men,

---

πλέον, τὴν τυραννίδα παρεστήσω, τοῖς ὑπὸ σοῦ παρασκευασθεῖσι στρατοπέδοις παραταξάμενος.

[52] Amm. Marc. 21.16.15 for Constantius's triumphal arches in Pannonia and Gaul, where he had defeated Magnentius; Mayer 2006, 141-55.

[53] Julian Or. 2.53B.

[54] Amm. Marc. 14.11.13.

[55] Amm. Marc. 14.11.11-15.

"soldiers whom Constantius had chosen because they were under obligation to him for favors, and could not be influenced by bribes or any feeling of pity."[56] The *fibulae, solidi, largitio* silver, or promotions received by these troops cemented their connection to the emperor, and Constantius used their loyalty to snuff out a civil war before it began.

The fall of Gallus reveals the importance of winning over and rewarding soldiers in the civil wars of the fourth century. Mastery of these two aspects of intra-imperial conflict permitted Constantius to eliminate Gallus without recourse to the battlefield, a rare triumph in an age of protracted struggles. Even when aspiring emperors did not equal the off-the-battlefield effectiveness of Diocletian and Constantius, regional solidarity could stiffen soldiers' resolve, as it did for the army of Licinius in Thrace. Such cohesion left its mark upon the rewards, such as Constantine's *solidi* for the Gallic army. Distinguishing civil war opponents as non-Romans seems to have been a common tactic, and Magnentius and Constantius extended it to matters of policy in intra-imperial conflict. Incentives for civil war were vital because they offered the possibility for swift, nearly bloodless triumph, and the ensuing competition in promoting intra-imperial conflict contributed to the instability of the fourth century. Exploring the intersection of late Roman civil wars and incentives thus fills an important gap in the history of warfare in the later Roman Empire.

Figures

Figure. 12-1. Solidus of Constantine, Trier mint, c. 317 (*RIC* VII, 192). Image courtesy of Numismatik Lanz München (Auction 112, Lot 866, 25 Nov. 2002).

---

[56] Amm. Marc. 14.11.19.

Figure. 12-2. Solidus of Constantine, Siscia mint, 317. (*RIC* VII, 28) (ANS 1001.1.22131; photograph by author).

Figure. 12-3. Valerius Victorinus' Funerary Inscription, Ulmetum, after 324. (*AE* 1976, 631) (Histria Museum in Istria, Romania; photograph by author).

Figure 12-4. Medallion of Magnentius, Aquileia mint, c. 351. (*RIC* VIII, 122) Image courtesy of Numismatica Ars Classica. (Auction 33, Lot 605, 6 April 2006).

Figure 12-5. Æ2 of Vetranio, Siscia mint, 350. (*RIC* VIII, 287) (ANS 1984.146.1096; photograph by the author).

Bibliography

Banaji, J. *Agrarian Change in Late Antiquity: Gold, Labour, and Aristocratic Dominance*. Oxford: Oxford University Press, 2001.

Barnes, T. D. *Constantine and Eusebius*. Cambridge: Harvard University Press, 1982.

Bihain, E. "L'épitre de Cyrille de Jérusalem à Constance sur la vision de la croix (BHG[3] 413)." *Byzantion* 43 (1973): 264-96.

Bird, H. W. "Diocletian and the Deaths of Carus, Carinus and Numerian." *Latomus* 35 (1976): 123-32.

Bruhn, J.-A. *Coins and Costume in Late Antiquity*. Washington, DC: Dumbarton Oaks, 1993.

Cahn, H. A. and Kaufmann-Heinimann, A. *Der Spätrömische Silberschatz von Kaiseraugst*. Derendingen: Habegger, 1984.

Carrié, J.-M. "Le système de recrutement des armies romaines de Dioclétien aux Valentiniens," *L'armée Romaine de Dioclétien à Valentinien Ier*, 371-87. Lyon: Université Jean Moulin 3, 2004.

Dearn, A. "The Coinage of Vetranio: Imperial Representation and the Memory of Constantine the Great." *NC* 163 (2003): 169-91.

Elton, H. *Warfare in Roman Europe, AD 350-425*.Oxford: Clarendon Press, 1996.

Gregoire, H. "Deux champs de bataille: 'Campus Ergenus' et 'Campus Ardiensis.'" *Byzantion* 13 (1938): 584-86.

Heather, P. "The Barbarian in Late Antiquity: Image, Reality, and Transformation," *Constructing Identities in Late Antiquity*, edited by Richard Miles, 234-58. New York: Routledge, 1999.

Henderson, J. *Fighting for Rome: Poets and Caesars, History, and Civil War*. Cambridge: Cambridge University Press, 1998.

Ivanovski, M. "The Grave of a Warrior from the Period of Licinius I Found at Taraneš." *Archaeologica Iugoslavica* 24 (1987): 81-90.

Jones, A. H. M. *The Later Roman Empire, 284-602: a social, economic and administrative survey*. Oxford: Blackwell, 1964.

Leader-Newby, R. *Silver and Society in Late Antiquity: Functions and Meanings of Silver Plate in the Fourth to Seventh Centuries*. Aldershot: Ashgate, 2003.

Mayer, E. "Civil War and Public Dissent: the State Monuments of the Decentralised Roman Empire," in *Social and Political Life in Late Antiquity*, edited by W. Bowden, A. Gutteridge, and C. Machado, 141-55. Leiden; Boston: Brill, 2006.

Mirnik, I. A. *Coin Hoards in Yugoslavia*. Oxford: BAR, 1981.

Nicasie, M. J. *Twilight of Empire: The Roman Army from the Reign of Diocletian until the Battle of Adrianople*. Amsterdam: J. C. Gieben, 1998.

Noll, R. *Vom Altertum zum Mittelalter*, Katalog der Antikensammlung I, Kunsthistorisches Museum, 62-63.Vienna: Schroll, 1974.

Nutt, D. C. "Silvanus and the Emperor Constantius II." *Antichthon* 7 (1973): 80-89.

Richardot, P. *La fin de l'armeïe romaine: 284-476*[2]. Paris: Economica, 2001.

Schwinden, L. "Kaisertreue: Ein weiterer Fingerring mit Inschrift fidem
    Constantino." *Funde und Ausgrabungen im Bezirk Trier* 27 (1995): 39-
    45.
Southern, P. and K.R. Dixon. *The Late Roman Army*. London: B.T.
    Batsford, 1996.
Speidel, M. P. "The Soldiers' Servants." *Ancient Society* 20 (1989): 239-
    48.
—. "A Horse Guardsman in the War between Licinius and Constantine."
    Chiron 25 (1995): 84-87.
Woods, D. "Valerius Victorinus Again." *Chiron* 27 (1997): 85-93.
Wright, W. C. *The Works of the Emperor Julian*, vol. I. Cambridge, MA:
    Harvard University Press, 1913.

CHAPTER THIRTEEN

INDISCIPLINE IN THE SIXTH CENTURY HISTORIOGRAPHY OF GENERALS

CONOR WHATELY

In the last two decades or so, the late Roman army has garnered a lot of attention, though much remains to be done.[1] This is particularly true in regard to discipline and insubordination on the battlefield,[2] factors that some scholars argue contributed to the effectiveness/ineffectiveness of the army, and hence the stability, or instability, of the state.[3] Before anyone can reconstruct how those issues affected the army, we need to understand the way that discipline and insubordination are presented by the contemporary writers, who are by and large civilian—thus, although discipline and insubordination are issues faced on the battlefield, the writers who discuss them do so beyond the battlefield.[4] There are a

---

[1] I would like to thank Michael Whitby, Ed Bragg, Brian Campbell, and Shaun Tougher for commenting on various drafts of this paper.

[2] Discipline is a multi-faceted term that encompasses the somewhat disparate issues of the order of soldiers in battle; their willingness to hold the line in the face of enemy attacks; the actions of the soldiers towards the inhabitants of besieged cities and surrounding lands on campaigns; and the obedience of the soldiers to their commanding officers and the mutinies that can often evolve from disobedience or insubordination (which in turn is often caused by other serious problems such as a soldier's remuneration). In regard to soldiers and civilians, the most recent contribution is that of Fear (2007), who presents much of the evidence, though there are many points where I disagree with his interpretations. In regard to mutinies and military unrest, see Kaegi 1981.

[3] For recent views regarding the effectiveness of the sixth century army see Elton 2007a and 2007b, Lee 2005, Rance 2000, 2004, and 2007, Syvänne 2004, and Whitby 1995, 2000, and 2005. For some earlier views on the discipline of the sixth century army see Delbrück 1980, Grosse 1920, 272-320, and Jones 1964, 668-679.

[4] Both Jordanes, whom I do not discuss at any length in this paper, and Procopius, who is discussed, spent a significant part of their lives on the staff of important

number of authors, from a plethora of different genres, who could be used in this discussion. I have selected five writers who describe warfare from the 530s through to the 620s, partly because they place a heavy emphasis on war, partly because they stick to traditional Greco-Roman genres, namely historiography and military handbooks.[5] In what follows I shall highlight some of the patterns that surface when we look more closely at the descriptions of indiscipline and insubordination found in the accounts of Procopius, Syrianus, Agathias, Maurice, and Theophylact Simocatta, with particular emphasis on Procopius and Maurice.[6] What emerge are connections between how generalship and discipline, and—perhaps less surprisingly—generalship and insubordination are represented in literature;[7] furthermore, didacticism is also an important part of the discussions of discipline found in these works, and this is largely due to the significant role that these works, both the secular histories and the military treatises, had in the "training" of would-be generals. Thus, the following discussion is less concerned with discipline and insubordination on the battlefield than it is with generalship—a much discussed issue at the

---

military officials. Jordanes was a secretary for the Master of Soldiers Gunthigis (*Getica* 50.265), and Procopius was a secretary for Belisarius (*Wars* 1.12.24). Procopius in particular was also involved in some of the action that he describes in the *Wars*, though, more often than not, his duties were administrative, and so he was essentially a civilian. We know less about Jordanes' combat experience, for he effaces himself more fully from his texts, so any suggestions about his role would be speculative.

[5] There is a diverse body of material that could be used to analyse warfare and discipline at the end of the late Roman period such as the poems of Corippus, the ecclesiastical history of Evagrius, and the law codes of Justinian. I briefly discuss the significance of using five authors who were working in traditional Greco-Roman genres at the end of this paper. For a provocative discussion of war in classical era literature, see Hornblower (2007).

[6] Kaegi 1983, in his essay on Byzantine strategy and military thinking, focuses on Procopius and Maurice, the two most important works for the study of warfare in the sixth and early seventh centuries. Given the restrictions on the length of this paper, I have in many cases been forced to skirt a detailed treatment of some of the issues that are raised. Cf. Kaegi 1990.

The translations used are those referred to in the notes. Where no translator is listed, the translations are my own.

[7] This is perhaps an unsurprising conclusion for the histories of Procopius, Agathias, and Theophylact, given their interest in characterization.

conference[8]—and its relationship to discipline and insubordination in sixth century historiography beyond the battlefield.[9]

Procopius, who as a member of Belisarius' staff was an eyewitness and participant in much of what he describes, wrote his *Wars* in the 550s. In the preface to that work Procopius says that he recorded these events for the benefit of those men who might find themselves in a similar situation (1.1.1).[10] He also says:

> For those who plan to wage war or are preparing themselves for any kind of struggle might benefit if there is a narrative of a similar situation in history, as this reveals the outcome for those who came before and were involved in a similar contest, and hints to those who plan best what sort of outcome the present events are likely to have.[11]

This is an important point, and one that is often overlooked by those who mine Procopius for evidence of problems in the sixth century Roman army. Interestingly, we are reminded of this point at the beginning of the *Vandal Wars* when Belisarius finds himself bemused in the face of a new enemy of which he had no experience: "As soon as Belisarius disembarked upon the island [Sicily], being at a loss he started to feel uneasy and it drove him mad not knowing what sort of men the Vandals whom he was attacking were, or how capable in war they were, or what

---

[8] In this volume, see Asmonti, who investigates the career of the Athenian general Conon, and Levithan, who explores the imperial presence on the field of battle (a situation not found for much of the period of this paper).

[9] Some similar historiographical issues to those explored in this paper have been raised in two of the other papers of this conference; namely moralizing and generalship in historiography, and the process of selection and omission in the composition of an historical narrative. Hau explores the moralizing that often accompanies the victorious general after battle, while Nevin suggests that ethical concerns and atrocities were only included in a narrative when they might provide a useful example.

[10] For more information about Procopius see Evans 1972; Cameron 1985; Brodka 2004, 14-151; and Kaldellis 2004, among others. For a fairly concise look at the development of Greek historiography, see Hornblower 1995.

[11] 1.1.2. Procopius was certainly not the first historian to suggest that his work might have a didactic element, nor the last. Thucydides, for example, says: "It will be enough for me, however, if these words of mine are judged useful by those who want to understand clearly the events which happened in the past and which (human nature being what it is) will, at some time or other and in much the same ways, be repeated in the future" (1.22, trans. Warner). Frontinus' treatise, *Stratagems*, of course, was aimed, at least in part, at would-be generals.

tactics to use or from where they would launch their attacks".[12] Thus, as I go through some of the cases of indiscipline in the *Wars*, I shall point out how the examples are by and large framed by Procopius' concern with generalship, part of the didactic aim of the work.[13]

In Evans' brief monograph he notes that discipline was an important concern of Procopius'.[14] And sure enough, indiscipline rears its ugly head early on in the *Wars*. While setting the scene for the war between the Romans and Persians, Procopius includes some "historical" background material about the Persians themselves, including a narrative of the battle in 484 between the Ephthalite Huns and the Persians.[15] Discipline plays a key role in that battle, and in this case it is the Ephthalites who fare better. Earlier, the Persians had deceived the Huns, and so the Huns were keen to launch an immediate and severe attack in retribution; furthermore, they bitterly reproach their king. This unnamed king, however, who also happens to be the commander-in-chief of the Hunnic army, cautions his troops against such rash behaviour and calms them down. As a result, the Huns win the battle and "enslave" the Persians.[16] When we first encounter the Roman army in the narrative we are reminded almost right away of the importance of a general. One Roman army under Patricius and Hypatius is caught unawares and routed by the forces of Kavad (1.8.11ff). Procopius then tells us that another Roman army came to the scene shortly thereafter, but accomplished nothing of note because they lacked a commander-in-chief (1.8.20).

Discipline plays a huge role in the first major battle of the *Wars*, the Battle of Dara (530). In the exhortations found before the main phase of the fighting the theme of discipline is constantly stressed.[17] Peroz, the

---

[12] 3.14.1. For a good study of the information available to a Roman commander in Late Antiquity see Lee 1993.

[13] Indeed, when reading any ancient historian—and Procopius is no exception—it is important to be mindful of the goals that he sets out for himself in the preface as this often guides the narrative in more ways than might be at first apparent.

[14] Evans 1972, 47-76, esp. 65ff.

[15] In fact, this battle serves as something of a proto-battle, laying down some of the important elements of the battle-narratives to follow.

[16] For an argument that the theme of "freedom and slavery" underscores the narrative of the *Wars*, see Pazdernik 1997.

[17] Contrary to some recent assertions, the battle exhortations found in Procopius' *Wars* do serve an important function in the narrative. In the respective speeches the generals lay out the factors that will be crucial to their sides' success; these speeches also incorporate some of the details from the preceding narrative. Once the action commences, it is the mastering of the relevant factors that leads to victory. Cf. Kaldellis 2004, esp. 21ff.

Persian general, goes to great lengths in his exhortation to condemn the Romans' record on discipline.[18] He says the following: "in the past the Romans have not been used to going into battle without confusion and disorder", "they were not thrown into confusion, because they had not yet encountered the dangers of war", and "fear and inexperience will seize them and throw them into disorder". In Belisarius' and Hermogenes' reply, which is closely modelled on Peroz's speech, Belisarius assures his troops that they will be successful in this battle if they obey the orders of their commanders. The two generals assure their troops that it was only their disobedience that led to their previous defeat (and not, by proxy, any deficiency in their ability to fight), "defeated...being quite disobedient to your officers". If those same troops choose to follow orders ("so if you wish to obey the orders given") and take courage despite the seemingly unfavourable conditions ("the multitude of the enemy is particularly frightening", "thus be brave men in the presence of this danger"), it is the Persians who will find themselves defeated, "for they are coming against us confident in nothing other than our former disorder".[19] As it turns out, it is Belisarius and Hermogenes who have a better grasp of the situation, for it is the Persians who end up turning tail and fleeing while the Romans perform a number of manoeuvres that could not have been affected without strict discipline.

There are a number of other occasions in the *Wars* where discipline is described in terms of generalship. The Battle of Callinicum (531) turns largely on the failure of Belisarius to control his men. What had initially been a successful operation, in which the Romans had managed to keep the Persians at bay without forcing a confrontation, became a battle, and then a defeat, once Belisarius gave in to his men's overzealousness.[20] A

---

[18] Invariably, battle exhortations are works of fiction created by the author to add greater structure to the narrative, to highlight some important points raised in the narrative itself, and to identify some of the ideas that might have been relevant to the respective characters giving the speeches; this is particularly true for Procopius. That is not to deny the existence of speeches before the start of battles, for we have countless examples where generals are described riding through the ranks encouraging troops before, or at the start of, a battle. The point is that what was said by the generals is unlikely to be what is claimed by the historians. See Hansen 1993.

[19] Caesar, too, had rebuked his troops for failing to follow his suggestions, see Caesar *BG* 1.39-41.

[20] Shahîd has wrongly claimed (1995, esp. 134-142) that Procopius blamed the Romans' Arab allies, when in fact Procopius lays most of the blame on Belisarius and the unruly Anatolians who urge him to battle. Evagrius, for example, based on

similar situation occurs in the Battle of Nisibis (530), and it, too, involves insubordinate officers (2.18.1ff). Belisarius tells his men not to camp too close to Nisibis, and most follow his instructions, though Peter and some others do not. As a result, they are nearly routed by the Persians and are only saved thanks to the foresight of Belisarius.[21] In the Battle of Anglon (543) the general Narses becomes enraged over some conflicting intelligence and, as a result, it spreads to his troops and they end up moving about in a disorderly manner (2.25.10ff). In the *Vandal Wars*, two Massagetae kill one of their own men and Belisarius ends up crucifying them in order to set an example (3.12.8-22). Not long after this, Belisarius again takes immediate and harsh action when he catches his men taking some fruit from a local field (3.16.1ff).[22]

There is one further example of indiscipline that I want to highlight from Procopius' narrative, this one from the *Gothic Wars*. In the early stages of the siege of Rome around 537, the Byzantine soldiers are elated by their success earlier and so decide that they want to engage the Goths again in open battle (5.28.1ff).[23] Belisarius refuses, reasoning that the relative size of the two armies would not work to their advantage. But the soldiers continue to harass Belisarius with the aid of the Roman populace, and so he eventually concedes—again—and, according to Procopius, convinces himself that an open battle is preferable to a sudden sally. Not surprisingly, the Romans are routed. If Belisarius had followed his instincts and held firm in his position—that is, had he not caved in to the insubordination of his soldiers—at the very least the Romans would not have suffered the casualties that they did. Thus, it is clear that, in those passages where Procopius presents the issues of indiscipline and insubordination, they are invariably tied to Procopius' presentation of

---

his reading of Procopius, believed that the defeat was due to the indiscipline of the troops (Evagrius *HE* 4.13). See Greatrex 1998, 200-212.

[21] Of course, if Belisarius had managed to keep those men under his control to begin with, he would not have been forced to engage the Persians unprepared and thereby risk a serious setback in his campaign.

[22] With these two cases we are reminded of Narses' handling of a similar situation in Agathias' narrative of the Battle of Casilinum [2.7.2ff], which took place in 554; it is possible that Agathias was intentionally alluding to Procopius' discussion of Belisarius' actions. On Agathias see below.

[23] Generally, I use the terms "Byzantine" and "Roman" interchangeably; however, given the context of this example (the siege of Rome), I have used "Byzantine" to signify that I am referring to East Roman soldiers, and not soldiers from the city of Rome. Despite this point, I am very much in agreement with the conclusions of Kaldellis (2007, 42-187) concerning the Roman identity of those whom scholars generally call Byzantines.

Belisarius, the text's didactic purpose, and the structure of the narrative at large.

Most of the examples above have been drawn from that part of the *Wars* where Procopius is generally supposed to have presented a favourable picture of Belisarius. Instead, we see that Procopius has presented a balanced view of the general who dominates the narrative.[24] Wherever indiscipline and insubordination are an issue in Procopius' text, a general, and usually Belisarius, is responsible for their elimination. Indiscipline is included in the narrative as one way of highlighting Belisarius' qualities as a general.

Agathias, a well-educated lawyer, poet, and historian, who was writing in the last third of the sixth century and narrated the years 552-559, is often cited in support of the apparent decline in military standards.[25] To be sure, there are a few places in the text where the discipline of the Roman army is brought into question; however, they are used to illustrate one of the broader aims of the work and the writer's concern with individuals.[26] Agathias devotes a sizeable chunk of his preface to the merits of praising, or slandering, individuals, and the relationship between such characterizations and the truth (16-20); we must bear this in mind when we examine the allegations of indiscipline in the text.

Towards the beginning of his *Histories*, the eunuch Narses, in an exhortation (composed by Agathias) in which he is trying to play down the enemy's numerical superiority, says: "...we shall prove very much their betters in regard to our disciplined behaviour, provided we keep our heads".[27] Agathias also claims that "Narses ordered them to train much more vigorously for war and strengthened their resolve by daily drill."[28] A few chapters later, Agathias says that Narses was blessed with excellent generalship (2.9.1). Indeed, Narses' efforts continue to pay off throughout the text, and are particularly apparent in the Battle of Casilinum in 554.

---

[24] Procopius did, after all, state in his preface that he would do as much: "In accordance with this principle he has not concealed the failures of even his most intimate acquaintances, but has written down with complete accuracy everything which befell those concerned, whether it happened to be done well or ill by them" (1.1.5, trans. Dewing).

[25] For further discussion of Agathias see Cameron 1970; Kaldellis 1997; 1999; 2003; and Brodka 2004, 152-192.

[26] Agathias is also concerned with morality, which explains why we find what are at times pretty stark contrasts between "good" characters such as Narses and Belisarius and "bad" characters (in the sense of evil), such as Justinian.

[27] 1.16.9, trans. Frendo, with revisions.

[28] 2.1.2.

This Roman victory over the Franks, a "famous and brilliant victory" (2.10.1), is in Agathias' eyes largely a result of the work of Narses. Even though the Franks found themselves in dire straits prior to the engagement, Narses' mettle was still tested. The Franks has worked themselves up into a fervour, and just as the Romans are proceeding to battle, Narses learns of the transgression of a Herul chief (2.7.2ff). Narses dutifully stops the march to address the issue and exact the appropriate punishment; he then continues to the field of battle, ignoring the reproaches of the Heruls. Just before the fighting itself begins, two renegade Heruls tell the Franks that they will find the Romans "suffering from confusion and disorderly behaviour, with the Herul contingent embittered and refusing to take any part in the action, and many of the other troops terrified by their defection."[29] Immediately following that statement, Agathias assures us that the allegations of the traitors are false: "Doubtless because that was what he wished them to be, Butilinus had little difficulty in accepting these words as true."[30] As noted, victory belonged to the Romans, thanks in no small part to the generalship of Narses, who marshalled his line to take account of the possible absence of the Heruls.

In the latter part of book five, Agathias paints a fairly gloomy portrait of the army's conditions. But this description is presented in relation to Justinian's poor leadership. Agathias claims that Justinian had allowed the quality of the armed forces to deteriorate (5.14.1), that officials had been depriving the soldiers of their pay (5.14.2), that they were deprived of their food (5.14.3), and that the soldiers had been neglected to such a degree that they were forced to abandon the military profession entirely (5.14.4). Despite the miserable state of the army, Belisarius is able to appear and make an important contribution. Shortly after Agathias' tirade against Justinian, Belisarius is put in charge of Constantinople's defences in the face of a Hunnic approach. In an exhortation prior to an engagement with the Huns outside of Constantinople in 559, Belisarius says:

> But if we keep our heads and use our traditional discipline and act with prudence, they will learn that if you are to succeed and move forwards it will be through experience, which is always to be preferred to the situations in which you are forced to make difficult decisions in the heat of battle.[31]

---

[29] 2.8.6, trans. Frendo, with revisions.

[30] 2.8.7, trans. Frendo.

[31] 5.18.11, trans. Frendo, with revisions.

The Romans end up winning the battle despite being outnumbered, and, according to Agathias, the casualties that they suffer are negligible (5.20.1).

Taking any of these passages individually will yield a skewed picture of the situation. On the one hand, the excerpt from Belisarius' exhortation would suggest that the army was well-trained; on the other hand, the comments about Justinian would suggest the opposite. However, if we take these passages, and the work, together, a different picture emerges. The problems which accrue for the army later in the *Histories* are attributable to the neglect of Justinian and his top officials; this is what puts Constantinople in such trouble in 559 and leads to Belisarius' recall. Conversely, when an able "good" general is left in charge, order is maintained, or, in some cases, restored. Narses, the eunuch and general, is very much the focus of the first two books of the *Histories*: he is referred to more than any other character. And Narses' achievements and the state of the armed forces are much starker once we read on and learn of the scale of Justinian's negligence. Agathias is hostile towards Justinian, and one particular arena which he felt deserved censure was the military. With Narses in charge, the army had been quite successful (Casilinum 554), but once he is no longer part of the narrative, and Justinian was left to his own devices with the change in theatre of operations—Lazica for example— chaos reigned. It was only with the recall of another eminent commander, namely Belisarius, that the army could succeed again. Agathias is selective in his references to indiscipline, and tends only to refer to it when it is pertinent to his objectives, namely the slandering of Justinian or the praising of a general such as Narses.

Theophylact Simocatta, who wrote a universal history during the reign of Heraclius (610-641), makes frequent reference to military discipline and mutiny.[32] Like Agathias, he too was probably a lawyer, and was possibly born in the 580s; we know less about him than we do about Agathias. In one passage, Theophylact says that "when everyone had been assembled by the general, the soldiers poured insults and abuse against Theodore".[33] Yet, only a few lines earlier, at the beginning of chapter 9, he had said that "on the following day…an uncontrollable terror deranged the general and drove him in a frenzy to inexplicable flight".[34] At 3.12.7 Theophylact gives us a rather familiar pronouncement: "And so the general attentively corrected the former lack of military training in the armies, moulding the

---

[32] For a detailed study of Theophylact see Whitby 1988. Cf. Brodka 2004, 193-227.
[33] 2.9.14, trans. Whitby.
[34] 2.9.1, trans. Whitby.

unformed and transforming the undisciplined into good order."[35]
Something similar was written by Agathias, as we just saw, and this is, in
fact, a common *topos* of ancient writers; it applies to the armies of both the
early and the late empire, as Wheeler has demonstrated.[36] To be sure, an
important facet of this episode is the appointment of Justinian (not the
emperor who reigned while Procopius was writing) to the rank of general
in the east in that same year, 575, in which Theophylact asserts that he
restored discipline (3.12.6). There are several further places where
Theophylact seems to refer to the indiscipline of the Roman army;
however, in all of these cases the charges are presaged with information
about the poor service conditions. This includes the intermittent
breakdown in the payment of the troops, and occasionally the failure of the
general in question to adhere to traditional standards of behaviour. So, for
example, we learn that in 587 or 588 the following occurred:

> "An ancient custom was honoured in the camp, that the man who was
> about to assume the reins of generalship should, when the soldiers came to
> meet him, dismount from the horse, walk through the middle of the
> soldiery and favour the camp with his salutations. When Priscus did not in
> fact do this…the army did not bear the insult with moderation…when the
> third day had passed and the reduction of the soldiers' remuneration was
> no longer in concealment…extreme anarchy made its entry: the masses
> converged on the general's tent, some carrying stones, others swords, as
> the occasion served each man."[37]

A little later, perhaps in 593, "mutiny visited them and confusion
reigned",[38] but only once it became clear to the soldiers that Priscus, the
general was depriving them of their share of the booty (6.7.6). Towards
the end of the *Universal History* in the section relating to the revolt of
Phocas in 602, we learn that this most serious of mutinies arose only after
the troops had learned that they were to winter in the territory of their foes,
the Slavs (8.6.2). Theophylact opens his *Universal History* with a speech
that highlights the qualities of leadership. Indeed, for Theophylact it was

---

[35] 3.12.7, trans. Whitby.
[36] Wheeler 1996, *passim*, esp. 248ff. In his 1996 paper, Wheeler questions the
charges of laxity often brought against the Syrian legions of the early and high
Roman Empire and suggests that these legions were no worse than those
elsewhere. Cf. Lendon 2005, who speculates that in the Roman army's earlier
years some lapses of discipline, and the competitive spirit that went along with
them, actually worked to its benefit.
[37] 3.1.7-9, trans. Whitby.
[38] 6.7.7, trans. Whitby.

up to the general to restore order once indiscipline reigned in the camp. It was upon his shoulders that any blame rested, for when discipline lapsed it was attributable to him alone, and it was his responsibility to re-establish the balance.[39]

The three authors that I have looked at thus far are classicizing historians who all stress the connection between generalship and discipline. This same connection is also drawn in the technical military treatises to which we shall now turn.

In an important article on the morale of the Roman army from the mid Republic to the fourth century, Doug Lee identifies three factors which influenced discipline and morale, the third of which is leadership.[40] Other scholars, both those who have argued for and against a disciplined Roman army, have also pointed to the connection between generalship and discipline, while also acknowledging a connection between remuneration and discipline.[41] This is also the assessment of the writers of the two principal military treatises of the sixth century, Syrianus and Maurice.[42] Syrianus, who was probably an amateur and likely writing in the middle of the sixth century, ties the general explicitly to strategy—the focus of his treatise, the *Peri Strategias*—which is, for him, the chief means by which a state can defend its land and defeat its foe.[43] In addition, as regards the general's most important qualities, Syrianus says that, "he should instil fear in the disobedient, while he should be gracious and kind to the others".[44] Syrianus even devotes a section to how orders should be conveyed to the officers and men (14.24-26). Even though Syrianus' interest in the issue does not extend much beyond those few comments, it was still present, and suggests that he too believed that there was a strong connection between generalship and discipline.

---

[39] See Whitby 1988, 311ff for some similar pronouncements about Theophylact's focus on leadership and the role of the individual (or more often than not, lack thereof) in historical causation.

[40] The other two factors are honour, fear, and shame on the one hand and group identity and cohesion on the other (Lee 1996). Cf. Lee 2005, 122-123.

[41] Rance 1993, 157, 250ff; Whitby 1995, 104ff; Southern and Dixon 1996, 171ff; Wheeler 1996, 236; Haldon 1999, 229ff, 264-265.

[42] Syrianus and Maurice were not, of course, the first writers of treatises to recognize this connection between generalship and discipline. Onasander, who was writing a manual on generalship in the first century, also stressed some similar points. Rance (2007, 343-348) offers a useful, and concise, overview of late Roman military treatises.

[43] The ancient understanding of strategy is different from modern conceptions. See Kaegi 1983.

[44] 4.22, trans. Dennis.

The other major military manual of the century, the *Strategikon*, was
written in the 590s. The treatise, which combines Greek military theory
with the exigencies of contemporary warfare, may have been an official
document, and though it was probably not written by the emperor Maurice
himself, it may very well have been commissioned by the emperor.[45]

In the preface to the work Maurice concludes with some points about
discipline in the army. Without a doubt discipline plays a much more
conspicuous role in Maurice's work than it does in Syrianus'. Yet, this
need not imply that discipline had deteriorated and that Maurice was eager
to see it restored, as is too often assumed. Granted, early in the preface he
does claim that "the state of the armed forces has been neglected for a long
time and has fallen completely into oblivion";[46] but he qualifies that
pronouncement with the statement: "those who assume command of
troops do not understand even the most obvious matters and run into all
sorts of difficulties. Sometimes the soldiers are blamed for lack of training,
sometimes the general for inexperience".[47] Only a few lines later he sets
out what it is that he has written: "We have, then, devised a rather modest
elementary handbook or introduction for those devoting themselves to
generalship, which should facilitate the progress of those who wish to
advance to a better and more detailed knowledge of those ancient tactical
theories."[48] Thus, he clearly believes that the responsibility for any
deficiencies in the armed forces actually lies with its commanders, and it is
to them that this treatise is addressed. Maurice also felt the need to justify
his work; if the contemporary army was not in need of reform, then there
would be no point for him to write his treatise.[49]

If we take a closer look at those parts of the *Strategikon* that refer
specifically to the discipline of the soldiers, we see that they are included
with instructions about what the general ought to do in the situation in
question. Indeed, Rance has convincingly argued that much of the
language of the treatise is standard for the genre, and need not represent
any real decline in standards.[50] In book 1, which is based on official

---

[45] Few scholars would attribute the work to the emperor Maurice, and so many
have opted to use "Pseudo-Maurice;" however, for simplicity's sake, I have used
the more traditional moniker "Maurice."

[46] 10-11, trans. Dennis.

[47] 11-14, trans. Dennis.

[48] 21-27, trans. Dennis.

[49] Vegetius makes similar pronouncements about the late fourth century army and
is constantly looking back at the glories of the earlier Roman army. See Milner
1993, xiii-xliii.

[50] Rance 1993.

material, there is a list of twenty military regulations divided up into three sections. Although at least a quarter of the regulations are devoted to discipline and insubordination, an equal number is devoted to injuries caused to the soldiers themselves. In point of fact, if there is a common theme among the military regulations listed, it is the importance of maintaining morale. Book 8 is entitled "General Instructions and Maxims". Among the one hundred and forty-five instructions and maxims listed, there is a little more than a handful that relate specifically to discipline. What is more, the connection is also made between discipline and morale. Maxim 8, for example, opens with the line: "courage and discipline are able to accomplish more than a large number of troops."[51] Thus, in this treatise, discipline is tied to morale, and morale is created by the commander, or, more specifically, the general. Admittedly, the instructions and maxims were probably not Maurice's own, and were in fact a typical trait of the genre. Regardless, Maurice still had to choose which ones to include, and so those that do comprise the list were surely significant, at least to Maurice.

One important observation that Rance makes, based on his analysis of the works of Syrianus and Maurice, concerns the amount of knowledge that a general needed to have.[52] Rance speculates that the general of the sixth century had to know considerably more than his Republican or Early Imperial counterparts; while this point is open to debate, the question of how a general prepares himself for a campaign, or any military operation, is an important one.[53] A fundamental issue that has been tackled by a number of scholars is the training and education of the generals of the Roman army.[54] It should be clear that this was one of the primary aims of Maurice.

The same may also have been true of ancient historiography; there is some evidence that late Roman generals used historical literature while on campaign.[55] One such example comes from Eunapius. In fragment 44, which chronicles some of the events leading up the battle of Adrianople, Eunapius says the following:

---

[51] 8.2.8, trans. Dennis.

[52] Rance 1993, 263.

[53] In an age when there were no military academies to provide the requisite training for a commander, literary works such as histories and treatises would have had additional value beyond their literary qualities. See Rance 1993, 264.

[54] See, for example, Campbell 1984.

[55] Kaegi 2003, 58-121 and *passim* suggests that Heraclius used treatises such as Maurice's extensively when he was at war with the Persians.

"That occasion illustrated how a literary education has value in war and how those who aim at a goal directly, economically and without a fight are aided by the experience of events gained through reading history. For there is much evidence from many occasions, and experience from olden times shouts out that one ought not, with forces either large or small, do battle with those who have come to despair of their lives and are ready to face danger."[56]

Ammianus Marcellinus claims that Julian, while on his ill-fated eastern campaign, read Scipio Aemilianus and Polybius (24.2.16). Theophylact includes a similar tale about the general Philippicus who was active around 585: "A story was current that the general [Philippicus], who was very fond of learning and who drew his military knowledge from the experts of the past, had acquired this aptitude for wise strategy from the shrewdness of Scipio, the perfect general."[57] Theophylact based that statement on "the reports of those who have set down the histories in writing".[58] Now, all of these statements are found in historians, and so, perhaps, we should not be surprised to find episodes in which other historical works were used by pre-eminent men. Nevertheless, it is an important point that, whether or not historical literature was used to teach a would-be general, many historians wrote their works with this didactic purpose consciously in mind. It is for this reason that, as we have seen, all of the authors discussed emphasize the connection between generalship and discipline. At the same time, those same authors also put considerable stress on the didactic qualities of their works, whether they are works of history, or proper military manuals.[59]

Over the course of the preceding pages I have suggested that the cases of indiscipline and insubordination of the army as presented in the chief military authors of the sixth century are not as clear as has often been supposed. Instead, the respective authors' inclusion of examples of indiscipline and insubordination in their texts is invariably tied to their didactic aims and the (or a) central theme of their works; invariably, generalship is that theme. Whether an ancient writer was an historian or the writer of a treatise, the processes of selection and arrangement played an important role in the construction of their respective texts. They chose

---

[56] Eunap. frag. 44, trans. Blockley.

[57] 1.14.2, trans. Whitby.

[58] 1.14.2, trans. Whitby.

[59] See Kaegi 1990 for the value of history for generals as well as a useful survey of Procopius' military qualities.

to emphasize those points that they felt were most pertinent.[60] If Maurice was concerned with providing a manual to aid would-be generals, he would certainly want to ensure that his work did, in fact, serve such a purpose; and what better way was there to accomplish this than to stress some alleged problems with the army? At the same time, Procopius, Agathias, and Theophylact are concerned with personalities in their narratives and, to a certain degree, with presenting a balanced picture of those same personalities.[61] Where there are references to indiscipline and insubordination in the literature, they are usually found in the sources most closely associated with the classical tradition,[62] and they are invariably framed within discussions of the successes or failings of a general (or, less regularly, an emperor) or his officials.

Bibliography

Agathias. *Histories*, edited by R. Keydell. Berlin: Walter de Gruyter, 1967.

—. *Histories*, translated by J. D. Frendo. Berlin: Walter de Gruyter, 1975.

Blockely, R. C. *The Fragmentary Classicising Historians of the Later Roman Empire. Volume II: Text, Translation and Historiographical Notes.* Liverpool: Francis Cairns, 1983.

Brodka, D. *Die Geschichtsphilosophie in der spätantiken Historiographie. Studien zu Prokopios von Kaisareia, Agathias von Myrina und Theophylaktos Simokattes.* Frankfurt am Main: Peter Lang, 2004.

Caesar. *The Gallic War*, translated by H. J. Edwards. London: Harvard University Press, 1913.

Cameron, A. *Agathias.* Oxford: Oxford University Press, 1970.

—. *Procopius.* Oxford: Oxford University Press, 1985.

Campbell, J. B. *The Emperor and the Roman Army.* Oxford: Oxford University Press, 1984.

---

[60] Of course, while the historians would choose which elements to include, they would also choose which elements to exclude. Thus, there are invariably numerous cases of indiscipline which they have passed over in their discussions. This does not, however, affect my argument.

[61] Whether they succeeded or not is another question beyond the scope of this paper.

[62] John Malalas, who wrote a Christian chronicle, and Pseudo-Joshua the Stylite and Zachariah of Mytilene, who both wrote works in Syriac, are much less concerned with discipline on the battlefield than the authors discussed here. For a good overview of late antique historiography, see Croke (2007), whom I want to thank for sending me an advance copy of his paper.

Croke, B. "Late Antique Historiography, 250-650 CE." In *A Companion to Greek and Roman Historiography, Volume 2*, edited by J. Marincola, 567-581. Oxford: Blackwell Publishing.

Delbrück, H. *History of the Art of War, Volume II, The Barbarian Invasions*, translated by W. J. Westport: Renfroe Jr. Greenwood Press, 1990.

Elton, H. "Army and Battle in the Age of Justinian (527-565)." In *A Companion to the Roman Army*, edited by P. Erdkamp, 532-550. Oxford: Blackwell Publishing, 2007a.

—. "Military Forces." In *The Cambridge History of Greek and Roman Warfare,Volume II: Rome from the Late Republic to the Late Empire*, edited by H. van Wees, P. Sabin, and M. Whitby, 270-309. Cambridge: Cambridge University Press, 2007b.

Evans, J. A. S. *Procopius*. New York: Twayne Publishers, 1972.

Fear, A. "War and Society." In *The Cambridge History of Greek and Roman Warfare,Volume II: Rome from the Late Republic to the Late Empire*, edited by P. Sabin, H. Van Wees, and M. Whitby, 424-458. Cambridge: Cambridge University Press, 2007.

Frontinus. *Stratagems,* translated by C. E. Bennett. London: Harvard University Press, 1925.

Greatrex, G. *Rome and Persia at War, 502-532*. Leeds: Francis Cairns,1998.

Grosse, R. *Römische Militärgeschichte von Gallienus bis zum Beginn der Byzantinischen Themenverfassung*. Berlin: Weidmann, 1920.

Haldon, J. *Warfare, State and Society in the Byzantine World, 565-1204*. London: Routledge, 1999.

Hansen, M. H. "The Battle Exhortation in Ancient Historiography: Fact or Fiction?" *Historia* 42 (1993): 162-175.

Hornblower, S. "Introduction." In *Greek Historiography*, edited by S. Hornblower, 1-72. Oxford: Oxford University Press, 1995.

—. "Warfare in ancient literature: the paradox of war." In *The Cambridge History of Greek and Roman Warfare, Volume I: Greece, the Hellenistic World and the Rise of Rome*, edited by P. Sabin, H. Van Wees, and M. Whitby, 22-53. Cambridge: Cambridge University Press, 2007.

Jones, A. H. M. *The Later Roman Empire*. Oxford: Oxford University Press, 1964.

Kaegi, W. *Byzantine Military Unrest, 471-843*. Amsterdam: Hakkert, 1981.

—. *Some Thoughts on Byzantine Military Strategy*. Hellenic Studies Lecture for Ball State University, Brookline, 1983.

—. "Procopius the Military Historian," *ByzF* 15 (1990): 53-85.

—. *Heraclius, Emperor of Byzantium.* Cambridge: Cambridge University Press, 2003.

Kaldellis, A. "Agathias on History and Poetry," *GRBS* 38 (1997): 295-305.

—. "The Historical and Religious Views of Agathias: a reinterpretation." *Byz* 69 (1999): 206-252.

—. "Things Are Not What They Are: Agathias Mythistoricus and the Last Laugh of Classical Culture." *CQ* 53 (2003): 295-300.

—. *Procopius of Caesarea: Tyranny, History, and Philosophy at the End of Antiquity.* Philadelphia: University of Pennsylvania Press, 2004.

—. *Hellenism in Byzantium, the Transformations of Greek Identity and the Reception of the Classical Tradition.* Cambridge: Cambridge University Press, 2007.

Lee, A. D. *Information and Frontiers: Roman Foreign Relations in Late Antiquity.* Cambridge: Cambridge University Press, 1993.

—. "Morale and the Roman Experience of Battle." In *Battle in Antiquity*, edited by A. B. Lloyd, 199-217. Duckworth: London. 1996.

—. "The Empire at War." In *The Cambridge Companion to the Age of Justinian*, edited by M. Maas, 113-133. New York: Cambridge University Press, 2005.

Lendon, J. E. *Soldiers and Ghosts: A History of Battle in Antiquity.* New Haven: Yale University Press, 2005.

Maurice. *Strategikon*, edited by G. T. Dennis. Vienna: CFHB, 1981.

—. *Strategikon,* translated by G. T. Dennis. Philadelphia: Pennsylvania University Press, 1984.

Onasander. *Strategikos*, translated by Illinois Greek Club. London: Harvard University Press, 1923.

Pazdernik, C. F. *A Dangerous Liberty and a Servitude Free from Care: Politicial ELEUTHERIA and DOULEIA in Procopius of Caesarea and Thucydides of Athens.* Unpublished PhD dissertation, Princeton University, 1997.

Procopius. *Wars*, edited by J. Haury, revised by G. Wirth. Leipzig, 2001.

Rance, P. *Tactics and Tactica in the Sixth Century: Tradition and Originality.* Unpublished PhD dissertation, University of St. Andrews, 1993.

—. *"Simulacra Pugnae*: The Literary and Historical Tradition of Mock Battles in the Roman and Early Byzantine Army," *GRBS* 41 (2000): 223-275.

—. "The *fulcum*, the Late Roman and Byzantine *testudo*. The Germanisation of Roman Infantry Tactics," *GRBS* 44 (2004): 265-326.

—. "Battle." In *The Cambridge History of Greek and Roman Warfare, Volume II: Rome from the Late Republic to the Late Empire*, edited by P. Sabin, H. Van Wees, and M. Whitby, 342-378. Cambridge: Cambridge University Press, 2007.

Shahîd, I. *Byzantium and the Arabs in the Sixth Century, Volume I, Part 1: Political and Military History*. Washington: Dumbarton Oaks, 1995.

Southern, P. and Dixon, K. R. *The Late Roman Army*. London: Routledge, 1996.

Syrianus. *On Strategy*, edited and translated by G. T. Dennis. Washington: Dumbarton Oaks, 1985.

Syvänne, I. *The Age of Hippotoxotai*. Tampere: Tampere University Press, 2004.

Theophylact Simocatta. *The History of Theophylact Simocatta,* translated by M. and Ma. Whitby. Oxford: Oxford University Press, 1986.)

Vegetius. *Epitome of Military Science*, translated by M. P. Milner. Liverpool: Liverpool University Press, 1993.

Wheeler, E. L. "The Laxity of Syrian Legions." In *The Roman Army in the East,* edited by D. Kennedy, 229-276. Ann Arbor: Journal of Roman Archaeology, 1996.

Whitby, M. *The Emperor Maurice and His Historian: Theophylact Simocatta on Persian and Balkan Warfare*. Oxford: Oxford University Press, 1988.

—. "Recruitment in the Roman Armies from Justinian to Heraclius (ca. 565-615)." In *The Byzantine and Early Islamic Near East III: States, Resources and Armies*, edited by A. Cameron, 61-124. Princeton: Darwin Press, 1995.

—. "The Army," In *CAH XIV*, edited by Cameron, A., Ward-Perkins, B., and Whitby, M. 288-314. Cambridge: Cambridge University Press, 2000.

—. "War and State in Late Antiquity: Some Economic and Political Connections." In *Krieg, Gesellschaft, Institutionen*, edited by B. Meißner, 355-385. Berlin: Akademie Verlag, 2005.

Epilogue

Edward Bragg, Lisa Irene Hau, and Elizabeth Macaulay-Lewis

The goal of this volume has been to demonstrate the wide lens through which young scholars have begun to study ancient warfare and its impact on society. The wide ranging topics of this monograph reflect the rich amount of postgraduate research on this subject as budding scholars find new ways of approaching what has often been seen as a traditional, conservative field—the bastion of military historians. The papers in this volume demonstrate that the field of military studies in antiquity can be, and must be, expanded into ever new areas.

The various papers in this volume have approached military history by drawing upon the full range of evidence from the Graeco-Roman world—material culture, literature (historiography, oratory, and epic poetry), epigraphy, numismatics, and garden design—in order to understand the scope of the importance of warfare in antiquity and the depth of its impact on ancient society and culture. The genres of historiography and oratory have been shown to provide insight into the practical issues of recruitment and intelligence gathering as well as into the literary portrayal and self-promotion of a number of generals and victors, from the fifth century BC to the sixth century AD. The correlation between internal political power and military success abroad (or the lack of it) has been explored both for Classical Athens, on the background of literary sources, and for late Republican Rome, in the context of the use of plants for propagandistic purposes. Two thoughtful interpretations of the very different genres of epic and epigraphy have demonstrated how the idea of peace was an integral part of an otherwise militaristic world. The correlation between death and honour has been explored both in the literary realm of epic and in the visual realm of Athenian black figure vases.

The other aim of this volume has been to set the stage for new lines of enquiry into ancient warfare and society. There is still much work to do be done; however, we see both the conference and this resultant volume as a springboard for future productive interdisciplinary work in this field.

Fruitful topics for exploration could be the study of peace and its representation in history, literature, and material culture. Likewise, further examination of the defeated and prisoners of war, as well as death brought about by war (though not necessarily on the battlefield), could allow greater insights into a society that was more violent and militaristic than the world most classical scholars live in today. These themes are very rich and can be explored from various different avenues—allowing for continued dialogue and cross pollination between the disciplines of history, archaeology, art history, philology, and literary criticism. For both the scholar and reader, this work and future research should also prompt reflection about modern conflict, its representation, effects, and aftermath.

Bibliography

Dillon, S. and K. Welch. (eds). *Representations of War in ancient Rome.* Cambridge: Cambridge University Press, 2006.

CONTRIBUTORS

Jeremy Armstrong is completing a doctorate in Ancient History at the University of St. Andrews. His research focuses on the development of the early Roman state and the changing character of Rome's armed forces during the late Regal and early Republican periods.

Luca Asmonti is currently a sessional teaching fellow at the University of Reading, having received his doctorate in Ancient History from Kings College, London in 2007. His research focuses on the relationship between military leaders and voting citizens in late-fifth century Athens.

Edward Bragg has submitted a doctorate in Ancient History at Wadham College, Oxford, as well as following a PGCE in Classics at Kings College, London. His research focuses on the methods that Roman commanders employed during the Republic to promote their military achievements in the city of Rome.

Craig Caldwell is a visiting Professor at the department of History, University of Furman, South Carolina, having completed his doctorate in History at Princeton University in 2007. His research focuses on the effects of civil war in the later Roman Empire, particularly in the region of Illyricum.

Brian Campbell was educated at Queen's University Belfast and the University of Oxford and is Professor of Roman History at Queen's University, Belfast. His main research interests lie in the area of the Roman army, ancient military writers, Roman imperial politics, and land survey. In August 2002, he took up a Leverhulme Major Research Fellowship to pursue a project on rivers in the ancient world. In 2005, he was a Visiting Fellow at All Souls, Oxford.

Lisa Irene Hau is a teaching fellow at Bristol University, having completed her doctorate in Classics at Royal Holloway, University of London 2007. Her research focuses on ancient historiography as literature, specifically on moralizing themes and techniques in historiography.

Lynn Kozak is completing a doctorate in Classics at the University of Nottingham. Her research looks at trust as an element of construction for Homeric characterization and how that construction changes in fifth-century tragic re-workings of Iliadic characters.

Carsten Hjort Lange has completed his doctorate in Ancient History at the University of Nottingham. His research focuses on the Triumvirate and the Battle of Actium in Augustan ideology.

Josh Levithan is an assistant professor of Humanities at Kenyon College, Gambier, Ohio, having completed his doctorate in Ancient History at Yale University in 2007. His research focuses on social and cultural aspects of the Imperial Roman army, with special attention to siege warfare.

Elizabeth Macaulay-Lewis completed her doctorate in Classical Archaeology at St John's College, Oxford in 2008. Her research focuses on the archaeology and history of Roman gardens, architecture and art, with particular interests in garden design, ancient plants, and the construction of space.

Sonya Nevin is completing a doctorate in Classics at University College, Dublin. Her research looks at military ethics in Classical Greece with particular interest in sacred spaces during times of war and how Greek historians dealt with issues of sacrilege.

David Saunders is the Anissa B. Balson curatorial fellow curatorial fellow in the department of European Painting and Sculpture at the LA County Museum of Art, having completed his doctorate in Classical Archaeology at Lincoln College, Oxford in 2006. His research focuses on depictions of dead and dying figures in Greek vase-painting, with reference to warriors and the idealisation of death in battle.

completing a doctorate in Classics and Ancient History Warwick. His research focuses on war, historiography, century, with special emphasis on the *Wars* of

his doctorate in Ancient History at Cardiff currently a part-time teaching fellow at the His current research focuses on illuminating the infrastructures of the Persian Empire.

Hans van Wees is Professor of Ancient History at University College, London. His main areas of interest are the social and economic history of early Greece, archaic and classical Greek warfare, and the use of iconographical and comparative evidence in the study of the ancient Greek world; subjects on which he has published widely.

Index